the perfection campaign

the perfection campaign

a daughter's search for acceptance

JILL VANNEMAN

SHE WRITES PRESS

Copyright © 2026 Jill Vanneman
All rights reserved. No part of this publication may be reproduced, stored in a retrieval system, or transmitted in any form or by any means, electronic, mechanical, photocopying, recording, or otherwise, except for brief quotations in reviews, educational works, or other uses permitted by copyright law.

Published in 2026 by
She Writes Press, an imprint of The Stable Book Group

1569 Solano Ave #546
Berkeley, CA 94707
https://shewritespress.com
Library of Congress Control Number: 2026904447
ISBN: 979-8-89636-326-2
eISBN: 979-8-89636-327-9

Interior Designer: Andrea Reider

Printed in the United States

Names and identifying characteristics have been changed to protect the privacy of certain individuals. These true stories are faithfully composed based on memory, photographs, journal entries, and other supporting documents. Conversations between individuals are meant to reflect the essence, meaning, and spirit of the events described.

No part of this publication may be used to train generative artificial intelligence (AI) models. The publisher and author reserve all rights related to the use of this content in machine learning.

All company and product names mentioned in this book may be trademarks or registered trademarks of their respective owners. They are used for identification purposes only and do not imply endorsement or affiliation.

For Sara and Ren

Shame is the birthplace of perfectionism. The antidote is empathy. If we reach out, and share our shame experience with someone who responds with empathy, shame dissipates.

—Brené Brown, *Atlas of the Heart*

CHAPTER ONE

STEERING THE CAR

AS WE WALKED away from her old friend's house in North Tacoma, the one with the expansive view of Commencement Bay, my mother's expression caught my eye. In a single flicker she surveyed me, top to bottom. *Oh, shit*, I thought, *here it comes*. I slid into my Pinto Runabout, Dad beside me in the passenger seat. My mom got into the back of the car. I heard the click of her purse opening as she pulled out a cigarette.

What was it this time? My clothes? Lack of makeup?

My mother, of course, looked coiffed and composed. She wore a navy blue and white linen skirt and chic white top. Her Elizabeth Arden cherry red lipstick and pink blush were just so. Mom didn't wear a lot of cosmetics, but she never went anywhere without her lipstick—or her cigarettes, for that matter.

"Why couldn't you at least have put on a skirt or dress?" My mother's clipped voice floated up from the back as we set off for Seattle where they were staying with my aunt and uncle.

"I'm twenty-six now, Mom. I know how to dress myself." I'd put on a nice pair of cords and a tailored, non-iron, navy blue shirt with gold stripes from Saks that my mother had bought for me. I knew this line of criticism, yet her words still stung. "You're so focused on appearances," I told her. "I mean, I know your friends are rich. But surely, they are more interested in me as a person than in what I am wearing. Besides, the visit wasn't about me. It was about you catching up with your old friend." We had just left the house of her best friend from graduate school. Dad stretched his legs in the front seat and continued to stare out the window. Who knew what he was thinking?

The smoke from Mom's cigarette filled the car. I glanced back and saw Mom rolling her eyes and twitching. I wanted to change the topic to something else other than my attire. But I wasn't sure I wanted to go to where my mind was taking me. I wanted to tell them I was gay. While I'd rehearsed coming out to my parents with my therapist, I hadn't specifically thought about how or where on this visit I would tell them. As I was driving, I thought, *why not now?* But I was tense from this anticipated conversation. I began sweating. The bottoms of my thighs stuck to the vinyl seat. The car windows remained closed against freeway traffic noise. Dad had taken his suit jacket off, but his tie remained knotted. I wondered if he was as warm as I was.

I looked out the window and gauged how much time I had before we reached Seattle. We buzzed past the War Pony Smoke Shop—a feature of my daily commutes from University of Puget Sound law school to Seattle—and I knew I had about thirty minutes left. I didn't have a speech prepared, although I remembered my therapist, Ruth, cautioning me that my parents might already know I was gay and refuse to talk about it. She'd steered me away from using a label like *gay* or *lesbian*. Instead, I should say I was a "woman-loving woman," or simply that I "preferred women." While her words sounded good in her office, now I wasn't so sure. *Let's just say "gay,"* I thought. "Gay" captured it all and left no room for doubt. "Woman-loving woman" sounded too feminist and would alienate my parents.

My parents already knew or suspected I was gay. They knew about my close friend Leslie in college. They had recently met Jude, my first lover. I also knew they didn't want to talk about my relationships with women. My impression, which came primarily from their never asking me about my private life, led me to think they only wanted to hear about "successes" that didn't include romance. When I spoke to them on the phone—as I did sporadically since their last visit to Seattle and after meeting Jude—we spoke about my career: law school and my part-time job as an intern with the Seattle city attorney's office. Our phone conversations steered clear of me previously sharing an apartment with Jude.

I gripped the steering wheel tighter and watched the sign loom for Federal Way. I glanced up at the rearview mirror to see what my mother was doing. She seemed to be fussing, maybe even wringing her hands. I took a deep breath and said I had something to share. I did not tell them that I was a woman who loved other women.

"Mom and Dad, I have something to tell you." Neither of them asked what. My heart pounded in my ears. I wasn't sure I could go through with it. Anxiety leaked through my sweaty hands on the steering wheel. A hamster wheel of questions ran through my mind. *Was I going to lose my parents for good? Would they still love me? Why did I think I needed to be honest with them?* Mom was already upset with me. *Why rock the boat?* But here in my car, sailing down the I-5, they were a captive audience. I was tired of carrying the weight of their expectations. I would never be the person they wanted me to be. By living a lie, I couldn't tell them about my new girlfriend or the joy of feeling like I finally belonged somewhere. I wanted to share all of my life with them. I just wasn't sure they wanted to hear what I had to say.

I had wanted to tell them last summer when I first started going to law school at night, but a trip to my doctor's office changed my mind. I had gone back to the family home for a visit. Nothing was out of the ordinary about that visit except for my appointment with our family doctor. I had decided to schedule a physical with Dr. Wedell in the hopes he could give me a preview of how my parents might react to my coming out. Our family doctor was not just our doctor—he, his wife, and their four boys were family friends. My parents played bridge with them, partied with them, and our family had even gone on a vacation with theirs.

I drove out to Glenview, Illinois, north of Evanston, to Dr. Wedell's office. We talked about law school and I asked about his tennis, a passion of his as well as mine. After the medical exam concluded and he pronounced me fit as a fiddle, I asked, "Hal, how do you think my parents would react if I told them I was gay?"

He looked at me with such fierce intensity that I suddenly felt my temperature drop and I knew it wasn't the air conditioning.

He said, "Jill, I think they would rather that you had cancer." There wasn't an ounce of deadpan levity in his voice. He was serious. I looked back at him blankly. I couldn't find the words to respond. While many positive things were happening in areas like New York City, San Francisco, and Seattle for gay people, there was still widespread homophobia in the United States about people coming out as gay. It was not accepted and people lost jobs, friends, and even housing by coming out. It was still a felony to have sex with a same sex person. I apparently lived in a bubble in Seattle.

I left his office on wobbly legs and gingerly walked to my car. This was not at all the answer I thought he would give. I had expected him to say that my parents wouldn't like my news, but that in time, they would get over it. Telling Hal had been the test drive for telling my parents that summer. However, after my friendly little chat with Hal I decided that no way in hell was I coming out to them then, or maybe, ever. We could all just go on pretending that someday my prince would come and the rest of my life could then begin. The problem was that I was already living the rest of my life—and for the first time, I'd begun to like it.

I had brought some books home with me that summer that I had planned to give to my parents after we'd had my coming-out conversation. One of them was *Now That You Know: What Every Parent Should Know About Homosexuality* by Betty Fairchild and Nancy Hayward, published just two years earlier, in 1979. At the time, there were not many books on this topic. I thought this book's frank tackling of the subject might be helpful. My appointment with Hal had shaken me to my core, so I went home to Seattle, still in silence. I found the three books I had brought with me and shoved them into a sweater storage chest under my bed. I buried them underneath some clothes where I hoped they would never be found. Now, given Hal's reaction, I never wanted to tell my parents. I had tried to bury Hal's words and enjoy the rest of my trip with my parents. But Hal's revelation tore into my sense of self, a state of mind that already had holes poked into it since birth. The message was that there was something wrong with me.

Until I left home for college, I had thought of my childhood as privileged, even idyllic. I never wanted for material things; I got new clothes for school, I was able to take piano and guitar lessons and even ice skating lessons. We took vacations to resorts, national parks, and educational sites like Gettysburg. My parents did set greater limits than those of the other kids in the neighborhood. When the streetlights came on, my brother and I were the first kids to say we had to go home. That was the rule in our house. My mother was involved in the minutiae of my school life through the PTA and as a leader of my Brownie troop. Outside of his demanding job and political aspirations, my father volunteered with my brother's Cub Scout baseball team. As I continued to plod through that first year of law school, the knowledge that my parents would prefer I had cancer ate away at me. My ability to focus on law school classes—already shaky—became even shakier. The closet in which I was hiding my true self from my family grew even darker. Now, here on I-5 with my mother's criticism still stinging, I just spat it out: "I'm gay." *Oh, my God. I said it.* I felt my mother flinch even though I wasn't looking at her. I could sense sudden, frantic movements coming from the back seat. I could hear her reaching for her purse on the floor and the clasp of her purse being undone as I imagined her fumbling for her cigarettes. I heard her shifting in her seat and her shoe bumped the back of my seat as she uncrossed her legs. My words were simple and true, but my mother wanted to shoo them away. I glanced in the mirror. Her right hand holding her cigarette darted about abruptly as if it was an angry firefly. She wouldn't meet my eyes in the mirror; instead, her gaze bounced all over the car as if looking for an escape.

"Jill, stop the car!" my mother yelled. "Stop! We're going to have an accident. You need to pull over—now."

Dad said nothing again. I was concentrating on my mother.

"Mom, I'm fine." I looked at the speedometer. I was going sixty, keeping pace with the other vehicles, and my hands were at ten and two on the steering wheel. My spine was straight. I was so relieved to have gotten the words out. "When I was home last summer, I left behind some books about homosexuality and one is about what parents need to know. You might want to read them. They're in my sweater chest."

"When . . . when did you leave these?" she asked. "Why are you telling us now?" I told her that I'd been wanting to tell them for some time, and that, here in my car, we had privacy. *If I had told you I was gay in an unconfined space, like a room*, I thought, *you might have walked out.*

She grew more frantic. Her hazel eyes, including her wandering left one, seemed to bulge out of their sockets and she screamed and pleaded with my dad. "Ed, say something! We've talked about this. Why aren't you saying anything?" I thought, *Whoa, wait . . . they've talked about this? They knew or suspected that I'm gay and they have never brought it up?* Maybe they were waiting to hear from me, but I wondered if we ever would have talked about this crucial part of my identity if I hadn't brought it up.

My father, who had been sitting mute in the front seat during my mother's hysteria, did not turn around when he spoke to her.

"Shirli," he said with a sigh, "I think when we get back to Evanston, we should read these books." He spoke calmly while my mother continued to twist and turn, her face an ugly, blotchy red. I realized I was experiencing firsthand my father's famous political unreadability. Dad had been entangled in Evanston politics as an unpaid civil servant for all of my life, even while he worked full time as a corporate attorney. His tone of voice gave me no idea what he thought or felt. He sat staring out the front window, not looking at either of us. I had heard that both political foe and friend would leave his office thinking that they had him on their side.

But my mother would not be placated. She placed another cigarette in her mouth, fumbled for the car lighter, and nearly missed igniting its tip. When it was finally lit, she jabbed the cigarette into the air to punctuate her points, waving its burning end dangerously close to the back of my seat. Her furor and the smoke from her cigarette so consumed the car that I imagined my little Runabout would implode. I had not expected my announcement would merit a detonation. Her emotion was so raw. I had never seen agitation like this from my mother before.

"Who knows about this in Seattle?" she demanded, jabbing her cigarette toward some unseen enemy.

"W-what... what do you mean, 'who knows'?" I answered. She didn't elaborate. I guessed she wanted to know if any of her friends from college or my relatives knew. I didn't even know what friends she could be talking about. She had left Seattle at eighteen.

"Why did you pick my hometown to do this in?" she moaned. While she had been born and raised in Seattle, she'd accepted a scholarship to Northwestern University in Evanston to get her master's degree in journalism. She met my father and stayed in Evanston to raise her family, never returning to her Seattle roots, except for the occasional visit.

"It's all that Leslie girl's fault. That girl from college. I never liked her, you know," she said. *What the hell?* I thought. And then, I got worried. Maybe they knew the whole truth about Leslie. But this conversation was not about Leslie. My mom went on in a voice that now sounded like a sheep separated from its flock, bleating on and on. "Why would you pick this lifestyle?" she wailed while I tried to keep my eyes on the road.

With each of my mother's insistent and biting judgments, I felt a searing heat around my scalp. My brain was on fire and my nerves were singed. It was as though someone had sawed the top of my head off, gone in with a cauterizing instrument, and with the persistence of a surgeon, knocked against every nerve ending.

"Mom, it's not a choice or a lifestyle. This is *who* I am. It's not a flavor of the day," I said. "I just really don't have any interest in men sexually. It's not that I dislike them. I just don't click with them in that way." I wished in that moment I could be braver, that I could have said being a lesbian wasn't about her.

I couldn't read my mother's mind, but as someone who had donned a new skin when she married my father, my mother knew about being an outsider. Her blue-collar, Democrat, union-dues-paying roots held no place in the conservative, white-collar, upper-middle-class Republican part of Evanston she'd married into.

I had not expected my mother's rage. What was this anger about? Was she afraid or ashamed? If I had to guess, I'd say it was a mixture of both. I don't know what kind of experience or knowledge my mother had about lesbians. I doubt she even knew any. I wonder if she thought my coming out meant that she'd been a bad mother, that somehow her actions planted some bad seed called "lesbian" in me. Or, perhaps, she was afraid for me. Perhaps she thought I would end up lonely and discriminated against by the rest of society. Then again, neon lights might have flashed in bold before her mind reading, "No wedding! No children!"

This was supposed to be my moment of freedom. I was scared but also excited to finally share a part of me that was just about me, and not about fulfilling some sort of punch card of societal expectations. I wanted them to share my excitement, but I knew that what they wanted for me was to do what everyone did. Succeed in school. Get married. Have children. Those were the expectations they'd grown up with and I was expected to march in that straight, orderly line. But, even in high school, I'd known I needed to get out of Evanston. To me, Evanston and my parents were intertwined, and if I was going to establish my own identity, I needed to escape them both. When I left, I hadn't known I was a lesbian. At the time, I didn't realize how risky establishing my own identity would be.

As far as my parents were concerned, choosing a college two thousand miles away showed my independence. They were proud of me forging my own path, at least in that way. I don't know if they wanted me to come back and settle eventually, but I had no intention of doing that. Although Evanston was a town of eighty thousand, many people knew of my parents through their civic activism. Maybe I would follow in their footsteps. But when I first left at seventeen, I wanted the freedom to choose my own future.

And then, while I was ruminating, came the coup de grace in a loud voice from the back seat. "It's that bull dyke we met on our last visit, that woman Jude," my mother spat out. At those words, I finally snapped. Couldn't she at least say she loved me—even though she didn't understand or required time to digest the news? Her need for reflection I could have understood, but this outright attack on me and people I cared about crossed the line. I'd done everything my parents had wanted me to do for most of my life. My God—I was still *me*. My announcement should not have changed that.

"Mother," I said, "don't you dare call Jude a 'bull dyke.' You don't even know what that word means. And, you are talking about a woman I loved and still care about." I was still processing the shock of hearing that word come out of my mother's mouth. Shocked that she even knew that word. My father said nothing. He neither came to my defense nor commented on our interaction. In a way, I was relieved by his lack of involvement. Dealing with my mother's hostility while driving took all of my concentration. I just brooded about what his silence meant.

Then I heard my mother's last desperate cry, the one I would still hear years later: "Why? Why would you do this when we tried so hard to make you perfect?"

And there it was, the truth. Their campaign—at least up to this point—had failed. I presumed my mother was acting as the spokesperson. To her mind, their efforts to address my limitations had been for naught. I tried to tuck her dissatisfaction into some mental-corner-equivalent to the sweater chest where I'd hidden all the books, but in that sense, I was bound to fail as miserably as my mother.

CHAPTER TWO

THE VANNEMAN NAME

THE DECISION to come out to my parents on that car ride at twenty-six is a decision that so many self-identified gay people make at some point in their lives. But as I was learning in all the progressive literature I perused, coming out was not just one event but a lifelong journey, both for me and my parents.

My coming-out journey was lifelong because I incorporated my parents' shame into my own view of myself. Coming out to them was not as freeing as I had hoped it would be. I no longer had to hide who I was, but my parents' unwillingness to hear that truth—let alone accept it—kept me in a cage. The cage let me come and go, but its steely perimeter glinted back at me. I would soon discover that my declaration could neither release me from my desire to please them nor their efforts to contain me.

Parental expectations had governed my childhood. I thought I knew what those expectations were pretty early on. I was around eight when I grasped the unspoken checklist. It went like this:

1. Earn good grades
2. Do not throw temper tantrums
3. Be involved in activities like student government, clubs, church, and youth groups
4. Do not—under any circumstances—bring down shame upon the family name

I became adept albeit imperfect at following these rules. And I might have tried harder to be perfect if I didn't have so many strikes against me—if nature hadn't given me a cleft in my palate and a love for women. I was destined to bring shame down on the family name. Yes, the *family name!*

Vanneman. The name I inherited from my father. It comes from the Dutch name of my forebears, "Van Imen," and means "leader of men." I wish it described me. It's a name that I hate and love at the same time, a tug of war inside me, because that name is me and not me. A name that I want to disown and yet take pride in every time I have to spell it out for someone. I can hear my father's voice every time I'm asked to sound it out countless times the way he would for restaurant reservations, newspaper reporters, and hotel clerks during family vacations. "V" as in Victor—"A"—double "N" as in Nancy—"E"—"M" as in Mary—"A"—"N." That name exists in the annals of Evanston history. Not on a building, not on a park or a school, but in results. The results of efforts by a man who simply wanted to give back to his community. And those results so overwhelmed me I eventually distanced myself two thousand miles away from the name. But, of course, *Vanneman* followed me all the way to the west coast of the US. The name, after all, is in my blood, my genes, and my ideals—even if it holds me tenuously in its grip.

I want to say, "Oh, that name doesn't apply to me, that applied to my dad," the man I didn't even realize I revered until I discovered one day in my forties that I'd acquired many of Ed Vanneman's habits. I was just going through my usual morning routine before going out the door to work when it hit me. Those habits I inherited include making sure I had enough time in the morning before work to sit with my coffee and read the paper, getting up early even on the weekends, because I could not turn my inner work alarm clock off, sitting the way he did with an erect back leaning slightly forward with his bottom slightly pushed back, pursing his lips while concentrating, my smile, my love of music and history: these, I attribute all to him. The leadership bit, probably not so much. But the tendency to shy away from others' exuberant expressions of love—that part I've got down pat.

Both of my parents possessed the gift of leadership in spades. They didn't just focus on improving their offspring, they wanted to make things better in their community. My mother did it through countless hours of volunteer work with the Junior League, the local library board, the Chicago Volunteer Nurse Association, Easter Seals, the United Way campaign, Donald Rumsfeld's first campaign for Congress, and other Republican campaigns. When she died at sixty-nine, her obituary appeared as a news item on the *Chicago Tribune* obituary page and took up five inches of space in the *Evanston Review*. It helped that fifteen years earlier, my father had been the mayor of Evanston, a cozy, respectable town that hugs the shore of Lake Michigan and is the closest suburb north of Chicago.

My father, Edgar Jr., chose to make things better through his work in politics. It was not his full-time job. No—the job that provided my privileged childhood was Dad's work for Brunswick Corporation. His political life, however, was his passion. A corporate attorney by day, he turned into civic superman at night. Right after dinner, he would rush out the door to perform his civic duties: city council meetings as an alderman, the zoning board to weigh in on what sort of development Evanston would allow, the young Republican party, the school board, the mayor's office from 1971 to 1978, and the list goes on. The list is so long that when I read the obituary he had prepared before his death to spare his children I had to sit down and take a breath. The accomplishments filled at least three columns above the fold of the *Tribune*'s obituary page.

The betterment campaign began when I was born. While I don't remember the details, I imagine what my parents saw. The doctor would have held me upside down by my ankles, swatted me, and made me cry. The three of them would have counted my fingers and toes. *Yup, ten in each place, all the right numbers*. But a hole—something not quite right—existed where my upper lip met the cleft beneath my nose. Most people don't think about that part of their anatomy, but mine would play a starring role in my life and that of my parents, despite cleft palates being garden-variety birth defects.

In the early days, I just knew my condition made me special. I got out of classes and went to visit all of these different doctors. My throng was impressive: an orthodontist, ear doctor, in-school and after-school speech therapist, and a plastic surgeon. I was proudest of the plastic surgeon, because seeing him required going all the way down to the Loop or downtown Chicago and my father would come too. That's how I knew that doctor was important, because Daddy would leave his attorney job at Brunswick Corporation in the middle of the day. Dr. Slaughter was his name. I guess his name didn't matter to my parents. He was going to "fix" their daughter and make her look like everybody else—or at least make her look less different.

Dear Mr. Vanneman:

Jill was born (1953) with a cleft of the left side of the lip and the posterior palate

March 8, 1954, surgery completed left cleft lip was repaired to narrow the cleft

Oct. 19, 1955, the posterior portion of the cleft of the palate was closed

May 7, 1956, on recent examination she still has a small opening in the palate which was not closed at the initial procedure which we can improve later

Nov. 7, 1956, the final operative procedure was carried out and a small opening in the palate was further closed

I assure you, everything possible will be done to make this a smooth experience for Jill.

Klo;/ The Office of Wayne B. Slaughter, MD

Three surgeries by age three.

After almost sixty-five years, I remember my first trip to see Dr. Slaughter. I was around three when I started making regular treks to his office in the Pittsfield building on East Washington Street, close to Michigan Avenue and Lake Michigan. I stood gawking at the brass highlights on the building's exterior and tried to touch them, but my mother's white-gloved hand clasped mine as she tugged me back. "Let's go inside and wait for your father, okay?" she said. I suddenly felt the wind from Lake Michigan brush against my neck. When we went inside, I stared up at the ceiling, which was made out of some bright, shiny material that I learned later was coffered gilt. And then the most important man in my life appeared. "Daddy, Daddy," I cried out as he strolled through the lobby of this 1920s Chicago skyscraper and I ran across the marble floors toward him in my patent leather Mary Janes. The pretty building and the fact that Daddy accompanied me were the best part of these visits.

My speech—hampered by my cleft palate—was the other thing my parents wanted to fix. My mother shuttled me back and forth to a speech pathologist near St. Francis, a hospital near the Chicago-Evanston border where Dr. Slaughter had privileges. She liked to keep herself occupied, but I don't know what she did while I was there. She might have gone to the Junior League thrift shop where she volunteered. Throughout grade school, I also got pulled out of regular classes to join kids who needed help with their speech. During these sessions, I was awarded a black plastic flute to play that somehow helped me make the "s" sound without an accompanying nasal tone. I just thought it was cool to have this instrument. Nobody ever said anything about being unable to understand me and my friends seemed okay with my speech. But this shortcoming must have been a source of pain for my mother in particular. One day, she told me a story about a woman she called "That Ms. Miller," my kindergarten teacher. That Ms. Miller had the temerity to equate my taciturn behavior at school with the possibility "I didn't know how to talk." And my mother said, "Well, Jill talks just fine at home—and she talks a lot." My mother put Ms. Miller in her place and made herself feel better in the process.

Along with the speech lessons came braces. The shape of my palate made my lower jaw stick out, so braces for my teeth started at five. My mother wore her navy-blue tweed suit with the big blue buttons, and clasping my left hand in her white glove, took me aboard the "L" to the Loop. *Wow, it was like taking the train, only we were high above the ground.* She told me I could get finger paints afterwards if I didn't cry, and afterwards, I got the promised finger paints even though I cried. Nobody I knew had so many doctors. Lucky me! Well, maybe not so lucky in retrospect.

The betterment campaign acted as the Formula 409 shame cleanser in our household. Shame was a postwar era parenting tool that pediatrician Dr. Benjamin Spock was unlikely to have discussed in the baby and childcare bible sitting on our living room bookshelf. Future thought leader Brené Brown's denunciation of that word would take decades. My introduction to its subtleties were just beginning. I couldn't know then just how powerfully shame had seeped into the walls at home and into my parents' psyches—too deeply to be erased by any old cleaning agent.

At six, I began to run bases while older boys in our neighborhood played baseball and practiced hitting. When the bats came out, I ran across the street to the playground and eagerly stood in a line of like-minded kids (almost always boys) waiting to run the bases. Alternatively, I would go with my three-years-younger brother, John, and take turns throwing the ball against the exterior school wall while one of us stood with a bat on the shoulder waiting for the right pitch. One day, I was the pitcher and my wind-up went wild, the ball soaring and smashing one of the tall, second-floor windows of my elementary school. This was not good. I tried to play it cool when we went home, but John kept a better poker face. Dad asked me what was wrong. How did parents always know these things? The words about my mishap came tumbling out.

"What do we need to do, Jill?" my father asked.

"I don't know."

"Maybe we should go talk to Hank, hmm?" my father said. "The school is kind of like Hank's house."

Hank was the kindly janitor and he always seemed to be at school, even on weekends. I actually thought Hank lived there. I just knew Hank would be mad, but I didn't like that insistent look on my dad's face. He rarely expressed his displeasure with me and this was my first memory of being caught. Butterflies fluttering in my stomach. My dad's lesson was that I had to own up to my mistakes. That's what people were supposed to do. That's what Vannemans were supposed to do.

CHAPTER THREE

COOL LAKE BREEZES

THE SUMMER between my freshman and sophomore years of high school ramped up the betterment campaign by a notch. It was humid, as Evanston summers tend to be, but living two blocks off Lake Michigan brought us the cool lake breezes at night. We didn't have a view of the lake, but one of my father's friends had one of "those" houses on the lakefront—with a swimming pool and private beach too—if we were lucky enough to receive an invitation from the Bates. Usually, I went with a friend or a group to Lighthouse Beach, known for its famous huge landmark, Grosse Point lighthouse, built in 1873. We were less interested in lighthouses and more interested in lying on the sand for hours trying to work on our tans, accompanied by the smell of alewives. I wore a two-piece and tried not to compare myself to my skinnier friends. I spent hours trying to acquire a tan rather than a burn, no thanks to the fair skin gifted me by my Swedish ancestry. Somebody would have their transistor radio playing, and we'd lie there listening to the 5th Dimension harmonizing its classic, "Stoned Soul Picnic," or the Rolling Stones strumming "Jumpin' Jack Flash," or Herb Alpert crooning "This Guy's in Love with You." That June, Robert Kennedy was assassinated. We had all wanted him to win the presidency because he was so cute. Well, not everyone had wanted him to win. My parents clung to their staunch Republicanism.

It was during this summer that Dr. Slaughter reappeared in my life. I had last visited him when I was in junior high for some dental work. I had graduated from braces to a retainer that often had its own misadventures. One time at a movie, I took it out to eat popcorn and then I couldn't find it. When my friend Susie's mother came to pick us up, she found it tangled in my fisherman knit sweater. Speech correction class had stopped in junior high, and now my parents told me it was time for one more surgery: a cosmetic one to "straighten out my lip." To me, the word "cosmetic" sounded like no big deal. It was scheduled for the end of summer so I would have time to recuperate before going back to school.

I lay on the operating table, freezing, waiting for the gas mask and the familiar ether smell from my toddler days of cleft-lip-correction surgeries at St. Francis Hospital and the Pittsfield building. Instead of gas, the doctor proceeded to inject Novocain into my face. I was trying to be good, I really was, but after the first shot, tears began trickling from the corners of my closed eyes. They were closed because I couldn't watch the needle come down again and again, piercing into the tender skin around my nose and upper lip. I don't recall being knocked out, but the last thing I remember before waking up in the recovery room was a rubber mallet swooping toward my nose. Rather than waking up in a private room, I woke up in a bed on an open floor, and nobody from my family or the nursing staff was there. My mother was not there. Where was she? I felt sick to my stomach and I wanted my mother. She finally appeared.

"Where were you?" I demanded.

She seemed surprised by my question. "I've only just been told that you were awake. I came as soon as they told me I could see you."

Within a few minutes, Dr. Slaughter appeared. "Now, that wasn't so bad, was it?" he said.

Wanting to be the good girl I'd been trained to be, I shook my head, "no." Yet I cannot begin to describe the pain of those Novocain shots. Not tiny pinpricks but more like a thick sewing machine needle puncturing my face. Nobody had told me what to expect. I was just a fourteen-year-old girl, after all. Nobody had bothered explaining that they were going to break my nose to create more symmetry between the lateral halves of my upper lip. I spent several days in the hospital and went home with packing up my nose and deep, black-and-blue circles under my eyes. My parents noticed an "improvement" in my appearance and in my speech. I didn't. But then, I wasn't asked for my opinion.

I recuperated in the family den on the sofa watching TV for two weeks, covering my injured nose as I watched the Chicago police assault Vietnam War protesters during the Democratic National Convention thirty miles from my house. Years later, I learned that my corporate attorney father volunteered his services to the protesters at their bail hearings. My Republican corporate attorney dad was wearing that cape again. I knew he didn't agree with the protesters, but I'm sure he believed they deserved representation. I know that he certainly disagreed with the Democrats' and Mayor Daley's decision to violently quell the protests. My father was a peaceable man. He would never have condoned the use of force to stop people from speaking their minds. The strongest language I'd heard him use was the occasional "damn" when he hurt himself.

My father wasn't an autocratic leader. Yet in answering my own questions about my father and what kind of leader he was, I struggle at times. The most common remarks I heard from people he worked with on committees and in the political arena pointed to his fair-mindedness. "He ruled by consensus. He wanted every voice at the table," they said, along with, "you never knew where he stood on an issue," and, "he never expressed his own belief about an issue." I would never hear directly how he felt about my decision to live as an openly gay woman, either.

Dad's inscrutability was a constant in our household. The occasions he got mad could usually be attributed to his impatience. Once, he lectured me about my eating habits. My parents already liked to talk about my weight. When I asked for seconds at the table, for instance, it would prompt deep discussion. My brother loved these talks, because it took the heat off him and how he wasn't working hard enough at school. It's true—I liked to eat. In fact, my paternal grandmother Fern, whom I adored, told me at one point: "Jill, people eat to live. They don't live to eat."

Grandmother, Dad's mom, was a tiny woman, around five feet and constantly watching not only her weight but her husband's. He had formerly played center for the Illinois State football team and no longer got much exercise. She and I shared a fondness for Fannie May double-chocolate-cream-filled candies and sweet things in general. I suspect Dad might have picked up some of his mother's guilt about overeating, but I'm not sure why weight mattered so much to my mother.

I can still hear her asking why I was having seconds at dinner, or worse, her calling out from the living room, "Jill! What are you doing in the kitchen?"

My underarms would moisten, and I would hate myself and my parents at the same time. And it wasn't just her. My father in his kidding-but-not-kidding voice would ask about the potato chips on my sandwich plate. Diet Rite sodas populated our refrigerator. My brother could have Coke or Mountain Dew, but those remained off-limits for me.

The stairs from our basement exited into the kitchen, and one day when I was in the kitchen and had probably just snuck a cookie, I heard my mother interrogating me yet again as she made her way up from the basement.

I didn't think. I just reacted and yanked my arm back, my hand making a fist. As she reached the landing, I shot my arm forward as if to punch her, then momentarily withdrew, but couldn't draw back fast enough before my hand connected with my mother's stomach. She let out a cry that caused my father to come running.

He took one look at my mother's face and jerked my arm away. "Don't you ever touch your mother that way again!" It was a rare glimpse into my dad's fury.

Years later, after I had moved to Seattle, my mother called and asked the question she always did, "How's your weight?"

I didn't know where the words came from, but I replied, "I am an adult. I am thirty years old, and you don't ever get to ask me that question again." She followed my command but continued eyeing me up and down every time I got off the plane or she came to visit. And in that gaze—before she could tear her eyes away from my midsection—I knew what she was looking for.

I have never figured out why my weight caused such concern. But I had so internalized my parents' obsession that years later, when I looked back at photos of my younger self, I was shocked to find a relatively normal-sized me reflected back. I looked for other photos that told me the truth—my parents' truth—but I could not find them. Sure, I wasn't model-thin. Perhaps the goal of slimming me down was just another strategy in my parents' campaign.

Senior year ended and the move to Whitman College in Walla Walla, Washington—the birth-state my mother had ironically run away from—couldn't come soon enough. I spent the summer mapping out tour routes at the Chicago Motor Club, representing the American Auto Association in Evanston. After work one night, my mother asked me to pick up some fresh ribs from the meat market across the street. En route by simply running across the street I broke my fifth metatarsal—a bone in my pinkie toe. For six weeks, I wore a half-cast from my knee to that toe.

One day at work still recovering, an older woman came into the AAA and we made small talk for about twenty minutes while I put her maps together. Before turning to leave, she looked straight at me. "Oh," she said, "my granddaughter has one of those—you poor thing." I later realized she was commenting on my lip and not my cast. It threw me. I had gotten used to being around people who had known me since I was a small child. They knew my cleft lip was a part of me. I didn't even know it was open for discussion.

The prospect of leaving behind my place in Evanston, with its familiar habits and touchstones, didn't really occur to me. Whitman was calling. I yearned to shed the yoke of my do-gooder, community-minded parents. I wanted a fresh start where no one knew the Vanneman name. A good old-fashioned landline shared with a floor of eighteen girls would be the only connection to Evanston and my parents. I could mostly choose when I wanted to speak to them. Of course, they could call me. But long distance was expensive. I knew at most we would only talk once a week.

I took a United jet from Chicago to Spokane and changed planes to a twenty-seater bound for Walla Walla. Walking directly to Walla Walla's single luggage carousel was the first of many shocks. Clusters of clean-cut guys were standing around saying, "Hi, I'm a Teke," or "I'm a Phi Delt. Let me help you with your bags." One of those fraternity boys drove me to campus. I stared in disbelief as a tumbleweed rolled across the road in front of the car while passing the lackluster strip mall—a mall housing the thirty-one-flavor Baskin-Robbins that I would soon become intimate with. During the twenty-mile-or-so drive east of the airport, we passed through a dry, undeveloped landscape. The town itself featured charming, turn-of-the-century houses. But Walla Walla in the '70s was not yet known for its vineyards but rather its prodigious wheat crops and farmers who drove Cadillacs. A trip to a small café called the Red Apple to get a chocolate sundae would rank as the height of excitement. The "Whitman experience" had begun, but I was already gauging the fit between my "sophisticated" Chicago suburban self and this rural town where going to the DQ was a treat.

I really liked my freshman roommate, Denny, who had sparkling blue eyes and long straight auburn hair. She was from Boise and I was impressed that her dad was an Idaho Supreme Court judge. I soon settled into the thrill of being away from home and making new friends. Friends who couldn't give a fig about my last name or my parents' choices. I hadn't been there even a month when I received a letter from my dad. He gave a snapshot of what was going on at home and then he wrote the following:

"What does one say to his only daughter and first-born child when she leaves the nest? The answer seems to be very little. I was unprepared for the emotion I felt in finally realizing that you had departed. On the other hand, we have been so proud of your work and responsibility and your general self-sufficiency that we could only look forward with anticipation to watching your progress during the next four years."

I had longed to hear these words from both of my parents for so long. I remembered sitting in Dad's lap the night before I'd left—something I hadn't done since I was a young child—and him saying nothing, though I could sense his emotions then. Later that night, my mother, who'd been sitting across from us, said, "I was almost jealous of you . . . seeing you in your father's lap." Odd words to your child who is soon to leave the nest. Perhaps my mother was sad to see me go, but if she was, she saw no need to tell me so.

CHAPTER FOUR

LESLIE

WHEN MY mother blurted out those words in the car about never liking Leslie, she caught me by surprise. I wouldn't have admitted this out loud, but I was still trying to figure out what that relationship had been about. Had I been taken by a scam artist? Was I merely a victim of inexperience? College trailed so far behind me by the time I came out to my parents in the car, I no longer obsessed about Leslie twenty-four-seven. That's what I was telling myself at twenty-six. When you're five years out of college, you feel like you've put your childish first love behind—or so I thought.

Leaving suburban Chicago for the wheat fields and one-movie-theater town of Walla Walla required some cultural adjustment in my freshman year. I settled in and surprised myself by joining a sorority. During the early 1970s, however, the Greek system saw little action at most colleges and universities. Outside Walla Walla, my sophisticated peers spurned the relic social groups their parents had belonged to. They preferred to be independent. But Whitman was isolated from the national politics splayed across the front pages of US newspapers. We saw no anti-Vietnam protests and were offered no feminist or Black studies classes, and certainly none in gay studies. When President Nixon made a brief stop at the Walla Walla airport, the Whitman football team presented him with a football. I doubt that would have happened at Northwestern or the University of Washington, where they were more likely to protest Nixon's mere presence. In Walla Walla, '70s college life was just a continuation of the '60s. Only the clothes and music were different. Instead of the Beach Boys, we had groups like America and the Carpenters on our turntables and jeans replaced dresses for women. Whitman went on as it always had, churning out future engineers, lawyers, and doctors, seemingly unaffected by world forces.

Even the dorm I lived in my sophomore year seemed a relic, ever immune from societal change. The all-women's dorm of Prentiss Hall had been that way forever. Built in 1926, it was an attractive, red brick, neoclassical building with ornate doorways denoting each of the sorority entrances. In an earlier time, men arrived to pick up their dates after they were called downstairs via intercom. A tempered last kiss could only happen on the porch before the eleven o'clock curfew. In 1972, the dorm still had an actual Ernestine, a paid student who—much like the brash phone operator comedian Lily Tomlin impersonated—was responsible for making phone connections for each sorority by plugging lines into the correct numbers.

At first, I really enjoyed being a Tri Delta. I became popular in a way I hadn't been since elementary school, and many of my sorority sisters seemed to find me interesting and a willing listener. I relished sitting in the living room eating popcorn with them or walking down to Pizza Pete's on Issacs Avenue. I even learned how to bake my first apple pie with my friend Bev. I finally belonged somewhere and was accepted for being me. I didn't have to deal with friends who believed they had outgrown me but still carpooled with me, but otherwise snubbed me. And, I didn't feel the strictures of my privileged background. None of my new friends knew anything about that. I thought I'd assuaged my need for that special, best friend—that is, until I met Leslie.

I first met Leslie at sorority rush, a system of recruitment I now see as barbaric in attracting "just the right girls" to join a particular sorority and making them feel lucky to be asked. Rush offers a series of parties with different themes that allow the sorority to get to know you—and vice versa—to see whether you'll be a "fit." I chose the Tri Delts, because we played touch football at their "activity" party. I liked athletics and growing up, I'd identified as a tomboy, whereas the Delta Gammas, for instance, seemed more interested in physical appearances. But the sororities were really just cliques. Campus housed six sororities, and seventy percent of the student population belonged to a sorority or fraternity.

Leslie entered my life in the fall of 1972 on a Saturday, two weeks before I was to start my sophomore year. I arrived at Mrs. Ringhoffer's large, two-story, Tudor home in my powder-blue, mid-calf-length dress. Mrs. Ringhoffer was a Whitman music professor who also happened to be an alumna of the Tri Delt sorority and was hosting us for rush week. She'd prepared a formal tea service and laid out her best silver and crystal. Her stylish living room had a shiny, black grand piano as its focal point.

The freshman and transfer student candidates would be arriving soon to be paired up with one of the existing Tri Delt sisters. Leslie was assigned to be my sorority "date," the girl I was to spend the afternoon with in Mrs. Ringhoffer's living room. We'd received pictures of our assigned girls so I knew who Leslie was the moment she walked through the door. She was wearing a pastel pink dress with lace around the hem.

I walked up to her with butterflies flitting in my stomach. I knew it would be my job to maintain her interest in the Tri Delts by keeping the small talk going for two hours. "Hi, Leslie?" I proffered. "My name is Jill. I'm your date for the day." Leslie didn't meet my eyes but looked down and nodded her head slightly. "Hi." She spoke just above a whisper.

"Come on in. Can I get you something to drink or eat?" I gestured to the interior of the sitting room. She followed me in and we settled into a pair of folding chairs scattered around the room. We talked for a few minutes and I noticed her southern accent. "Where are you from?"

"Well, I'm originally from Alabama," she said. "But I spent my high school years in southern California."

"How are you feeling about rush?"

"I'm nervous," she admitted. "But I'm excited for school. Last year I was in *The Music Man* and I can't wait to try out for this year's musical at Whitman."

We talked about our shared love of musicals, and as we did, my previously subdued date grew animated—to the point where I worried that the delicate balance of Leslie's tea cup and plate of dainty cookies would spill on Mrs. Ringhoffer's pristine white rug. Leslie kept pushing her dishwater blonde hair back behind her ear so it wouldn't fall in her tea or brush against her plate of food. Her plate shook sometimes. I could see she was nervous. I felt the urge to reach out and pat her on the arm, to help her understand she wasn't the only outsider here, to reassure her that it was normal to be nervous. I had an overwhelming empathy for her because of my own loneliness through my high school years.

In her slight southern drawl, she said, "Why did you choose to come two thousand miles to go to Whitman?"

Everyone asked me that. "They had to fill their state quota," I joked. In its promotional literature, Whitman touted having students from thirty-five states. They weren't just some provincial, Pacific Northwest school. I was the one student from Illinois. "We have lots of people from California," I said. I tried to make her feel more at ease, but I'm not sure I succeeded. She would go on to other parties with the Tri Delts, but during the bidding process, my opinion was one of three that would carry the most weight. Leslie did end up getting voted in, but just barely. Somebody opined that she didn't seem sufficiently outgoing. "We can't all be rah-rah," I said. "We need some introverts." Another sister thought she was overwrought. And then Becky, one of the other sophomore Tri Delts, spoke up. "I went to high school with her. She was involved in drama and ran with the theater crowd. She'll be fine. I think we should vote to give her a bid."

"I agree with Becky. Let's give her a chance," I said.

I remember thinking at the time that Leslie wasn't so much painfully shy; she just seemed to wear her friendlessness on her sleeve: "Please select me, because no other sorority will." The way she kept her head down during the tea, barely looking at me when we weren't talking about musicals, made me think she was terribly insecure. I related to her insecurity and felt sorry for her. I would continue to feel sorry for Leslie throughout the rest of my "Whitman experience"—to my regret.

In contrast to the political fervor of other campuses and the relative calm on our campus and contrary to my initial perceptions, Leslie soon seemed hell-bent on creating a maelstrom. From the day she moved into the dorm's Tri Delt section, she expressed a seemingly nonstop hysteria, something more than the usual freshman jitters. Meltdowns and emotional overspill accompanied everything from her fear of not getting into Acting 101 to auditioning for the first theater production of the season. She didn't get a part in *The Corn Is Green* but she demonstrated great talents as an undeclared drama major offstage rather than on. Her personal dramas forced others to pay attention.

I would often find Leslie on the horrid, floral-patterned couch in the main hallway next to the bathroom. She liked to sit with her knees underneath her and splayed out to the side. She often wore a paisley scarf to keep her hair out of her face and a bright yellow T-shirt. Her voice was a high-pitched southern drawl, and loud. You couldn't avoid her, although many of my sorority sisters tried. I spoke to her briefly in passing. I marveled at the transformation from this shy person I'd first met at the rush tea.

She wore her clothes haphazardly, as if at the last minute she'd remembered she couldn't go to class wearing her fuzzy blue bathrobe. Her uniform was typically a large T-shirt covering her plump breasts and torso paired with snug, flared blue jeans. Occasionally she branched out to more feminine attire: powder-blue knit pants and a flowery blouse over a brightly colored T-shirt. On first contact, her overt emotions and neediness made me recoil. When she didn't get the part in the play, she cried out on the couch—in public. I was amazed she was so open with her emotions. But perhaps her neediness was like a radar for my own: my need for a special someone—not a romantic someone, just a close friendship—such as the ones I'd had in high school. Falling in love never occurred to me.

During the second half of my sophomore year, Leslie began sharing a room with me and my other roommate, Julie. I don't recall Julie and me particularly wanting that arrangement, but we did have another bed on offer. Our room was the only triple and consisted of an inner and an outer room. One room had three desks for studying and the other had one bunk bed and one single bed. The three of us agreed to switch beds on a rotating basis so that everyone got a chance at the choice single bed.

One Saturday night, Julie was out on a date and I was halfheartedly studying when I heard a low moan in the other room through the closed bedroom door. The moaning grew louder and I could no longer pretend to study. I knocked on the door. "Go away," Leslie said in a pathetic, sobby little voice. "I'm sorry I bothered you." But I couldn't do that and went in to find Leslie in the bottom bunk with the blankets pulled up over her head.

"What's wrong?" I said.

"Go away," she told me. But I was curious and concerned about her tears. She rolled on her side away from me.

"Come on," I said. "It might feel better to talk to someone."

"No, it won't," she persisted as she continued to cry. I was going to leave, but I then noticed she seemed to have her fist jammed in her mouth. *What on earth?* I thought. It wasn't in my nature to avoid others' pain. Throughout my school years, I seemed to instinctively recognize the new kid. I sought them out and extended my friendship. I understood the hurt of peers walking away. I felt compelled to comfort Leslie. I pulled the covers back to see her tear-streaked face and a hand indeed clamped inside her mouth.

"Please take your hand out of your mouth so I can talk to you," I said. She shook her head. I gently pulled on her hand to get her mouth to release it. What came out of her mouth was a hand with a precise sprinkling of teeth marks. Surprised, I released her hand. "Jesus Christ, Leslie! What are you doing?" *Whatever was ailing her must really hurt to make her want to add to her pain.* Years later, I wondered if she had been biting her hand before I came in or whether she'd done so afterwards to further get my attention.

"What on earth is wrong? Are you okay?"

Her eyes flinched as she vaguely pointed to her stomach. "It's my stomach," she said with a gasp. "I get this cramping."

"Should I call somebody like the RA?" I said. The resident assistant was the person responsible for students' well-being on our floor. Even though it was a Saturday night, and nobody was around, I wanted to get Leslie help or get her to the doctor. Leslie adamantly shook her head "no," and whimpered, "I'm scared." She stuck her hand back in her mouth, continuing to refuse outside offers of help. That should have been a clue. But I totally missed it. I volunteered to stay with her. These pains were Leslie's hook to get my attention and I grabbed for it with all I had. I didn't really understand my motivations, and I still don't. Perhaps responding to Leslie's need gave me a sense of power: I could help this poor girl. I could not only give her friendship, but I could give her release from this awful pain inside her. Perhaps I could help her feel less shy and awkward and help my friends see that her need for attention came from insecurity. Aside from my other roommate Julie, another sophomore Tri Delt, my fellow sisters seemed to avoid her. Julie hailed, with her guitar and songwriting prowess, from Los Angeles and she and Leslie bonded over their southern California roots. Julie's main preoccupation however was in how to get a boyfriend.

Looking back now I wonder if Leslie knew that I was the one who needed attention. During my last semester of high school, I was particularly lonely. My two best friends now had boyfriends and no time for me. That semester, my dad ran for and became mayor of Evanston for the first of two terms. It was a part-time job, but he treated it like a full-time, second job. My mother became "Mrs. Mayor"—which she abhorred while at the same time she loved being my father's political confidante. On top of her community activities and golf, she was now laser-focused on Evanston politics. In my mid-level popularity status circle of friends, everyone seemed to be paired off with a guy or trying to achieve that state.

I spotted Leslie's frequent trips to the bathroom. While I didn't see her put a finger in her mouth to purge, I did wonder years later if she had been bulimic. Her behavior elicited everyone's reluctant focus. My friends didn't believe her stories and tried to avoid her. They couldn't understand why I was friends with her. But those blue eyes of hers had a haunting look that first drew me in, much like an animal in deep physical and psychic pain. I was happy to play Sir Lancelot to Leslie's Guinevere. It made me feel important.

Our roommate Julie seemed oblivious to Leslie's pain. Around Julie, Leslie's behavior veered toward normal. I believe now that Leslie saved her pain for me. Curiously, I didn't speak to anyone else about Leslie's pain. It was special, just for me. I also thought nobody would believe me or care.

The sorority sisters would often congregate around the couches in the living area to socialize while waiting to go down to dinner or after dinner. Leslie often sat on the couch across from me. Frequently, while she was sitting there after dinner—or so it seemed—Leslie would experience this ambiguous, inexplicable pain and look at me with pleading eyes that begged me to follow her to our room. It wasn't a sexual look, at least not for me. I was not sexually attracted to Leslie. It just felt good to be needed. Sometimes, I tried to avoid her gaze, because I was enjoying my conversation with friends in the living room. But often, I couldn't resist. I was then happy to follow her, grab a chair, and hold her hand beside her bed so that she wouldn't try biting it to soothe herself. I would hold her hand until her arm relaxed and she appeared to fall asleep. Only then, would I leave her. That became our pattern.

I would often fall asleep in the chair next to her bed. She told me that she was on dialysis, but that it didn't do much for the pain. Several months later, I realized I never saw or heard her say she was going to dialysis. Yet I soon found that I couldn't do anything with anybody else, because what if Leslie needed me and I wasn't there? Over time, I became distracted from my studies, and began to forget about my other friends. Leslie appeared frequently in my letters to my parents, but in reference to our activities and not about her constant pain or my need for her friendship. This "mutual need society" did not go unnoticed by my fellow sorority sisters. Some tried to warn me—"Leslie's not good for you; you'd better be careful"—or even threatened to stop being friends with me if I didn't sever my ties with Leslie. But I couldn't pull myself away.

My junior year, I began avoiding seeing or talking to Leslie. I even tried moving into another dorm. I would see her trudge by in her green winter parka when the icy winds of winter came to Walla Walla, and my stomach would lurch from the clear sense of absence in my life. I knew I was hurting her with my childish snubs, and when I looked in her eyes, I saw bewilderment mixed with hurt. I attributed mistreating Leslie to my willingness to bow to my other Tri Delt friends' warnings about "Leslie not being good for me." I'm not sure what they meant, but I knew they didn't like Leslie. Every look from Leslie across the chapter room or while I was upstairs eating popcorn with the other girls, however, would melt my resolve. How could I treat my best friend this way? My grades went up that semester and I made new, non-Tri Delt friends. But I couldn't leave Leslie alone. She made me feel good about myself and my presence seemed equally important to her. I hadn't experienced the same intensity in previous friendships. My friends in junior high and high school were more socially advanced with fewer parental boundaries. They seemed to move on to the next developmental level and leave me behind. Instead, I spent many hours in my dorm room alone with my guitar pouring my heart and soul into learning the songs of Judy Collins, Joan Baez, and Peter, Paul and Mary. Music became my solace.

One day after Christmas break of my junior year, Leslie looked at me across the chapter living room and I just knew I needed to reconnect. She lured me like a drug. I couldn't stay away from her and we became inseparable. We wrote notes to each other, pumped each other up when one of us was down, and ate almost all of our meals together. When I didn't see her come into the dining hall, I was disappointed. I played songs on my guitar for her and she seemed to enjoy it. The new musical *Godspell* was popular and she loved the song "By My Side?" I taught myself how to play the song, practiced it over and over again, and presented it to her as a gift. She blushed when she expressed her pleasure. There was a line about taking a hand for it needed comfort which conveyed what I wanted from Leslie. I wanted to walk with her and talk with her and be by her side. The song encapsulated all of my longing. Not sexual longing, but a longing to belong to someone.

All the while, I never felt anything more than a deep, emotional intimacy. We sent cards to each other that quoted others such as Rod McKuen or *The Little Prince* or lines of free verse from publications printed by Blue Mountain Arts. I was fond of *Gift from the Sea* by Anne Morrow Lindbergh, the book my mother had given to me. I quoted lines that talked about loving someone but not all the time or in exactly the same way. Love was something that ebbed and flowed, Lindbergh wrote. To me, love was some sort of aspirational feeling that did not involve sex. I don't think I even realized that I was falling in love with Leslie.

During one of our month-long Christmas breaks, she sent me a card from home expressing her efforts to be such a brave, big girl. She was in the hospital again for another Christmas and the whole "show," she wrote, had been hard to carry. "Show" meant being in the hospital, I guess. *Was everything a show for drama major Leslie?* She hadn't even told me she was going to be in the hospital or had been in the hospital for other Christmases. She thanked me for a book I had given her and then said the best Christmas gift I could give her was "your smile, your laugh, and your friendship." Another short note she sent read "You made flowers of my hours. Today was a bouquet." My heart sang: she cared about me the way I cared about her.

After we rekindled our friendship in the second half of my junior year, I frequently ended up in Leslie's room. We usually went up there to study or talk after dinner. She now had a single room, because no one wanted to room with her. And while her notes were mostly thanking me for my friendship or encouraging me about studying for majors and writing my thesis, I sensed a strong, emotional undertone. Neither of us ever proclaimed our love, per se. But I knew the bond was mutual.

Leslie liked to study on her bed, a position I found uncomfortable. Her books were spread out and she propped up her head while talking to me. One day, I was sitting in the chair at her desk but had turned around in response to a familiar, moaning sound.

"What, what?" I said. "Not again. This must be so awful for you." She nodded and pinched her eyes shut. She rammed her hand in her mouth as she had on the first night. This move was as seductive as slow dancing with a lover on the dance floor. I hadn't known that sensation yet, that pull that turned my insides to mush. I felt it at that moment and my heart dissolved. Neither of us spoke, her pain seemed to fill the room and me. I went to her, sitting down by her on the bed and holding her hand to comfort her. I found myself clearing her bed and helping her settle. Then I waited until I thought she was asleep before helping myself into her bed. I guess I was afraid that she would say no, and I didn't want her to say no. When I crawled in next to her, I felt a barely perceptible shift as her body moved over to accommodate me.

What happened next seemed to occur from a great distance. I felt as if I was watching my hands move all over her body, tracing and caressing each curve through her nightgown. I didn't kiss her. I thought that, like Sleeping Beauty, she would awaken if I kissed her. I felt her body respond as I cupped her orange-sized breasts. She seemed to move, involuntarily, and she didn't pull away. If she, in any way, had said "stop!" or forcefully moved away, I would have stopped. But she didn't do that. Instead, she barely moved while my hands continued to trace imaginary lines down and around her stomach. I reached her pubic area and discovered she wore underpants to bed under her gauzy, flower-covered nightgown. I wondered what would happen if I touched her over her underpants. I began to caress her pubic area through her panties, and again, her body seemed to respond in some imperceptible way. She opened her lips and I heard a soft sigh escape. I felt a moistening as I rubbed that area and felt the same moistening between my legs, even though she was doing nothing to me. I didn't even know what I was doing, because I had never been in this situation before with a boy or a girl. I wondered to myself how I knew what to do. Whether I was doing it right or wrong didn't seem to matter. I knew I shouldn't stay. I stayed as late as I dared, then quietly left.

I was excited, ashamed, and scared—all at the same time. What had I done? Would Leslie be okay with what I had done? I thought I was expressing my love. Would she see it that way? The rest of the night in my own bed, I worried while also feeling exhilarated.

The next morning, I awoke exhausted, wondering if I had imagined the previous night. *Did that really happen?* I wondered as shame flushed my face. I got dressed in a daze and walked to Leslie's room. I hesitated outside her door before knocking. My nerves were jittery as though I'd already had three cups of coffee. I finally knocked when she told me to come in. "Do . . . do you want to eat breakfast with me?" I said. Leslie fixed me with her heavy lidded, still sleepy eyes and flushed face. "What were you doing last night?" she said. My heart stopped as I tried to think of how to respond. This was a point of no return for us, and we knew it. We couldn't admit that we loved each other in a sexual way, because what would that make us? Something abnormal. I had no role models to base my actions on. I didn't know if Leslie had any, either.

I sucked in my breath, felt my face go warm, and said, "Nothing. I wasn't doing anything." We never talked about it again. But the foreplay continued—not every night, but often enough. And Leslie continued to pretend she was asleep. We couldn't talk about this because—I assume—we were both scared to death. If we admitted what we were doing, what would the other sorority sisters say? I had never heard the word "homosexual" in high school, and my absence of knowledge probably convinced me that others would not approve of or condone what we were doing.

For me, nothing mattered but reliving those poignant, excised moments on a regular basis, savoring the dark quiet of Leslie's bedroom before I fell asleep at night in her bed. During that time, I came to know that my feelings were like none I'd ever had for any boy, or any girl, either. That I was in love with another female was something I didn't want to examine too closely. The replay always ended the same way—with the unreadable look on Leslie's face as I said, "Nothing, nothing happened last night." She didn't believe me. But she didn't tell me to stop, either.

The next Christmas, she came on a planned visit from southern California to Evanston to hang out and to meet my parents. I wanted them to meet this friend whom I'd written so much about. My usually charming father was hospitable, but my mother seemed wary and unfriendly. She would speak to Leslie in short, clipped tones and didn't ask her many questions. She probably asked her what on earth she was going to do with her theater major, but the conversation held no warmth. "Isn't she wonderful?" I gushed after Leslie's visit was over. My mother's reaction was tepid at best. She may have even said she wasn't that impressed.

Always an outsider—for as long as I could remember, really—I didn't mind the idea of being different, even in terms of my apparent attraction to a woman. I just wasn't sure if my attraction was a one-time thing or if this occurrence was telling me this is who I really was. I guess I was just a little unnerved by the possibility of being so markedly different from the person I'd always thought I was. I had never thought of myself as anything other than straight. I didn't know about same-sex relationships. I had never even heard the word "straight," except as applied to a line or an edge.

I now found myself up in the psychology stacks of Penrose Library looking up abstracts about homosexuality when I should have been up in American history, collecting abstracts about the progressive southern historian Comer Vann Woodward, who was the subject of my senior thesis. Woodward wrote broadly about the topics of southern history, populism, and race relations between the 1930s and his death in 1999. He looked at the historian's job as one of storytelling; one of the reasons I was so attracted to history and had chosen it as my college major. Woodward is probably best known for his book *The Strange Career of Jim Crow*.

But no, I was not focusing on this major project but odd psychology abstracts that mostly talked about gay men. I sat cross-legged in the stacks reading, because I didn't dare take these abstracts back to my study carrel where someone might see them. Only one abstract mentioned women loving women. Did that mean there weren't that many of us? Or just that we didn't matter? Although I had gone with a freshman dorm mate and her gay male friend to Shelly's Leg, the Seattle gay bar underneath the viaduct, I didn't think this word applied to me. What I read made me leery about identifying myself as a homosexual. But I was beginning to see the ways in which this word *might* apply to me. I was worried, therefore, since the literature made living openly as a gay woman sound like an unhappy experience. "These women tend to be mannish in appearance and have multiple, serial, monogamous relationships," one journal intoned. But I went on kidding myself.

Maybe I wasn't one. Maybe my relationship with Leslie was just an intense, schoolgirl crush.

Leslie continued to send me notes that extolled my wonderfulness and how she didn't deserve me. Surely, she knew we were having sex, but we never talked about it—and she never woke from her feigned sleep. Instead, the lies kept falling out of her mouth, like fish bait. Although she said she was on dialysis, she never went anywhere to access it. She had those mysterious surgeries during summer and Christmas breaks. The only time she seemed to acknowledge the physical side of our relationship occurred one spring break when we traveled down to southern California together. We shared a bed in a motel room. She didn't protest the absence of a second bed. Rather, she showed no compunction about us sharing the bed and even seemed to encourage it.

Another time, she said she had asked this guy Tom to the pledge dance, an annual sorority dance where women did the asking, allowing those of us who didn't normally date access to the field of allegedly desirable men. Tom was a blue-eyed, hunky tennis player I had my eye on and was working up the nerve to ask to the dance. I had never really spoken to him except as part of the women's tennis team. But here Leslie was, telling me she had asked him even though she knew I was planning to ask him.

For once, I didn't believe her. I didn't want to believe she could do this to me. So, I worked up the courage to ask Tom to the dance, and he said yes. Then I asked if my good friend Leslie had asked him and he said, "Who is that?" I'd finally caught her in a lie. *Why? Why would she do that to me?* I decided to confront her in her room. I was sitting on her bed and she was on the floor, sitting at my feet. "You don't even know him," I said. "You knew I wanted to ask him. I'd been talking about it for a week."

"I'm so sorry, Jill," she said. "I don't know why I said that. I'm not worthy of you." I felt confused but strangely vindicated by this forced apology.

"I don't know why you did that, either," I said. She began to cry, her bosom heaving and shoulders shaking. My heart melted. I, the "great benefactress," gave a maternal "disappointed in you" speech and ended it by saying, "I forgive you." I never did hear why she did it. We then continued our game of pretend in the bedroom.

During one of those nights in Leslie's room, Leslie seemed to be in so much pain that I called the dean of women students and the dean came to her room. Magically, Leslie's pain disappeared, and Leslie, using all of her dramatic skills, convinced the dean that I was mistaken. I stared in amazement as she convincingly delivered this message. All of Leslie's acting talent was better suited to our melodramatic interludes than it was for her never-ending auditions. Her playacting was superb. I even called her mother. But when I asked her about Leslie's continuing pain she said, "Oh, you mean those cramps she gets?"

"No, no . . . what about the dialysis?" I said.

"What dialysis?" her mother replied, and I began to wonder about everything Leslie was telling me.

She kept a powerful hold on me. People continued to notice and comment on my whirling around Leslie's orbit, although I did not. I noticed, however, that as the comments from friends dwindled, so too did their requests to spend time with me. I had originally thought of my friendship with Leslie as a sort of community service project. Through my popularity in freshman year, I'd thought I could persuade the other sorority sisters that Leslie was likable. My project was not turning out as envisioned. Leslie gained few admirers, while our exclusivity probably made matters worse. But it wasn't until long after my 1975 graduation—when I left Leslie to complete her senior year—that the significance of this relationship struck me broadside.

Four months after graduating, I sat at the built-in, '50s-style kitchen nook in my uncle's one-bedroom house in West Seattle. I missed Leslie—deeply and painfully. I was not in graduate school pursuing journalism as I had wanted, but rather trying to figure out what was next in my life. I had relied on a college adviser who claimed that a good liberal arts degree would set me up for graduate school. I'd started researching graduate schools in April of my senior year. May was far too late, but I had been busy fooling around with Leslie. That's when I found out that most journalism graduate schools wanted you to have a bachelor's in journalism. Rather than fretting about my education, I sat at the kitchen nook with my trusty, sixteenth-birthday, Smith Corona electric typewriter churning out resumes to try to land a job as a paralegal. The phone rang.

"Hi, Jill," said an almost inaudible voice. But, of course, I recognized the voice. I had been waiting to hear it for weeks. I so desired her presence I could almost smell the cloying White Shoulders perfume she favored.

"Well, I didn't want to call. But my dad made me."

Those words made me sit up. "What happened?" I said, my chest tightening around my heart. I was supposed to go down to Walla Walla in six weeks for homecoming. I was afraid she was calling to cancel our visit.

"Well," she said, "the second week of school, the regional Tri Delt rep flew in from Boise and summoned me to a local hotel basement."

"Okay," I said, totally confused about where she was going. For the regional Northwest Chair of the Tri Delts to come from Idaho was unusual. A moral breach in the code of conduct would have to have occurred. *Why was Leslie involved?*

"They asked me a lot of questions. For about two hours."

"Who else was there?" I said but didn't get an answer. "About what?" I continued.

"About us. And about sex."

I sat down on the floor with the phone pressed tightly against my ear.

"Oh, my god," I said.

The sorority had kicked her out because of her "lesbian relationship" with me. The evidence: other Tri Delt sisters' testimony. They claimed to have seen us do sex acts in all manner of public places—something that had never occurred. Leslie relayed all of this in a flat, unemotional voice. The tone of her voice alone surprised me. She didn't cry, she didn't sound angry, she just sounded flat—like a balloon bereft of air.

"I'll be down there today," I said, my blood boiling. They couldn't do that to her. She'd been asleep when I was touching her. I got on my knees and peered around the corner to make sure my uncle wasn't in earshot, and then I raised my voice just a little. “Leslie, I won’t stand for this! I’m coming to Walla Walla immediately to give them a piece of my mind.”

Leslie discouraged my valiant cries. I thought, *yeah, my actions might make matters worse*—although I desperately wanted to ride my steed down there to defend Leslie’s honor, throwing myself at the inquisitors’ feet if necessary. In the end, I couldn’t keep myself away. Six weeks later, in mid-October, I made the long, lonely drive down to Walla Walla. The radio was on and as the miles went by, my tears flowed to the hit song “Feelings” and perked up at Helen Reddy’s “I Am Woman.” I was not sure what I would find when I arrived. But I did not expect to be ignored.

Once I spotted Leslie on campus, I watched her stride across the lawn through the maple and cottonwood trees while I trailed behind, imploring her to speak with me. When I tried to catch up with her, she would only walk faster. She didn’t say she was mad; she just wouldn’t talk to me. Later that night, she finally relented. As we got farther away from campus, she slowed down. “What’s wrong?” I said. “Why won’t you talk to me?”

“What are you doing down here?” she almost hissed at me. “Why did you come?”

“What do you mean, ‘why did I come?’ I was concerned about you. You didn’t call me for six weeks after you told me. You never bothered to give me your number. I didn’t even know whether you were living on or off campus.”

“I don’t want to talk to you. But you can come in.” We were finally at her off-campus room and maybe she felt she owed me since I had driven five hours to talk to her.

I tried again. "Tell me what happened. Why did they kick you out of the sorority?"

Finally, she spoke. "I really don't want to talk about it." She had turned on the stereo and we just sat and listened to Billy Joel's album *Piano Man.* I remembered his song "If I Only Had the Words (to Tell You)." He didn't have the words and neither did I. When she refused to talk, I suddenly felt slammed into a cold, miserable room by myself. It occurred to me Leslie was prepared to shut me out indefinitely. *How could she switch off her need for me—just like that?* When I could not take another minute of her rebuff, I said, "What about all that happened with us?"

I didn't mention the sexual nature of our relationship, and Leslie refused to get into specifics as well. But what she did say in her veiled response was that "If it happened, it will never happen again!" She made this pronouncement on a Friday night and wouldn't see or speak to me for the rest of the weekend. I returned to Seattle, never to speak with Leslie again. It was as though our relationship had never happened. But in my heart, I knew what we'd had, and that all those months of whispered conversations and my reassurances and caretaking and even the reciprocal nature of our unspoken lovemaking had shattered into something unrecognizable—broken in pieces like one of my mother's finely detailed, beloved, Wedgwood china cups. Our love was so fragmented that each of the splintered pieces would represent for me a year of recovery.

Leslie froze me out and I still wanted to know why. I kept alive the possibility that one day she would call me out of the blue or appear at my door, that one day she would admit to our mutual attraction. *How could she pretend I didn't exist? As though our time together deserved to be erased, or—worse—languish forever inside me. That I would simply have to add this experience to my growing heap of shame and self-disgust.*

Devastated and depressed by Leslie's withdrawal, I finally called the only supportive people in my life: my parents. Somehow, I knew I couldn't tell my parents the whole truth, but I felt like I needed huge transfusions of love and support from them. I mean, they were my parents. Wasn't that their job?

I waited until my aunt and uncle left on some errand and nervously called my parents' number. How could I communicate my devastation without admitting the physical side of my relationship with Leslie?

My mother answered. "Mom, something has happened and I'm not doing so well," I said.

"Wait," she said. "Let me get your father on the line too." While I waited, I sucked in my breath.

"You remember Leslie, right?" I said once I heard my father clear his throat. "Some sorority people mistook our bond for something else. I really liked Leslie and we developed this intense friendship. But it's gone so terribly wrong and I don't know what to do. She's been kicked out of the sorority."

I heard a long pause while I waited for their response. Dad spoke first. "It's not that uncommon, Jill, that people have these mild infatuations with friends." Dad hadn't really understood my relationship with Leslie, but I had no desire to share the details. I intuitively knew this information would not go down well. I was glad he thought my interest had just been "mild." During the phone conversation, I wasn't even sure what my relationship with Leslie had been—except . . . complicated.

"You just need to try to move forward, Jill," Dad said.

"Yes." My mother readily agreed. "Friends come and go. Stay focused on trying to get a job." *They don't get it*, I thought, *but why would they when I haven't shared all the details?*

I would later receive a letter from my mother. "I'm not knocking your introspection," she wrote, "but I am saying you can psych yourself up or down, analyze forwards and backward, but onward and forward is THE GOAL!" Her capital letters, not mine. She carried on in this vein. "What's done is done. FINIS." Mom seemed relieved that Leslie was out of my life.

Perhaps she wanted to console me with the words that appeared further along in the letter: "Everybody has up and down times and wishing (sic) they had done it differently." She wrote about my generation, with all of its "love and peace and all that had made it so black and white, i.e., if you don't love, you hate." She went on to declare that each of us carried an element of heterosexuality and homosexuality. All these thoughts she'd carefully written in a letter she said she'd completed in the Ladies' room at Marshall Field's after a dental appointment in the Loop. The Ladies' room had an elegant sitting room and I could imagine her crafting these pearls of wisdom there. None of these pearls helped. I felt lonely and terribly misunderstood.

My father had also written along the same lines, claiming most people, from time to time, tended toward homosexuality and risked letting their feelings "get out of hand." He urged me to move on, while commending "your ability to identify and recognize your problems."

But five years after my anguish over losing Leslie, those "problems"—as my parents called them—could no longer be categorized as mistakes. They were a reality, now that I had told them that I was gay and owning that homosexual part of me. When my parents were confronted with these facts, much like Leslie, they did not want to deal with them or even acknowledge the existence of our relationship.

•

CHAPTER FIVE

FOOTPRINTS

DURING MY senior year of infatuation with Leslie—and months before the Tri Delts kicked her out—I somehow forgot that after Whitman I had no concrete plan. Scratch that: I did have a plan. There was just no concrete in it. The future involved Leslie, somehow, but that part of my future was vague. I just knew we would live together after she graduated—either in Seattle or L.A. Leslie was a year behind me and still had a whole year of Whitman to finish. I didn't want to live in Walla Walla and just wait for her. Somehow, I had forgotten to take the next steps, whatever they were. I had talked about going to graduate school in journalism, but it wasn't until May of my senior year that I realized I had forgotten to apply. My parents had not once asked me what was next after Whitman. Looking back, I find that odd. They had been so involved in my life, suggesting things and laying out expectations. But everything was quiet back there on the Midwestern front.

Until my mother called. "We're looking forward to graduation and then going to Seattle afterwards to visit Len and Rita. Then we have reservations at Salishan Lodge on the Oregon Coast. And then we'll come home together."

"But Mom, no, I can't do all that. I promised Leslie I'd drive with her back down to Orange County. That's a long way to drive by herself." There was no way I was going to this golf resort and back to Evanston.

"What do you mean? You most certainly are. We've already made the reservations." I could picture my mother sitting at the desk in the alcove by the windows looking out into the backyard. No doubt, she had a cigarette in hand with a little red lipstick smudge at the end. Her tone was one of surprise, but also a bit of "how dare you upset these carefully made plans." I was pretty sure Salishan was a golf resort, since my mother and brother loved to play. Now I knew why my parents hadn't asked me what I was doing. They'd just assumed I would come back to Evanston and figure out my next steps. My mother was clearly shocked that I had made plans on my own.

"Why didn't you give me more notice that you had these plans, Mom?"

"We . . . we just assumed . . ." she said. "We thought this would be our last opportunity to vacation as a family," she sputtered. "And after Orange County, then what?"

"I've been looking at paralegal certificate programs and I thought I would take the three-month summer program at the University of San Diego. It might help me decide if I want to go to law school." I didn't add that Leslie's grandparents lived in San Diego and that she lived only an hour away. My mother didn't respond, but, clearly, she was unhappy with my decision about not going to Oregon or coming home. At the same time, she probably thought that paralegal school wasn't such a bad idea. It offered me, and her, the hope of me having a "legitimate" career.

After I completed the three-month program, I moved up to Seattle to live with my aunt and uncle. I didn't have a job, but I knew Seattle was where I wanted to live. I'd known that since I was eight and visited Seattle for the first time during the summer of the 1962 World's Fair. We came for the fair and also to visit my mother's relatives, including her brother Len and wife Rita. The whole week we were there, the sun shone brightly on Puget Sound and Lake Union in a way it never shone on Lake Michigan. It seemed like the best of both worlds: lush, high mountains and sparkling, cool water. I fell in love and vowed that as an adult I would live in this beautiful, emerald land. I had never seen my mother so happy as she was on that visit. She had not been to Seattle since her last visit home while pregnant with me. I don't know if she knew that she would never see her mother again. My mother was thirty when her mother died of stomach cancer—soon after that visit.

Len was her only sibling. But she had lots of relatives, some of whom still spoke Swedish. My uncle and aunt contrasted wildly with my parents. Uncle Len was all of five-foot-seven with a hard, fat stomach; a commercial electrician deep into union politics. At four-foot-eleven, Aunt Rita was even shorter and a devout Catholic. She stayed at home and did not drive. I found that fact perplexing. All the women I knew drove cars. But she had to sit on a phone book to drive; that might have had something to do with it. She also smoked. But, like the cigarettes they smoked—Rita with her menthol Virginia Slims and Mom with her Kents—the two women had little in common. Len and Rita were working class Democrats and my parents were devout Republicans. Everybody got along fine outside of political conversations, and my father's easygoing nature kept the temperature down on these discussions. Len would bait my dad with some swipe at what Republicans were doing to the unions. My mother and uncle stayed up late drinking, talking, catching up, and reminiscing. My father went to bed long before they even thought about going to bed.

I fell hard for Seattle and its pristine beauty and visited my aunt and uncle occasionally while going to Whitman. In the fall of 1975, I was ensconced in my uncle's house, still licking my wounds over Leslie. I didn't have a concrete plan about Leslie, because the assumptions about our future had fallen through. I was alone in Seattle, without friends. I had tried to find out what prompted Leslie to get kicked out, but none of my sorority sisters would talk to me. I also wondered if they thought Leslie and I were lesbians. But I never got to ask since it was apparently assumed. My pledge daughter Bev was the one who told me the rumors about people seeing us rolling around on the floor in the sorority kitchen. I was stunned. That had never happened. *Who would make this shit up?* I wondered. "Let us steadfastly love one another." The Tri Delta motto no longer applied to me.

Another friend,Vanessa—with whom I had once roomed, and who had discouraged my friendship with Leslie—had more to say. Both Vanessa and I had participated in Intervarsity Christian events and she came from a Presbyterian background.

When I visited Leslie at homecoming, I sought Vanessa out. "I tried to warn you, Jill. People were talking."

"You just told me not to be friends with her," I protested. "You didn't tell me that people thought we were lesbians or anything like that."

"The Bible is against homosexuality, Jill. Look at Genesis where it talks about Sodom and Gomorrah. And look at

Leviticus and one Corinthians six, verses nine and ten. It's wrong, Jill. What you and Leslie did was wrong." Vanessa's face was red with moral indignation.

I had looked at her in disbelief, this friend whose home I had been to and whose parents had been kind enough to share trips to Yosemite with me. "I love her, Vanessa," I said. "I'm not going to argue Bible verses with you. That's not the Jesus I know." If Vanessa thought I was a hopeless sinner, no wonder the other, former friends and sorority sisters wouldn't talk to me.

I was alone and friendless in Seattle, but I had my relatives, who graciously asked me to stay while I looked for a job as a paralegal. What I didn't know was that the semiprofessional paralegal vocation was relatively new. Seattle was not Los Angeles or Chicago, so while I got several interviews, it was clear that the Seattle legal field just didn't know what to do with a paralegal.

I churned out resumes at the kitchen nook in my uncle's house and tried desperately not to think about losing Leslie or all my friends lost to hypocrisy, lies, and fear. I was still wracked by guilt about Leslie, and while I knew she was unlikely to call, I kept hoping she would.

Temporary jobs as a "Kelly girl"—a low-paid office worker—helped fill the days. One of those jobs involved typing letters on carbon paper for a solo insurance broker with an office in Pioneer Square. Because the carbon paper was so unforgiving of typos, accurate typing was a must—a skill I hadn't yet perfected, requiring me to invariably start over. One day, while looking for more letterhead stationery, I pulled out the bottom drawer of the old wooden desk I was occupying. Inside it was a sheaf of stationery, but it didn't have his insurance company name on it. Instead, the letterhead featured the "Dorian Society." I quickly tucked it away. A few years later, I would learn that the Dorian Society was the first gay organization for men in the Seattle area, founded in 1967 to support gay rights and foster a more respectable image of the gay man. The man I was temping for was Charlie Brydon, a leader in the Seattle gay community. After I came out, I would learn more about the Dorian Society's role in promoting gay acceptance. But when I saw "Dorian Society" at the top of the page, my first impulse told me it was something I shouldn't know about. That day in Mr. Brydon's office, I was still trying to figure out the notion of acceptance around homosexuality—and I was pretty sure society remained pretty intolerant.

I kept writing resumes to lawyers and law firms in Seattle and Los Angeles, still hoping to work there. Leslie would be returning to Orange County and me once she graduated, and I blindly fostered hopes of that relationship continuing. At Christmas, I went home to Evanston and stayed a few months. I certainly wasn't getting anywhere as a Kelly girl or a paralegal in Seattle. I got a job working as a volunteer clerk for an Illinois circuit court judge in Chicago.

While I was there, I received a letter from a law firm in Los Angeles inviting me out there for an interview. No, they would not pay for a round trip flight from L.A. to Chicago. I talked it over with my parents that evening. I asked them whether or not I should go.

"Do you want it?" my father said.

"It seems like such a risk to go all the way out there, and maybe get rejected." Perhaps I was still smarting over my rejection from Leslie and the Tri Delts.

"It's your decision, Jill," he said.

That response floored me. I wanted my parents to make the decision. I never expected them to leave that one up to me. But it was the right thing for my dad to say.

Soon I was in Los Angeles working for an entertainment law firm called Mitchell Silberberg & Knupp in Century City, the splashy former backlot of 20th Century Fox. In this ethereal world, I was clearly on my own. I knew no one in Los Angeles, but I knew the city had good live theater. A lot of my income funneled into seeing names like Katharine Hepburn and a cherubic young Richard Dreyfuss on the stage.

The work itself was interesting and the monthly pay seemed huge. The clients ranged from a big, local dairy company called Arden-Mayfair to the singer Phoebe Snow. One day, we heard a big announcement: actor Warren Beatty was coming and no one was to walk through the lobby to gawk at him. All of the women, including me, wanted to do exactly that. Country singer Willie Nelson also came to our office, but he didn't have the same cachet.

I worked with three other paralegals: Gerri, Michelle, and Marylou. They were about six years older than me but seemed older. I wanted them to teach me how to be an independent working woman. Each one would play a different role in my social development.

Gerri had brassy red hair and a personality to match. She knew how to dress her shapely figure to her advantage and impeccably put on makeup to set off her big red lips. I'm sure every male associate and partner had his eye on her. "Gerri," I eventually got up the nerve to ask, "can I apply lipstick to make my lip look more normal?"

"Easy-peasy," she said, pulling out her lipstick liner, carefully painting a curve near the cleft where there wasn't one, and filling in the curve with lipstick. I saw no cleft, but I also didn't recognize myself in the mirror. I thought maybe a salon could help and I went there for blonde highlights and to learn how to apply makeup. Some of the makeup tips stayed with me, but I couldn't get the eyeliner on straight, and the way Gerri wanted me to do the lipstick just wasn't me. It felt fake.

Michelle and Marylou were seemingly inseparable and I worked on various projects with one or the other from time to time. They took me under their collective wings, knowing I had no friends in town—Marylou more so than Michelle. They were clearly straight and seemed to sense I was struggling to find my place in the world. After pouring my heart out to empathetic Michelle a few times, I soon developed an unrequited crush that left me feeling embarrassed and inclined to avoid her. One Monday Marylou took me aside and tried to explain the nuances of love, intimacy, and friendship.

"Love and intimacy are not the same, Jill," she told me. "The baring of the soul's secrets do not bind eternally the two sharing those secrets." This is what she told me after I left flowers on Michelle's front porch one Saturday morning. At twenty-one, I still had a lot to learn. The fact that Michelle and

I shared our vulnerabilities didn't necessarily mean that a love relationship was the inevitable next step.

Conflicted, I realized that my sexual identity dilemma remained unresolved. I decided to try out both sexes.

Los Angeles was sort of a strange beast in 1976. Strange to me, because Walla Walla carried such a different vibe by comparison. L.A. let me feel like I was finally meeting the decade head-on, albeit six years late. Frequent sights on the streets in Westwood and Santa Monica included free love and hippie beads, along with guys in bare feet with bandanas wrapped around waist-long hair who made the peace sign at me and had this glazed look in their eyes. It was time to find out more about myself, investigate myself and my desires. Here I was: still a virgin at twenty-one. I was sure there was a rule about that—a rule requiring you to lose your virginity before graduating from college. That hadn't happened and now I felt behind.

I had read *Looking for Mr. Goodbar*, about a repressed teacher who cruises singles' bars at night. I would do what she had done. I would lead that double life, going to bars and picking up men. The protagonist had made it look easy. But I was from the Midwest and couldn't easily shed Midwestern values. What's more, I hadn't ever had intercourse with a man, and the sex I'd had with Leslie, well, I wasn't sure that constituted sex. I had a boyfriend during my sophomore year for eight months at college and although we fooled around, we did not have intercourse. When I broke up with him, he had hurled an insult at me: "You're a lousy French kisser!" I thought he was blaming it on my lip.

In Los Angeles, I went to bars and felt inept. I would buy a drink and find someplace inconspicuous to stand. But then I got impatient, thinking I was too inconspicuous. I went up to a guy and spoke only a few words before asking him if he wanted to come home with me. He was older, much older. I couldn't really tell, maybe eight to ten years older. Sex wasn't at all what I had imagined. I had seen the scientific films in fifth grade, and again in junior high, that showed illustrations of a penis and a vagina, but I didn't really get it. I had never talked to my parents about it. My mother had given me a slim volume in fifth grade that explained the mechanics of reproduction, but contained no details about the emotional side. This was years before *Our Bodies Ourselves*, the seminal book about women's health and sex filled personal stories. I had fooled around with my college boyfriend, but we never had intercourse. All I knew was that sex was something that was supposed to happen between a man and a woman, definitely NOT two women.

So, I didn't really know what to expect with this guy I had just picked up

We made perfunctory small talk on the way back to my studio apartment in Westwood. The couch doubled as my bed, but we didn't even bother with that. There was no more talk, no getting to know each other, and certainly no foreplay. All I remember is disrobing and lying on my back on my couch, its rough fabric scratching my bare bottom and back. He seemed to tower above me as he began his rapid descent. I closed my eyes. I didn't really want to see what happened. Suddenly I felt him thrusting and I wanted him to stop because it hurt like hell. There was no lubrication and no rubber. I wanted it to be over and I wanted him to leave. But that's not what he had in mind. He was only just beginning. He could tell that I was a virgin and he told me I "needed instruction."

He sat in my armchair and asked me to suck him off. I was repelled by his penis and the last thing I wanted to do was put it in my mouth. *People actually do this and enjoy it?* I wondered. It just seemed like too much for my mouth, and at some point, I felt myself exit my body. Even though I was facing him I could see myself hovering above on the ceiling, looking down on this sordid scene. He didn't care about me or my feelings. I hadn't yet figured out that for me, whether it was sex with a man or a woman, I needed to have some sort of intimacy with them.

Yes, I wanted him to come home with me and have sex. And now here he was but he wanted more than what I thought I had consented to. Yet I couldn't ask him to leave. I thought some sort of bargain had been struck. *If you invite a guy home you have to put up with everything and wait it out.*

And then the coup de grace. He wanted me to sit and watch him masturbate. *At least it wasn't in my mouth, thank God for that.* He must have thought that was enough tutoring in the ways a man could be pleasured because he finally left after what had seemed like hours.

We went out two more times. He played tennis and I thought having a tennis partner—and maybe even a relationship—would be fun. But he only wanted sex. The second time, I demanded he take me to a movie, where he fell asleep before following me back to my tiny studio apartment for what he wanted. This time I said, "no," and told him to get out. As he hastily exited, I threw the book at him, one he had loaned me called *The Inner Life of a Tennis Player*. I knew what his inner life consisted of and I wanted out. He didn't care about me at all. That was pretty clear. I was a sex plaything to him, a way to get easy sex.

The next guy, Paul, was nice and into making films. He seemed to actually want to get to know me as opposed to using me as an object. He took me to two different films at Nuart, an independent art movie house in Santa Monica. I enjoyed talking to him, but invariably, he wanted to have sex. This time it wasn't so much the sex, but me again discounting myself: telling myself he was "too intellectual" for me. He talked a lot about films. He analyzed everything about the films we saw together and what type of films he wanted to make. It was clearly a passion of his but I couldn't keep up with his analyses and theories. I was afraid he would find me lacking in those areas and think me an imposter. So, before he could break up with me, I broke it off. I was beginning to see the limitations of picking up guys at bars as a way to explore my sexuality.

I was still curious about "my possible homosexual side" and went to two different lesbian bars I'd found in the L.A. gay newspaper. I tried a place called The Palms in West Hollywood. I drove around the block a couple of times, not only to find a parking place but to scope out the women going in. I dropped my keys as I got out of the car, my nerves getting the better of me, and debated going in. *Whoa, this is scary shit, Jill.* I had never been to a lesbian bar and had no *Looking for Ms. Goodbar* to guide me. Did patrons require a secret handshake or signal? I didn't have a clue. Women were dressed in jeans or chinos and Hawaiian shirts or muscle T-shirts. A cloud of cigarette smoke hung over their heads and I wished that I smoked to give me something to do with my hands. Music pulsated from a jukebox. Women's eyes glanced and darted away. I took a seat at the bar, ordered a glass of wine, and surreptitiously gawked, wondering if I belonged in this world. No one came up to me, and really, it could have been any bar but for its only occupants being women. I finished the wine and left. Where was the rule book? I didn't know how to dress, how to pick up women, or even how to flirt. No amount of higher education could have prepared me. I also tried a bar down in Newport Beach, hoping I could gather more clues. This bar provided more varied attire and types of women. I felt like an interloper researching some vague sociology paper. Some patrons wore heavy makeup, much like Gerri, with high heels and stylish pants as well as the chino and polo shirt variety. I felt as uncomfortable as I had in the heterosexual bars in Westwood Village. I sensed something different for me in picking up men as opposed to picking up women. I slowly realized that more was at stake for me in lesbian bars.

I bemoaned ever meeting anyone—either female or male—outside of work. Recalling my long-ago summer camp experience, I realized southern California offered plenty of hiking trails and outdoor fun. I knew I would find peace in nature. That childhood camp in Colorado—High Trails—had nurtured my independence and an unshakeable affection for the outdoors.

It was in the woods of Colorado, after all, that I had learned about the importance of footprints. I'd gone for six-week stretches over three summers starting at eight, then as a junior counselor, and finally, as a counselor. It was my happy place, a place my mind went to later when asked to conjure my most joyful memories during meditations. And I *was* happy there, a place where at 8,900 feet you could see Pikes Peak among the other fourteen-thousand-foot mountains, one of which I got to climb for an overnight backpacking trip and then glissade down on a slicker. Aspen trees and pines dotted the six thousand acres of camp, along with big boulders: a place where a young girl could run free and do things she had never done—river rafting, backpacking, archery, riflery, acting in silly skits, and listening to folk songs sung by counselors who looked like Mary of Peter, Paul and Mary—and just be content.

That contentment and sense of pure joy was something I had never felt anyplace else. Sitting atop the saddle of a horse six hands high gave me a new perspective. I experienced what it meant to be "tall in the saddle." My self-confidence grew while sampling each activity. It was even exciting to almost drown during the junior lifesaving class, but I passed and just kept going. With each new step, whether it was cleaning the cabin in groups or learning cooperative, campcraft skills, I learned about teamwork (and how you could get things done quicker that way).

But it was the smell of pine trees and being alone with nature that stayed with me, a girl from the Chicago suburbs who otherwise never got to feel that sense of peace and contentment. It's one reason I would later grow to adore the North Cascades area in Washington. It is my adult happy place for the smells that take me back to being most at ease with myself.

As I walked from the pool to the cabin I shared with ten other girls at camp, those footprints I left in the dusty hiking trails or the wet ones I left with my flip-flops left their traces on my heart. There were also the footprints my western cowboy boots left as I trudged up the hill from horseback riding to the dining hall when the dinner bell rang. So many footprints that helped walk me into a new me, one who dreamed at eight of living in a place like Colorado. Someplace with scenery and mountains and wide-open spaces and blue skies and the fresh smell of rain, the beauty of aspen and pine trees. The footprints led me to a part of myself I wanted to hold onto forever.

The summer ended, and, unfortunately, the footprints inevitably took me home to the house of my parents, where it felt wildly different. They were perfectly formed prints that my shoes could not fit into, and I made a mess of the ones I tried to create on my own. Still, I kept trying to fit into them with a sense of hopelessness, and sometimes, despair.

My Chicago footprints seemed so big, so deep. How could I begin to walk in them? I wanted to at least take baby steps through their diverse shapes. Because I knew that was expected of me. I had no such footprints in the bars of Los Angeles, but perhaps I could find them again with the Los Angeles chapter of the Mountaineers. I signed up for the Basic Mountaineering Training Course. This filled up my weekends and my soul for several months. But this dabbling in nature would turn out to be insufficient, and I returned to Evanston for graduate school in journalism at Northwestern University. I would put my search for my sexual identity on hold. Or so I thought.

CHAPTER SIX

WHO NEEDS SEX OR EMOTIONS?

BEING A PARALEGAL had been interesting, but dealing with the attorney-sized egos of my superiors made me rethink becoming a lawyer like my father. My father didn't have the swagger of these L.A. lawyers, but maybe he was just unique. The entertainment lawyers I worked for often mistreated their staff, finding others at fault, for instance, when they couldn't find the brief that already sat on their desk. I didn't want to be a law firm slave, working long hours into the night and on the weekends. I wanted a more balanced life.

My father had visited me in Los Angeles before. Brunswick Corporation had business dealings with southern California's McDonnell-Douglas aircraft, allowing him to combine business with the pleasure of visiting me at least once or twice during the year I lived there. I remember the thrill of taking him to Disneyland, where he got off every ride exclaiming, "Oh, that was simply marvelous," with a huge grin on his face. His favorite ride was the submarine ride. It was fun to see my father's face full of wonder and joy. It was as though the boy inside the man had been let loose.

During that same visit, we went to a Japanese restaurant in Orange County and I had sake for the first time. Both of us got a little tipsy. I saw my father in a different light. I'd never seen him affected by alcohol in an unguarded way and it led to us both getting silly.

Back in Evanston, I thought I would live at home and save some money. I thought my mother would be pleased, but when I shared this idea she said, "I'm not sure I'll let you. I've got things in your room." Surely, she was joking. I thought she'd be happy, even thrilled, to get reacquainted, but my mother never seemed to say what I longed to hear. She had gotten used to having an empty nest since my brother was in his senior year of college and soon to be in grad school at the University of Iowa. She had her volunteer activities, her golf, and her bowling, and I had school—along with my intensifying need to clarify my sexual orientation.

I could have titled this year, "How many times one girl can escape getting pregnant." Several . . . apparently. All of my sexual experimentations didn't include thinking about birth control. They were focused on me trying to figure out my sexual identity. I was still trying to fit into the heterosexual costume, trying on men like shoes. To be other than straight in the 1970s was still not okay. During my internship with the Jackson, Michigan, paper in graduate school, I had sex with my neighbor. He had just gotten out of Jackson Penitentiary. He offered me a joint after he invited me over. We both knew why I was there. We started to make love, but I got scared. I told him he couldn't enter, that he had to pull out, and he said he would, but he didn't. That was me—so naïve at twenty-two, thinking I could rely on a man to do as he was told. I worried for the next month about whether or not my period would come. I worried about what my parents would think of a Black grandchild. I didn't know what would be worse. Learning I was a lesbian or me having a Black baby? Either way, I was screwed, literally and figuratively. But my period came and I was so relieved. That experience, however, didn't teach me to consider birth control pills or at least make guys wear a rubber. No, I just started to date women.

Nancy was in Jackson. She was a Northwestern journalism undergrad in the same newspaper internship program. Three years younger than me, she possessed a soft vulnerability. I thought I just wanted a friend. One night, she needed to borrow my car to cover a night meeting. When she brought it back the next evening, I invited her in for a drink. We talked for a while and I asked if she would give me a backrub. I was sure she would say no, but she didn't. After she finished and I was feeling flush from someone else's gentle touch, I wanted to kiss her. Instead, I told her, "I don't mean to be cryptic, but one of these nights I'm going to lose control." It wasn't the first night we had spent talking.

She didn't jump or blanch. "Don't worry about it," she said. "Just let things happen." *Now who was being cryptic?* We continued to do things off and on outside of work: eating dinner together, going to the laundromat, even going to the high school girls' basketball game I was covering for the paper one night. Nancy confused me. She seemed straight and I knew Ron at the newspaper was trying to date her. At the same time, I found her refreshingly honest and felt I could be that way in return. But I sensed an unspoken limit. Any time I got too candid or intense about my feelings, she sidetracked the conversation. I kept remembering what she had said that night in my apartment about "letting things happen." I clung to hope but certainly wasn't going to make the first move. My experience with Leslie had taught me the painful consequences of taking risks on my own behalf.

Then we decided one night to go to the Rubaiyat, a gay bar in Ann Arbor, a good forty-minute drive each way. Nancy's willingness to go seemed like a bold statement. I had high hopes for the evening. What we didn't know was that Rubaiyat wasn't just a gay bar; it catered to college students and had a great sound system and a DJ. Only one night a week, the bar tolerated women dancing with women and men with men.

We ventured there on a cold October night and the drive seemed unusually long and contemplative. Despite the cold, my hands grew clammy and my imagination went into overdrive wondering what the night might bring. I was also focused on getting us there in the dark without a map. My shoulders tensed as I drove and my nerves were doing the jitterbug. Nancy spoke little. *Was she nervous too? Or busy asking herself why she had agreed to come?*

It was ten-thirty by the time we got there to find only a small number of patrons. A few couples were dancing on a mostly empty floor, offering no opportunities to hide in a corner. I became shy about asking Nancy to dance. I certainly didn't want us to be the only two out there. I also wanted her to ask me first. *Such a gesture would signal something important*, I thought. We went through the ritual of getting something to drink. We slowly sipped our drinks and I shifted from one leg to the other. Jimmy Buffett's "Margaritaville" started to play, and more couples wandered out to dance. Some were same-sex couples, but most appeared heterosexual. A few more songs went by, and then the beginning strains of Fleetwood Mac's "Dreams" drifted in and the tension broke. "Wanna dance?" I said, turning to Nancy. She did and we joined more couples on the floor. Finally, I was out in the open—dancing with another woman. I couldn't believe it. We danced to the next song, but then along came another that neither of us knew. We drifted back to standing against the wall. I felt like I was at junior high. But then a guy came up and asked Nancy to dance and she accepted. I tried not to show my dismay. She had never said she had come here to dance with me, though. She'd just agreed to come check the place out.

Nobody asked me to dance and I didn't ask anyone else. I wanted to dance with Nancy. She came back alone after a few dances. The tightness began to drain out of me and dregs of disappointment took their place. The night was not going as I had envisioned. Ever the eternal optimist, I still held out hope for the slow dances, hoping that Nancy might ask me, but that didn't happen, either. So much for my first experience in a gay disco bar and becoming a participant rather than an observer. Now I was even more confused about Nancy's mixed signals. But in the end, nothing happened.

I continued my risky explorations with guys while I was in grad school, but not with other women. I should have talked to someone about my struggles, although I didn't know who to talk to about having safe sex, let alone having sex with women. Who would have told me? Certainly not my mother, who had given me a book about how babies were born. Okay, I understood conception but not how to stop it. Schools didn't teach that in the 1960s during students' single sex-ed class in fifth grade. Sex? In fifth grade? It certainly was the furthest thing from my mind. But I had friends whose interest suddenly soared in sixth grade. They talked about meeting some hot guy down at Lighthouse Beach and making out. *Braggadocio* or truth? I never knew. It would have been too embarrassing to ask then, or even later. I just assumed everybody had gotten some message about sex but me.

During my second internship that summer, I found myself working in Washington D.C. as a news service stringer for three Montana newspapers. A male press aide for one of the Montana senators expressed an interest in me. But his interest turned out to be self-serving and our sex was lackluster. Another grad student also found his way into my bed. *Something is wrong here*, I thought. I started to look through the white pages for a doctor to give me birth control pills, but I was too embarrassed to go through with it. My roommate in our Georgetown basement apartment, a childhood friend, had gone to Stanford. When I asked her if she knew about Holly Near, a lesbian feminist singer who was just beginning to become famous in the Bay Area, she looked at me like I had accused her of being homosexual. Why was this so hard? This whole sex business seemed to happen fairly naturally for almost everyone but me. I didn't know anything about people being late-bloomers. I just felt that if I didn't take some initiative, life was going to pass me by.

In the fall of 1978, I graduated and left Chicago, carrying my history in its large backpack. On my journey to twenty-five, I had tried several times to lose that baggage. First, I had tried to address my own struggle and confusion by overfocusing on other people's crises, in the land of golden wheat and Blue Mountains, Walla Walla. Then I had tried to change my history of the dutiful upper-middle-class daughter during my "wanton woman of the world" phase in a city that couldn't have cared less—Los Angeles. I had managed to lose my virginity there, but not my history. Next, I tried to revise the narrative by going back to live with my parents. Reliving this history with them, unsurprisingly, didn't relieve the burden; it only intensified it. Revisiting the burdens of the Vanneman name propelled me back across the country to the evergreens—*A symbol of growth and resilience?* I wondered—in the hope of finding myself at last.

CHAPTER SEVEN

THE CRESCENT

I WAS SITTING at the bar in a tavern called the Crescent Lounge—or as locals called it, "the Crescent"—when I saw her come in. Jude had on what I would later come to recognize as her usual outfit: green army fatigues and an untucked plaid flannel shirt over her T-shirt top. I checked her out, made a silent note (*oh, her, she's here a lot*), and went back to the Miller longneck I was nursing. No one appeared to drink Miller Lite at the Crescent. I did, because my parents' obsession with my weight had traveled across the country with me.

I was new to bar-sitting. I was new to my sexual orientation. I was new to gay Seattle. Jude didn't look new. I was trying desperately not to appear new, but that's pretty difficult in a neighborhood bar where everyone knows everyone else. Seattle's version of a queer female *Cheers*. No men were allowed, at least I never saw any. I don't know if they weren't welcome and knew it or if they'd officially been banned.

Even though I'd been to the Crescent a few times, I hadn't met anybody except one woman who'd tried to pick me up three months earlier. I'd walked out to my car and she'd walked to hers and given me a certain look, but instead of following her, I'd driven back to my uncle's house where I'd been staying, scared to death that I had been propositioned. I wasn't ready to have sex with a stranger. I had tried that with men a couple of times and it hadn't worked out well.

After that failed pickup, I didn't go back to the Crescent for a while.

But eventually I went back, because I needed to hone my bar-sitting skills. What I had figured out thus far was that this type of sitting was an art form, and that you didn't go to eat at the bar. A cigarette was a good prop. Somebody might offer you a light and then slide her beer over and start talking to you. Or, if you were more adventuresome, you tried to attach yourself to a group and listen to the banter, hoping your yearnings weren't obvious.

Jude was a real regular. Lots of people seemed to know her. She sometimes came with her friend, Boo. The two of them would shoot pool, a game I had never played, although the bumper pool table in our Evanston basement made me familiar with a cue stick. Jude and Boo were both pretty good from what I could tell. I mean, if you can still get balls in pockets after a few beers, that counts as pretty good to me. They never appeared drunk, but they sure drank a lot of beer. They ordered pitchers and it didn't seem to affect their skills. No slop-playing for those two.

"Gloria," or maybe it was Heart's "Dreamboat Annie," pulsed out of the jukebox. Jude leaned over the pool table, cue stick in hand, tucked a still-burning cigarette behind her ear, and took her shot; the red two ball banked off the opposite bumper and dropped into the side pocket. She stuck the cigarette back in her mouth and lined up her next shot. She missed, and Boo laughed. It was rare for Jude to miss a shot as easy as a straight one into the corner pocket.

It was then that I put my quarter on the table, signifying that I would play the next game against the winner of the contest between her and Boo. Jude sunk the orange ball, then the purple one, until the last one left was the eight ball, which Jude missed. Then Boo scratched and it was Jude's turn again. She sunk it and it was my turn.

She looked at me, taking in my blue pantsuit and brown turtleneck, and a smile danced on her lips. "Haven't seen you before. You new?"

"God, it shows that badly?"

Jude nodded her head. "You wanna break?"

"No, you do it. I'm not that good." I chalked my stick while she expertly broke and sunk a ball in the process.

"Looks like you've got the stripes," she said.

It was a quick game. I got one for every four she pocketed. She offered to buy me a beer and I readily accepted. We chatted and got the particulars out of the way. She seemed genuinely interested and impressed by my master's degree in journalism. "Not too many women come in here have master's degrees. More likely to be graduates of the school of hard knocks," she said.

Jude had been in the military but got kicked out for being a lesbian, moved to Spokane with her lover, and then moved to Seattle. The lover was no longer in the picture. She took out a Marlboro and tapped it against the table. I searched through my purse for my True Blues. She said, "No one I know carries a purse."

"Oh, I didn't know," I said, blushing. "Are there rules?"

She laughed and said, "Are you for real? No, I just meant no one I know carries a purse. No one I know has enough stuff for a purse."

The jukebox was playing a tune I'd never heard before, Cris Williamson's "The Changer and the Changed." I asked her who Cris Williamson was. She told me Cris sang something called "women's music." I said I'd never heard of women's music. Boo came over and asked if Jude wanted to shoot more pool and she said no; she was busy educating me. I blushed again. I didn't know if she was making fun or genuinely enjoying what she was doing. The bar contained no windows and therefore no natural light. I didn't know until later that most gay bars had no windows back then. The artificial light in the bar created a glare for me so I couldn't see Jude's eyes behind her aviator glasses. I would see later that her eyes were a brilliant blue, and were her best feature, along with her sense of humor, which I would also discover later.

Jude started to say something, but I didn't catch it because of the uproar over one woman shouting at another woman by the pool table. The first woman picked up a set of keys lying on the pool table and threw them at the other one. "You whore, I don't want these anymore. Get out of here."

My eyes must have widened in amazement, because Jude said, "Oh, don't let them bother you. That's just Sue and Cindy going at it again. Cindy must have been making eyes at someone." The way Jude said it made it sound like no big deal: just another day at the Crescent.

How had I come upon the Crescent that fall of 1978? While I was looking for a job, I thought I should find my people. After all my sexual exploits across the country, I had a stronger feeling about who my people might be. But I didn't know where to look for them. It's not like they wore signs around their necks and walked up and down Pike or Pine Street in Seattle. Certain types did walk up and down Aurora Avenue, though, but those were not my people. I thought about looking for them in the phone pages but figured I'd find no listings there for "lesbian" or "gay." This was a strange dilemma. I remembered that man I had worked for as a Kelly girl with his Dorian Society letterhead. But somehow I knew that society would be closed to me. So, I sat in my aunt and uncle's kitchen nook churning out resumes and cover letters to various newspapers and trade journals and stewed about this other part of my life. I looked for a gay bookstore or at least an alternative bookstore with newsletters or leaflets, and somehow, somewhere, I found a copy of the *Seattle Gay News*. My prayers were answered—a resource that told me where to look. It was there that I found the Crescent.

With my newly minted master's degree in journalism, I planned to apply to a newspaper or magazine. Those options, however, were limited. Seattle had two daily newspapers and its magazines were mostly trade journals about the fishing and maritime industry. I started applying to major newspapers in Idaho, Montana, Oregon, and of course, Washington.

I hadn't considered freelancing. I hadn't considered it because it meant selling myself—myself as a sales item on the rack of life. I couldn't imagine. Even with the degree and all those pages of clippings I had written in journalism school for the Jackson, Michigan, newspaper and the three Montana newspapers in Washington D.C., I just didn't think that was enough. It hadn't helped that the news service editor in D.C. had told me I'd "never make it" in the newspaper world. I was too scared to ask why. He might have thought I wasn't aggressive enough in trying to find stories on the Hill. He was the very essence of the old school editor who smoked and chewed Tums like they were candy and barked out assignments. I sat in a world of self-doubt with those words of his ringing in my ears.

I'd started with an application to the Montana daily newspapers, because I had in essence written for three of them. Montana would be a great place to start, with its big open skies and mountain scenery. The scenery evoked in me a kinship of the heart, this small heart first filled by the similar mountain and river scenery of Colorado. Colorado, where I learned just how much I needed nature and wide-open space as opposed to the skyscrapers and concrete of Chicago.

Chicago was behind me, now. Now I had my scenery but no job—a job I needed to feel like I was a grown-up with money and self-worth. Discovering and owning my sexual identity along with a job would mean I had arrived. I had several interviews with various local papers, including the *Yakima Herald-Republic* and the *Coeur d'Alene Press*, but I just couldn't seem to land a newspaper job. Out of desperation, I ended up with the tantalizing offer of writing radio ad copy for two different merchants: a yarn craft shop called Rapunzel's and Ivar's seafood restaurant. It seemed like a sell-out to write for a corporation, to use my writing to sell things. I had gone to school to write well-crafted, human interest stories that would change the world or at least affect readers in some way. But, after the interview, my Smith Corona electric typewriter churned out two radio ads in a relatively short time one morning and I thought I was on my way. I got paid a phenomenal amount of money for a morning's work and the ads aired on the radio. I was in my car driving in the University District when one of the ads blared over the radio and hearing it was a rush. Maybe I could sell my soul to the corporate devil, after all.

But my ad copywriting days were short-lived and I was running out of options. More and more, it was looking like I would have to return home to Evanston and depend on my parents. I couldn't bear this thought. I ended up taking a retail clerk job at Waldenbooks in Northgate Mall. I spent hours at the Seattle Public Library researching freelance article ideas and reading the freelancers' bible, *Writer's Digest*, but working at Waldenbooks and assimilating myself into Seattle's lesbian culture consumed much of my time.

I met Jude and started hanging out at the bar with her crowd, but she was not the one who snapped the final puzzle piece into place. While hanging out at the Crescent and learning how to play pool and pinball, I met MaryJo. She was also on the recreational lesbian basketball team I had joined through the Lesbian Resource Center. She had shoulder-length, brown hair with unevenly cut waves, a thin frame, and breasts that barely accentuated the T-shirts she favored. She smoked and wore wire-rimmed glasses. At this point, I wasn't particularly interested in anyone—albeit I was lusting after Sue, a different player on the basketball team. I always seemed interested in males and females who had no interest in me. Yet within these circles, it was becoming increasingly clear that I had found my people but still needed validation. I heard about a feminist counseling service called Sister, Sister near the Green Lake Honey Bear bakery and thought I should go find out for sure.

It was my first visit to a therapist. She had a hippie name: Moon. The two of us sat on beanbag cushions as she gently probed why I was there and why I thought I might or might not be a lesbian. I'm not sure why I sought help to process this; for some reason I wanted someone's stamp of approval. This need to have my thoughts and opinions validated by others threaded through my life; I needed it the way a child yearned for her mother's approval in learning how to walk. I got what I came for, and when Moon said, "I think you already know the answer to your question," I knew she was right. I came out of her office a certified lesbian. I felt a huge weight lift and the self-doubt trickle away. I had an answer. I knew who I was. I wanted to run around Green Lake and tell every stranger I met. I felt that the world should throw me a party. I felt like I should throw the world a party. This was huge!

Shortly after this, I went to a concert at the University of Washington Women's Center where singer-pianist Margie Adam was to perform. She was part of a growing new music genre called "lesbian feminists." I saw many of these women perform in the '80s and '90s. Their music was the celebration of a movement that said lesbianism was something to be proud of, not ashamed of, not something to hide from. It was welcoming music that said, "Come out, come out of that dark closet." We deserved to be alive and to live the lives we wanted to live. Among the names that soon rolled off my tongue were Holly Near, Cris Williamson, Meg Christian, Sweet Honey in the Rock, BeBe K'Roche, Margie Adam, Joan Armatrading,

Teresa Trull, Ferron, k.d. lang, and Ani DiFranco. I saw MaryJo as the vehicle bringing me to the doorstep of this music. She was the one who'd asked if I wanted to go with her to see Margie Adam. A little bell rang in my head. *A date.* I was going on a date with a self-proclaimed lesbian and I was one too. *Hot damn,* I thought—*a part of my life was finally beginning.*

The concert was great and I was so taken with the music that I didn't worry about the "date" and what it might or might not mean. After the concert, MaryJo asked me to come back to her place. We smoked some weed, something she was accomplished at and something I had only tried once before—unsuccessfully. I was soon in a pleasant fog, my erogenous zones being touched in a wholly new way. She licked my nipples; she didn't just pinch and pull at them. She ran her tongue around my earlobes and down my arms, and then began caressing a part of me with her fingers that only I had previously found. She caressed me slowly at first and I felt a flooding in an area where I had last felt that sensation only with Leslie. Her finger began to more quickly stroke my clitoris and my body shook uncontrollably. Then I finally shuddered in one huge, orgasmic peak. That last jigsaw puzzle piece fell into place. My first and unforgettable orgasm. That's what all my high school girlfriends had been so excited about. It wasn't such an exclusive club, after all.

I started to drop by the Crescent more frequently. It was the only way to get in touch with Jude. Her house in Madrona, an East Seattle neighborhood, didn't have a phone. I wanted to be seen by Jude and I wanted to see more of her. Women gravitated to her. After the night we first played pool, she would flash that warm smile and wave me over to the pool table. She started to fold me into the group at the bar. I began to get better at pool.

I spent my days researching article ideas for possible pieces I could sell to the local press, but mostly I thought about Jude and how to tell her my attraction went beyond friendship. I had ditched carrying a purse and wearing makeup. I had never felt comfortable wearing makeup, anyway. Instead, I had found my tribe at the Crescent. I had found women only interested in other women. Men—they were best forgotten. I didn't hate men. I just felt more comfortable around women, perhaps because they were a more familiar species.

But I still felt at the bar like sixteen-year-old Liesl von Trapp nurturing a crush on the older and more assertive Rolf Gruber in *The Sound of Music*: ". . . timid and scared and shy was I . . ." While hanging with Jude and her friends felt comfortable, I didn't know what came next. I was worried about making a move on Jude and having it be the wrong one. I didn't want to lose my spot in this friendly tribe: my first group of lesbian friends. What were the rules when both people were of the same sex? The guy always made his interest known in high school and college, right? How did one date someone of the same sex? I moped; I pined. I waited for Jude to make the first move.

I continued to connect with Jude at the Crescent and joined her in playing on the same Crescent-sponsored, fast-pitch-softball team. I had never played fastpitch before, but Jude had played all her life and made a great shortstop, while I tried to catch the hard-and-fast zingers hurtling toward me at first base. "Not bad for the girl from the privileged background," Jude said one day after a game. I laughed, but her remark had hit a sore spot. I didn't want anyone to know about my affluent roots. With the exception of Boo, this new group came from more humble beginnings. I didn't want class to get in the way. We continued in this way for many weeks—me hanging out at the bar, hoping I fit in and getting used to my new way of being in the world. The Crescent seemed like my training grounds.

One day, I invited Jude and one of her housemates, Deb, for lunch at my aunt and uncle's West Seattle house. I proceeded to lay out tuna sandwiches and potato chips, which they readily devoured. Both of them were looking for work and money was scarce. Jude walked everywhere as she seldom could afford bus fare. I didn't care about any of that. I also entertained the two of them. *Yeah, I showed off a little and played the guitar and the piano.* Jude kidded me about these untold talents. Later, Jude told me that Deb had told her, "You know, Jude, that girl, Jill, she has a crush on you. She was flirting with you. Open your eyes. She's courting you. I don't know why you can't see that." Jude was used to being the one in control and the one doing the courting. Jude's attention toward me turned serious, leading to the night she asked me back to her house. She lived in a tiny room with a single twin mattress, a few books on the windowsill, and her clothes in a crate in the corner. One of the books was Rita Mae Brown's *Rubyfruit Jungle.* It was a groundbreaking book in the 1970s for its depiction of real lesbians living real lives and not some male writer's titillating fantasy. I had already loaned her my little portable TV. It was on the only chair in the room. We conversed on her bed for a while and then came the moment

I'd been waiting for. Afterwards, as we lay in her bed, she turned to face me and said in a somber tone, "Jill, I just don't know if I want to be the one to bring you out."

"What?" I sputtered. "Are you afraid I'm just some straight girl experimenting? I'm not! Let me show you I'm worth it." Corny as all get out, I know, but it's how I felt. Goddammit, I was insulted. *How dare she think I was just messing around?*

She exuded self-confidence and surety—at least in her sexual orientation. She had known that she was gay since she was five, she told me. I marveled, given my own bumpy journey toward self-awareness. How could anyone know that young? "I just did, Jill," she said.

Jude taught me practical things beyond the world of books. For example, one day she remarked that the price of gas had gone up. I hadn't paid much attention to gas prices when I'd lived in Los Angeles and had to navigate all those different freeways or when I drove back across the country. Jude cared about things like the price of gas. She taught me how to properly clean a windshield too. Her father had worked in a service station. Jude grew up poor and when I met her she was poor. She couldn't even afford to ride the bus up Cherry Street from downtown to her house on 32nd and Union. She walked everywhere in her green army fatigues, T-shirt, and open flannel shirt that doubled as a jacket. But while her economic means were scarce, her spirit was not. Her cerulean blue eyes and smirk of a smile let me know she knew things. That she could show me how to navigate this new world I found myself in. This new world of pool tables, Miller High Life, and smoking. These were things that Jude did. She smoked Marlboros and drank Miller High Life in a bottle. So many bottles I couldn't keep up. And while I smoked, I couldn't enjoy her brand. Marlboros were too strong. She laughed at me, at my inexperience in this new world. But it wasn't a mean laugh; it was an encouraging laugh, one I wanted to hear more of. But she was cautious and wasn't sure she wanted to help bring someone out.

I think she found my earnestness and naiveté refreshing. Some of the women she hung out with drank a lot and did stronger recreational drugs like LSD and mushrooms. I was willing to try marijuana, but it didn't like me and made me feel funny, even sick, sometimes. I thought I would stick with alcohol. I liked how it relaxed me and helped me let go of my shyness and my inhibitions. The problem was that no one else in this new bar scene was like me. No one had a college education—let alone a graduate degree—and I soon learned to stay quiet about those things. I wanted to fit in, so I got rid of my pantsuits and jewelry. I soon began to wear men's Levi's and green army pants. All those things I had tried so hard to learn in Los Angeles did not suit my new life, even though my parents had been pleased by L.A.'s temporary effect on my appearance.

Jude's perspective on how people lived and grew up was a striking contrast from suburban Evanston. Bringing that perspective into my parents' life was a different matter.

Now pool, the Crescent, beer, and pinball machines were my world.

I was trying to avoid thinking about my two different worlds when my mother called. I mentioned to her that I might be moving and needed a full-sized mattress. What I was hoping for inwardly was Jude and I finding our own place and moving in together. "Why do you need a full-sized mattress?" she asked, her tone suspicious.

In her mind, there could only be one reason for my bedding request. During the '60s, she and my father had been one of the few couples with a full-sized mattress in their bedroom. All the other neighbor kids' parents just had two single beds. My grandparents, who lived about ten minutes away, also slept on two twin mattresses. I remember my mother proudly telling me that when I was two and they'd moved into a new house, she had asked my father for a full-sized mattress. The mattress had to be hefted up two sets of ladders with ropes on the side of the house in order to get it into their second-floor bedroom. A full-sized mattress was only for couples. My mother had reason to be suspicious.

It was now the spring of 1979, and after staying a few months with my aunt and uncle, I was ready to move to an apartment on Capitol Hill. About six weeks later, the Bon Marche delivered the full-sized mattress my mother had been loath to provide for me. My uncle offered his brawn and his truck to move my few belongings. My mother called again to see how the move had gone. She reminded me that her family had once lived on Capitol Hill and offered other details about the area's origins. But it was her announcement that she and my father were coming for a visit that got my attention. My father had business to do with a Seattle marine company owned by his employer.

It had been thirty-plus years since my mother had been back to Capitol Hill. The neighborhood had changed and I had changed. My way of living had radically altered from the last time I had seen them in Evanston. Not only had I begun to eschew dressing up, but with all the beer I was consuming, I had put on weight.

"You're not staying with me, are you?" I blurted out. "I don't have the room."

"No, of course not," my mother said. "We'll stay downtown, or with Len and Rita." I hoped she couldn't hear my sigh of relief. "But we would like to see your apartment." When I got off the phone, Jude rolled her eyes.

"Oh, great, Shirli and Ed are coming for a visit," she said. To say Jude was less than thrilled was an understatement. She had heard about my parents and knew about our dissimilar backgrounds. She likely expected the visit would not go well. I had not yet sat in the car and told my parents that I had jumped out of the closet. But I was excited and happy about this jump. I belonged somewhere. I wanted to tell everyone the good news. Despite my utter joy about this self-acknowledgment, I knew instinctively that my parents would not like Jude. Her clothes were all wrong, her hair was all wrong, her background was definitely all wrong, and she, in their estimation, would be just all wrong for their daughter. The whole scene was far from what they had envisioned for me.

I was not using my graduate degree and I was not living in a small, two-bedroom house with pretty flowers and two-point-five kids. For a while, Jude had short hair with bangs. She'd gotten it trimmed to a buzz cut. She had not discussed this drastic haircut with me. I was surprised but I was also in love. The haircut rather suited her and made her eyes pop. I hoped my parents would see what I saw in her, a highly intelligent woman who, through no fault of her own, lacked the advantages that I'd had growing up. Jude was not close to her parents, and she spoke little about her growing-up years, although I'd always suspected they were fraught with the challenges my parents might otherwise refer to as "character-building."

Mom and Dad arrived. They came up the stairs and Mom's nose wrinkled. "Eeew," she said . . . "what's that smell?" as I knew she would.

"A lot of South Asians live here," I said, "and I think you're smelling onions and curry." I knew she wanted to ask me, "Why here?" Why had I moved to this apartment? *Why Mom? Because the price was right.*

As my parents opened the door, I could see their eyes fall upon the mattress. *Yes, the infamous mattress.* It was neatly made up, but on the floor rather than propped up on a frame, and it took up much of the living room. They also saw our clothes—Jude's and mine—piled in neat stacks atop student-type bookcases, the kind with cinder blocks between the shelves. Jude was hovering or hiding in the kitchen and their eyes took her in. Awkward introductions were made. They didn't ask if she lived there too. That part was obvious.

My dad walked over to the window and apropos of nothing said, "Where's the fire escape? Do they have one?" I didn't know where it was. I don't think I had given it a thought. Dad said, "I guess you could jump out this window to the roof of this building, below." He did not sound happy. They invited Jude for dinner, because that's what they did, hide their dismay behind a cover of politeness. They wanted to find out more about this woman and how we had ended up being roommates.

On their plane ride home, I'm sure my parents speculated about what their daughter was doing living with a woman with no hair in a rickety apartment with what my parents considered to be foreign smells and a building with only a rooftop to jump onto in case of a fire. Nevertheless, I had found my new home at the Crescent and with Jude. As someone once said, home is where we belong—and belonging was everything to me.

CHAPTER EIGHT

EVOLUTION OF A YOUNG LESBIAN

MY LIFE with Jude had settled into a homey relationship. When I first met Jude, she'd been working at a 7-Eleven in Ballard. Then she heard about a job at CC Grains and began working in the warehouse and doing deliveries. CC Grains, or just "Grains," was often viewed as a collective of hot-blooded, radical feminists. Yes, it was women-owned and women-run. All of the employees spelled women with a "y" instead of an "e." At that time women were trying to eradicate men from all aspects of their lives, even in the spelling of words. By the summer of 1979, Grains was a thriving cooperative on Capitol Hill with about fifteen, full-time female employees.

Jude frequently came home after a day hefting fifty-pound bags of millet or wheat berries onto pallets, extolling her appreciation for this kind of work with other politically minded *womyn*. She loved the camaraderie and working for the common good. "I just feel so lucky, Jill, that I get to work with other lesbians and have fun doing so," she told me. I loved seeing Jude happy. CC Grains also employed straight women, but they were in the minority. Not that it mattered: they all shared a radical feminist foundation.

Sometimes I would go to Grains and feel in thrall with all these womyn using their intellects and brawn to show the world that we did not need any stinkin' men to help us move the earth and create a new dawn. I wasn't sure I hated men, per se. I just thought my world would be fine without them. Feminism and even separatism were in full bloom. Lesbians were even buying land and creating women-only communes, similar to the hippies of the 1960s. I wasn't sure I would go that far in my beliefs. Just six years earlier, Betty Friedan saw the burgeoning growth of women leaping out of the closet as a threat to pure "feminism," and had labeled lesbians the "lavender menace." Friedan was wary about women who switched sexual preference as a political statement.

But me, I wasn't trying to be political. I wasn't reading Friedan or Susan Brownmiller or Simone de Beauvoir or Erica Jong. I was just following my lover into her world. Jude was political and anti-men. I was interested in seeing what a community without men might produce. I was being political without realizing that's what I was doing.

And yet, I came from a political family. To be political was a fiercely held Vanneman value. My father spent years as a politician—over and above his corporate attorney day job—trying to make the eighty-thousand-soul town of Evanston a better place. He reveled in that world. My mother was no slouch, either—from chairing the low-income housing committee and chairwoman of the United Way to playing my father's most trusted political confidante—she too modeled political activity and Republican Party activism. It's just that my politics were different in a way that my parents could not begin to comprehend. For many women at this time, being a lesbian was as much a political statement as it was about sex.

Me—I just wanted to be loved.

I had been trying to earn a living by freelance writing, but it wasn't paying enough. I soon decided that what Jude was doing looked like fun and I began working at CC Grains. On one of my sporadic phone calls to my parents, I told them about my new job. "What about being a journalist?" my mother said.

"I tried, Mom," I said.

God knows how many newspapers I had applied to and interviewed with across the Pacific Northwest.

"It's not working out. Learning how to run a forklift and heft fifty-pound bags of flour and wheat berries onto pallets is an experience I want," I continued. "Maybe I could freelance an article about it."

"Oh," my mother said. Her and my dad's disappointment could have flattened all the wheels on a cross-country six-wheeler. Privately, I thought I would mark my transition from privileged, suburban schoolgirl to feminist working woman. I wanted to drive one of those big pallet lifters that moved pallets from up high on the steel shelves and brought them down. That would be way cool. But instead, I got to load pallets and use the hand-operated pallet jacks. Way cooler! My job held no need for my fancy degrees and I felt a part of something that arose from my connection to Jude. Our social circle changed, and through working at CC Grains, we met MaryAnn and Carol.

MaryAnn and Carol had met as patients in the psychiatric unit at Harborview Hospital. Each of them had demons they'd tried to deal with. MaryAnn had tried to commit suicide. Carol had recently had a miscarriage and was not coping well with it, and she was having equally depressive and manic episodes about coming out. MaryAnn did not work at Grains, but we met her through Carol. Carol had juvenile diabetes and she resented it. She wore wire-rimmed glasses with lenses that she attributed to her diabetes. She didn't like following rules, she told me, so she took drugs her doctor didn't prescribe, but could cause her death. MaryAnn had survived an abusive hetero marriage and become a single mother of four. I asked Carol what drew her to MaryAnn and she said simply, "I like her butch energy and how she takes care of me."

We started hanging out, and Carol and I became best friends while loading pallets together. Jude was now driving a short-haul truck to a variety of small co-ops and natural-foods grocery stores in Washington State. Carol had an irreverent sense of humor and a class background similar to mine. She was trying even harder to disown her past. Carol's uniform of choice was a classic, white, wife-beater undershirt and army pants. We often challenged each other to see who could move the most fifty-pound bags in a day and took smoke breaks together. Me sticking with my True Blues and Carol with her Lucky Strikes.

She and MaryAnn and Jude and I went dancing or they came over to our place to hang out. Our socializing revolved around pot and alcohol and cutting loose on the dance floor. We frequently went dancing at either Eastlake East or the

Slipper until closing time. I loved the freedom of dancing: being able to let go. Eastlake East was a frenetic scene where sweaty men and women gyrated, song after song, to a thumping disco beat under a glittery disco ball. The bathroom contained women making out and taking drugs. Dancers openly took poppers on the dance floor. Sister Sledge's "We Are Family" often spilled from the speakers onto the floor, and finding a spot to shake or shimmy was challenging. I didn't care. Part of the joy was appreciating my body rather than accepting my parents' criticism. I could shake that off in a disco frenzy. Carol was uninhibited and needed no encouragement, and I often found myself dancing with her. Jude's idea of dancing was shuffling back and forth from one foot to the other. Don't get me wrong, though, I loved to slow-dance with Jude. I felt so protected in her embrace. I felt it on the dance floor and I felt it in our relationship. I wanted Jude to take care of me forever. I felt safe, much as I assumed Carol did with MaryAnn.

MaryAnn adored Carol. Anybody who interacted with them could see that. They had been together for a few years and the relationship seemed solid albeit dysfunctional. MaryAnn was a functioning alcoholic who held on to a well-paying administrative job downtown. One lunch hour, Carol and Jude disappeared together. I didn't think much of it. But when they returned and my eye caught them standing in the warehouse truck opening with the sunlight pouring in, their shaved heads glowed. "Oh, my God!" I exclaimed from across the warehouse. "What happened to your hair?" They both shouted, "We're free." Jude said her shaved head freed them from male oppression and from the notion of people liking her for the way she looked. I didn't want to shave mine.

I didn't feel the need. The four of us felt like family to me. I thought I had finally found a place where I was accepted for who I was. It didn't matter whether I wanted to shave my head or not. I could just be me without judgment.

The summer of 1980, I started attending law school at night and working for the city attorney's office as an intern. I had been with CC Grains for only three months, and while I enjoyed it, I saw that it wasn't going to be the rest of my life. Turns out that I couldn't quite shake off those parental expectations. Jude was widening her circle of friends at CC Grains that still included Carol and MaryAnn. The three of them decided to go to the Montana Womyn's Music Festival for the weekend and I would join them later in the week to go camping. I had heard of the Michigan Womyn's Music Festival and was sad I couldn't go to the one in Montana because of school and work. Women's music festivals started in the mid-1970s but always used a derivative spelling, such as "womyn" or "wimmin." They combined the politics of lesbian feminist rhetoric with the showcasing of lesbian singers, allowing these singers to grow their fan base. The event featured political discussion, but the big draw was the music and companionship of other lesbians.

After we came home from Montana, Jude seemed distant. "I don't know, Jill. We don't have to do everything together," she said one night, supposedly on her way to the Crescent. I wanted to go with her. I felt hurt but I didn't want to push it. I hadn't noticed Jude's withdrawals at first, though often I'd be done studying and getting ready for bed before she arrived home.

One night, the four of us were hanging out after deciding to stay in. We smoked pot, drank beers, and someone put some music on the turntable. We were dancing with our partners and then with each other's partners. I found myself getting turned on by watching MaryAnn's wiry body move provocatively across our living room. She had that glazed, stoner look that seemed to loosen her movements. While I knew I couldn't act on that arousal, I was turned on. I was surprised and scared. I hadn't felt this way about MaryAnn before. *Did it mean anything? Was I bad for getting aroused?* I felt guilty, but I also saw Jude and Carol standing and swaying dreamily with obvious affection for each other. I thought it was just the dope talking and didn't think anything more about it.

My relationship with Jude seemed pretty solid, but long-term relationships are like a house foundation that starts to crack. Solid until it starts to settle into the comfort. The cracks begin slowly, then splinter or widen. I didn't notice them at first. I would think, *oh, Jude's just having a bad day*. Then, perhaps, came a vocalized need for more space. Or, no vocalization but an icy cold distance that made me think I had left the door open. Jude was now working as a bookkeeper in the office at CC Grains and hanging out with her coworkers after work. I was busy studying for law school classes and doing my part-time job. We appeared to be drifting apart. I wondered where she was going, that person I'd poured my heart and soul into.

I didn't realize it at the time, but Jude was leaving me bit by bit. I had noticed we were making love less. One night, after some frustrating lovemaking, Jude said, "Let's stop. We're not getting anywhere." I just wanted to snuggle, but Jude wanted more and out of the blue asked, "Have you ever read any porn?"

"Pornography, no, why would I want to read that? Isn't that just for men?" I was aghast at the suggestion.

"I just thought it might help you be more adventuresome in our lovemaking," Jude said. "I've got some. I'll get them out for you to look at tomorrow." She turned over and turned off the bedside lamp. *Why did Jude need those books to get aroused? Wasn't our love for each other enough?*

The next day, I looked through Jude's porn. Naked women's bodies with unbelievably large tits and voluminous, hairy crotches, and the prose—if you could call it that—written obviously by men for men. I didn't like the books and was vaguely angry that Jude had asked me to look at them. What was she thinking? I thought it was adventurous to go down on her and have oral sex. But how could I know when Jude was my first real relationship with another woman?

"Jill, where are you? We need to talk," I heard Jude announce as she came in the door. I gladly closed my law book and turned toward her hoping for a kiss, but she walked around the table and sat across from me.

"Why the long face, honey?" I said.

"I don't quite know how to say this. B-B-But I need to break up with you." I felt as if I'd been punched in the stomach.

"What can I do, Jude? What happened? Did I do anything wrong?" I started to roll and spin a yellow highlighter next to my textbook on the table. I didn't want to look at her. I thought I would start crying. *Why? Why now? What am I going to do?* I thought this would last forever. My parents' relationship had lasted forever. The light fixture over the kitchen table suddenly seemed warm and I felt like I was in an investigation room under a detective's spotlight. My hands were twisting under the table.

"No, it's not that," she said as she fiddled with her shirt pocket where she kept her cigarettes. "It's just . . . it's just . . . well, for one thing, the way we make love. I want more than vanilla sex."

I looked up from my twisting hands, blinked at her, and looked away, the tears I'd been holding springing to my eyes. I tried to stay in the conversation. "What the heck is vanilla sex?" I said, knowing I should be embarrassed that I was asking. She'd made the term sound derogatory. "You're leaving because the sex isn't hot enough?"

"I need more excitement, Jill. You remember when I said I wasn't sure I wanted to be the one to help you come out. Well, it's not that. It's been great, but I want something more." She looked uncomfortable. "And there's one more thing."

"What else is there? I don't keep the house as clean as you like. Is that it?" I said.

"No, that's not it. Carol and I—"

I interrupted her. "Carol and you what?"

"We're in love. We realized it in Montana."

"Well, that's just great," I said. "Maybe MaryAnn and I should get together. That would solve everything, wouldn't it?" I was only half-joking, because I had felt attracted to MaryAnn that one night and thought rather naïvely we might just switch partners.

If she doesn't want me, I thought, *well, I'm not going to fight. I mean, that would be pathetic.* Maybe in this new world of lesbos, women partners did things like that. *What were the rules for breaking up? What would it even look like if I fought for her?* Jude suggested couples therapy. But she already seemed to have made up her mind. *Let her go*, I thought. I didn't know if MaryAnn would go for my fantastical idea, but it might make Jude jealous.

Jude and I continued to live together for six weeks as I watched Jude move on emotionally with Carol. Jude eventually moved out to be with her and I kept our apartment.

Desperation had made me suggest switching partners. I didn't want Jude to leave, and leaving me for my best friend was especially hard. That just didn't seem fair. Even though I should have seen the signs, I didn't really want to see what they meant. I figured MaryAnn wouldn't let go of Carol as easily as I was letting Jude go. Jude and I had only been together for eighteen months. Meanwhile, I waited pretty much in vain for MaryAnn to initiate something. I had been found wanting and my pride was hurt. For MaryAnn, it was more of a "screw you, Carol" response that propelled her toward me. I knew nothing about relationships or about the toxicity in Carol and MaryAnn's relationship. I just knew that I needed emotional intimacy before engaging in sex with someone. I didn't know how to use sex as a tool.

In my limited life experience as an out lesbian, I knew that women often hooked up with other people's partners or their best friends. The common joke was that you knew someone was a lesbian when, after three months of having sex with another woman, she packed a U-Haul so that she could move in. It was not the same kind of promiscuous sex that gay men were having in the 1980s, but women did jump around.

It was around this time that women started to play with sadomasochism. I began to see women at the bars wearing leather and collars and leashes. This was the non-vanilla sex Jude had alluded to. Women apparently liked to play power games as much as gay and straight men did. Who knew? All I knew was that I was repulsed by the idea.

Lillian Faderman, author of *Odd Girls and Twilight Lovers*, described this evolution in lesbianism as women giving themselves the permission to focus on what turned them on, rather than what was politically correct. She claimed that it was a way for lesbians to appropriate the lust and power hunger that feminist doctrine had deemed male. MaryAnn and I didn't have an S&M relationship. Our sex just reminded me of having sex with a guy. Thank god we only dated for three months.

I arrived at MaryAnn's rental house on my way home from night class at law school, the first time she'd asked me over when Carol wasn't there. Her place was a mess and her four kids were parked in front of the television. Leftover macaroni and cheese had begun to harden in a pan on the stove.

She took me into her bedroom. "You wanna fuck or what?" she said. *So downright romantic— how could I resist?* She started to undo my belt buckle, and I said, "What about the kids?" I'd agreed to come over but I wasn't expecting we'd go straight to her bedroom—the same bedroom she had shared with Carol. I'd thought that this was what I wanted: to prove Jude wrong and to do things beyond vanilla sex.

"Don't worry about them," she said, gesturing in the direction of her kids. "They're used to it. They know what a closed bedroom door means."

When I was growing up, I just thought my parents' closed bedroom door meant they were asleep. MaryAnn's kids had a much worldlier education. Once the niceties were out of the way, meaning our clothes were off, she said, "Carol likes to be fist-fucked. I bet you'd like that, huh?"

It seemed it wasn't going to matter what I said. She was drunk. As she blew smoke into my face from her menthol Virginia Slims I could smell the beer. I asked her how much she'd had to drink and she told me it was none of my goddamned business. I thought it best not to argue. She told me how big her ex-husband's penis had been and how that had gotten her to like fist-fucking. I hadn't ever been the recipient of fist-fucking. But since she seemed so keen, I thought, why not find out? She clearly wasn't interested in doing what I wanted.

We hardly had any foreplay, and after I was aroused, she went for it. I felt this huge object, her fist, in my vagina—like a battering ram. I kept telling her to stop whenever she paused from sticking her tongue down my throat, but maybe I was just telling her that in my head. She also kept asking me what that bitch Carol was saying about her.

I felt violated. I felt dirty and used. She was clearly using me to vent her anger. I didn't realize that women could do this to each other just as easily as men could to women. I had been living in some fairytale land of rainbows and unicorns where women believed in egalitarianism and cared about each other's feelings and pleasures. When we were done, I grabbed my jeans, not even bothering to thread my belt through the loops, strode through the living room where mercifully the kids' eyes were still glued to the television, and ran to my car. All I wanted to do was get home and take a shower.

The days seemed to pass in a daze. I went to work, studied for school, and went to my night classes. Jude and I saw each other infrequently. One night I heard the key turn in the front door lock and my heart jumped. Maybe Jude and I could talk.

"Jude?" I said, hoping my voice sounded relatively calm. "Is that you? Can we talk?" Jude was spending several evenings with Carol and I rarely saw her. I could hear her shuffling about in the bedroom and then I heard the shower. When she came out of the bedroom dressed, I said, "What about that therapy you suggested? I miss both you and Carol. I had hoped we could all stay friends, but that's not happening." I was trying to keep the whine out of my voice.

"I don't know, Jill. Our schedules don't seem to fit together," Jude said. "You're busy with work and law school and . . ." She mumbled something I didn't catch. "I've got to get going. Carol's waiting in the car."

That was like a right hook to my gut. I nodded. "Okay, then."

"Sorry Jill," she said and left.

The relationship therapy with all four of us never happened. I hadn't had much hope for it, anyway. I naïvely thought we all could stay friends.

A few weeks later, Cris Williamson and Holly Near came to town. This concert was huge: not to be missed. I hoped MaryAnn would go with me to mark such a big event for the Seattle lesbian community. I was sure Jude and Carol would be there, but I didn't care. Despite my excitement, I wasn't going to go by myself. MaryAnn willingly agreed to go with me.

We entered the 2,900-seat auditorium of the Seattle Opera House and I was overcome to see so many women. Some were in tuxes, and some, in jeans. I took a moment to just revel in the majesty of so many lesbian-identified women.

I had purchased really good tickets. When we found our seats in the main floor's fourth row, MaryAnn and I stood taking in the crowd. Just before intermission, though, she got up and left her seat. I thought she was avoiding the rush to the ladies' room. I waited until the song finished, not wanting to miss any of the music.

I later found MaryAnn arguing with Carol out in the hall—Carol's shaved head visible immediately. I didn't want to get involved and watched from a distance.

"Why are you doing this, Carol? It's time to come home, back to me. We belong together," MaryAnn said.

"No, MaryAnn. I just can't be with you anymore," Carol said. "Can't you quiet down? People are looking at us." I went back to my seat. I looked around for Jude but didn't see her. I thought the interaction between Carol and MaryAnn might explain why MaryAnn had seemed eager to come with me to the concert: she'd have a better shot at seeing Carol. This realization stung—to be used in this way.

On the drive back to MaryAnn's that night I was mostly silent. I wanted to connect again with that soft side I had first seen in MaryAnn. I wanted to say, *MaryAnn, don't you realize Carol isn't coming back? Take me. I can take care of you. I can make you forget Carol.* I knew my thinking was faulty. I wanted to be loved for me, not as a substitute for someone else. I had seen MaryAnn's soft side before the big breakup—how she treated Carol and touched her with affection—but that side rarely made an appearance. No, MaryAnn mostly tolerated me. She kept me around because she needed help with the kids. and she didn't like to be left alone with her feelings.

CHAPTER NINE

IDENTITY CRISIS

CAROL CALLED and asked if I wanted to come over to her place. I was glad. It had been a few weeks since we'd had one-on-one time together. I hadn't been sure if our friendship would continue after the big breakup. I didn't know where Jude was. Perhaps she was out of town doing a CC Grains delivery to Eastern Washington. Carol had found a studio apartment on the boundary line between Capitol Hill and Madison Valley, an old brick building with about twenty units built around a small courtyard. It wasn't Section 8 (low-income housing) yet, but certainly on its way there. Carol had outfitted it with her usual artsy flair. It featured an overstuffed red armchair from Value Village and a small, '50s-style Formica table and chairs in the kitchen. Carol no doubt slept on the blue couch she'd draped in an East Indian scarf. A couple of crystals on the windowsill completed her cozy little place.

Carol put on the tea kettle and asked me how things were going. "Not great," I said. "I miss you and Jude. Everything is so different now, like the world turned upside down." Carol nodded sympathetically. "Honestly, it's not going all that well. MaryAnn just wants you back." Carol smiled at that. I knew she didn't want to go back to MaryAnn but liked the fact that

MaryAnn still wanted her.

"Let's sit by the window," she suggested, "so we can smoke." She opened the window a crack to let the smoke exit. She gave me the teacup and settled into the armchair.

Carol told me she missed the kids. MaryAnn's four children ranged from ages six to twelve. During her relationship with MaryAnn, she had nurtured and cared for the kids while MaryAnn was either too busy or too burned out.

I told her I was worried about them. "With Scott, MaryAnn's oldest, left in charge, they seem to be mostly taking care of themselves."

Carol shook her head ruefully.

"She's angry, Carol. She's angry at me and at you and Jude, so she's turning inward and really neglecting the kids."

The subject then turned toward sex. "How's sex with MaryAnn?" Carol asked. I was taken aback by her invasive question. Even more awkward was the fact that the person she was asking about happened to be the one she had just left—a woman she'd made love to for seven years. I shook my head to signify my discomfort. But that didn't deter Carol. She went on in great detail about how she and MaryAnn had enjoyed fist-fucking and occasionally being tied to the bed. I was mortified. I hadn't experienced these sexual practices—at least, the fist-fucking part—until recently. MaryAnn and I hadn't had sex that many times anyways, and I thought it none of Carol's business.

And then we heard her out in the courtyard: MaryAnn. We couldn't quite see her as she was underneath the window we were looking out of.

"You whore," came MaryAnn's shouts. "How dare you talk to someone else about what we did in our bedroom. You left me, you bitch, and now you're sleeping with someone else. How dare you sit there, you princess, and talk about what passed between us."

Carol's head jerked up and her mouth turned into an "O." I was shocked that MaryAnn was out in the courtyard making all this private information public. I was also shocked that Carol had been discussing these details with me in the first place. Why would I care? But Carol was like that, sharing great intimacies that others would not dare to share. I shouldn't have been surprised.

We both peered out the window to get a glimpse of MaryAnn. She was dressed in blue jeans, a T-shirt, jean jacket, and cowboy boots, staggering all around the courtyard with a cigarette hanging out of her mouth. In her drunken state, I was worried about what she would do next. Then we heard her pounding on the door to Carol's apartment, so forcefully the cheap plywood door was vibrating. I was afraid it would break. "Should we let her in?" I said. Carol shook her almost bald head "no."

"She's being so loud, though," I protested. "Someone might call the cops." I reluctantly got up from the chair and turned the door handle. Carol moved from the couch into the kitchen to let her in. I knew immediately that letting her in was a mistake. MaryAnn staggered two steps toward Carol, cigarette still hanging out of her mouth. Her hair was disheveled, her eyes wild. She reeked of beer and cigarettes. Carol's eyes widened and she lurched back. I was behind the door watching the fear in Carol's eyes. I stepped toward MaryAnn in my stocking feet, thinking how easily she could take me down by stomping on my feet in her heavy boots. I took another step closer to MaryAnn and put out my hand as if to halt her. Carol was now near the kitchen entryway, having backed away to her own corner. MaryAnn brushed past me, advancing toward Carol. I moved again to block her, figuring I was bigger than MaryAnn and could take the brunt of whatever she had in store for Carol. I tried to yank her away from Carol but that thin, wiry, alcohol-fueled body was surprisingly agile. She fiercely elbowed me out of her way.

MaryAnn then pounced on Carol as if she were a large cat and Carol the prey. I tried to yank her off Carol—but was only partially successful—and then found myself in the middle of a violent fight. MaryAnn was clawing and Carol was yelling trying to get MaryAnn to back off, but she wouldn't. MaryAnn's fists knocked against my soft belly and occasionally her pointy cowboy boots thwacked my shins. And, goddammit, she even bit me. I'd landed in a melee and all I wanted to do was protect Carol and prevent anyone from getting hurt.

Finally, MaryAnn seemed to run out of steam, and with both Carol and me pushing her toward the door, we managed to maneuver MaryAnn out of the apartment. We were worried about her leaving and driving drunk back to Beacon Hill. I thought about calling the cops, but what would the cops do except laugh and call us a bunch of fighting dykes. It was 1980, and cops could be openly hostile toward lesbians and especially gay men. Domestic violence laws that required the arrest of the aggressor in fights among cohabitants had yet to be enacted. And besides, none of us lived together. As she pulled away in her car, I thought again about calling the police on MaryAnn for driving under the influence (DUI). But I didn't want to create more trouble for MaryAnn and her kids.

We let her drive away and Carol and I began to process what had happened. Finally, I roused myself. "Was she like this when you two were together?"

"She's got a temper, especially when she's drunk. But I've never seen her like that," Carol said. And then, perhaps realizing the physicality of the fight, she asked me if I was all right.

"Sure," I said, half-cocky. But inside, I wasn't so sure. I'd never been involved in a drama on that scale. I felt like Dorothy in *The Wizard of Oz*, landing in some foreign country whose cultural norms were so out of whack I longed for ruby slippers to take me back to Kansas. I had never been around angry, drunk people, especially those who got physical. I was pretty sure I didn't want to be around any more of them in the future. I had only seen those types on TV. I went home. The privileged lifestyle of my youth was not in sync with the life I was living. I was beginning to acknowledge the cognitive dissonance that Emma Copley Eisenberg writes of so well in her book *The Third Rainbow Girl: The Long Life of a Double Murder in Appalachia* when she describes what happens when "you have many of the advantages this life can bestow but have seen, up close and in slow motion, what they mean for those to whom they are denied. You start to think maybe you can abdicate your privilege like a crown, if only you try hard enough, and that maybe that will settle the score."

I didn't think I could give up my crown that easily, and little seemed to have been settled by talking to Carol. What's more, the evening had certainly ended on a somber note.

The next day at law school, I lifted my shirt in a women's restroom stall and examined the bruises and contusions on my midsection, and especially, my thighs and calves. MaryAnn's boots had left smaller marks around my ribs. The big, ugly bruises on my legs had started turning yellow and blue. I was horrified by evidence of bite marks. This experience just didn't jibe with going to law school. *Who had I become?*

I felt like some sort of double agent working as a paid intern in the city attorney's office by day, going to law school by night, and letting the lesbian out of the closet on weekends. I needed to settle down and do something constructive, perhaps along the lines of my parents' vision: getting a solid career and living "the good life"—whatever that was. But I was still a lesbian, albeit a covert lesbian. I didn't want to be in the closet most of the time. I ached to be me all the time. But I feared society's punishments. My parents' disapproval, coupled with my hidden status at law school, made me feel lonely and alone. I suspected the presence of other lesbians and gay men in my law classes, but I had yet to meet anyone like me.

In the summer of 1981, my first year of law school ended along with my relationship with Jude and my short-lived union with MaryAnn—the latter breakup occurring shortly after the three-way altercation with Carol. During this time, I received a letter from my parents about my coming out. I was excited when I saw the familiar handwriting on the envelope. *A letter from my mother, the one where she and my dad would apologize and tell me how much they loved me.* I soon saw that the letter was from both of them. It was, however, written in my mother's wonderfully clear penmanship. Her tone was equally clear. She started, "While we did not exactly hope for a Prince Charming, we certainly had not expected a frog." *Ooh, ouch*, I winced as I read the words. She again mentioned my masculine manner of dress and attacked my "mannish" friend,

Jude. "It's really important to put your best foot forward and appearances count," my mother went on. Lookism was my parents' native tongue. *Why hadn't I seen that growing up? Could it be that everyone I knew had looked and dressed the same way?* My shoulders caved and my insides seemed to crumble as I read on, because the letter contained no words of apology or acceptance, only words of defensiveness.

The topic turned to money in the next paragraph of the letter. "Are you supporting others on the monthly supplement we send you?" *They wanted to know if I was supporting girlfriends on what they sent to supplement my part-time job.* "And, we were wondering about a certain purchase on your credit card called 'liq.' Is this liquor? For you or someone else?" the letter said. I had purchased an item of clothing at a liquidation sale. *I'm sure they think I used it to buy liquor for some lesbian orgy.*

My mother mentioned they had gone to see a therapist about my news. I grasped at this hopeful tidbit. Therapy was almost a dirty word in my house. We Vannemans did not air our grievances to strangers and pay them to listen. When I told them I had started to see a therapist after the Leslie incident, they had been shocked. You didn't admit that you needed help. *They must have been deeply disturbed to want to see a therapist*, I thought. *Or, perhaps, lesbianism was such a foreign concept, they needed to learn more.*

"We went to Dr. Tomlinson three times," my mother wrote. *Dr. Tomlinson?* I had some vague recollection of this man from some of their parties and remembered his specialty was gerontology. I had hoped they might look into PFLAG, an organization that provides support for parents of gay and lesbian sons and daughters. The organization was mentioned as a resource in one of the books I'd left in my bedroom. My mom and dad said nothing about whether or not they had read these books. "Dr. Tomlinson told us that lesbians tend to be more monogamous than gay men," she wrote. That was it.

And then my father had a few lines at the bottom of the letter expressing his concern about my future and how they wanted the best for me, always. But his best piece of advice came toward the end. "Why can't you just masturbate?" This was their takeaway—my sexual orientation was all about having sex.

I shouted at the letter, "Yes, that's what it is all about, having FUCKING SEX!" I stood up, breathing heavily, and paced around the living room with giant strides. I picked up a few of my weighty law books and heaved them at the wall. They made huge, satisfying thuds when they hit, but the sounds didn't alleviate my anger.

A fence had been erected between my parents and me, dividing who I was before coming out and who I would be now that I'd come out. My parents, and especially my mother, had shown no interest in meeting me on the same side of the fence. The fence itself seemed insurmountable.

Now, I had to move on in some way. I felt stymied by what to do next. And that letter—*what on earth was I supposed to do with their hateful words and my anger?* I had no road map. I just stuffed it all in and tried to get on with my life.

I could no longer pretend my parents' betterment campaign was going to have the ending they wanted. But their shame would continue to mold who I was, how I interacted with them, and how I interacted with the world. Thankfully, I maintained our two thousand miles of physical distance. I could talk to them or not. I never found out if they read the books I had suggested to them when I came out. Perhaps my father did, because reading was how he processed things. What he thought of that information, though, he never shared.

Despite my fraught relationship with my parents, I needed to finish my first year of law school. I'd taken my first-year finals after the ill-fated, coming-out car ride and did badly. So badly that if I wanted to continue, I was going to have to petition the dean and apply for academic probation. I didn't want to admit that I couldn't hack it or make my parents think that being gay and becoming a lawyer were incompatible. Many ventures were like this for me. I had to do them twice before success arrived. Two tries at getting my driver's license. Two tries to pass my comprehensive major exams at Whitman. And now, two tries at becoming a lawyer. *What does that say about me? That I'm slow, dull-witted, lazy? No, I refuse to think of it—think of me—that way. My patterns say I'm persistent. Determined. Damn the torpedoes (as my father used to say), my family, and law school: I'm going to give it all my best shot.*

The prospect of meeting with Dean Fredric Tausend activated my anxiety. A former partner with a downtown Seattle law firm, he'd overseen the law school's transition from being located in a south Tacoma strip mall to becoming a world-class institution downtown. While waiting in reception on a September day, I crossed and re-crossed my legs, trying to contain my worry over being accepted back after such a rough year. I mused over why I'd let my self-imposed isolation become my undoing. The only academic success I experienced in the first year came from thoroughly detaching from other students. I thought we had nothing in common, that everyone else was fresh out of college, certain of their life's direction, and certain of their sexual orientation. Those orientations seemed to point them in the direction of high-paying jobs with Seattle's top law firms. My underlying insecurities got the better of me. I'd already wreaked tremendous self-harm by wrongly assuming people had the edge on me—assumptions that helped keep me in the closet. But societal pressures weren't my only reasons for staying stuck. I carted around my own homophobia. I feared the repercussions of being gay. Would people tell me I didn't belong in law school—or anywhere, for that matter? Certainly, my parents thought that way.

I learned that homophobia didn't just exist for straight people; gay people had it too. I had come out to my parents. I had also witnessed the fallout. When I wrote my best friend from high school, she wanted to know if I'd been interested in her. *Criminy!* We all—gays included—have homophobia, because we're so scared. Scared of other people's thoughts and judgments. It was those judgments that caused me to tie myself up in knots of self-doubt, wary of any help with the unravelling.

I threw myself a lifeline by sharing with the dean the story I'd rehearsed: I blamed gradual hearing loss on my poor performance. It wasn't a total lie. Wearing a hearing aid had indeed been a major adjustment my first year, and I only wore it for classes. He nodded, his face blank. I then surprised myself by speaking openly.

"Dean, there is one other thing. I'm gay, and my first long-term relationship broke up this year. I sought counseling but became depressed and almost suicidal." I took a big breath and sent up a silent prayer. "Two weeks before my property final, my parents responded to my 'coming out' with bizarre, personal attacks." I told the dean about the follow-up letter that spurred me to question my own judgment and values. I held my breath.

"You know Jill, I just recently divorced myself. It's hard seeing relationships end." He then proceeded to tell me how his recent divorce had affected him. "We had been married for a long time and the breakup was really rough. She wrote cookbooks about Mexican food and we took many memorable trips to Mexico for research." His speech was tinged with nostalgia. "I can see how a relationship breakup might make it difficult to concentrate on your studies." It was my turn to respond with a poker face. I struggled to believe the dean and I were having this intimate conversation in his office about our private lives. This was a far cry from the speech I'd rehearsed, let alone the subject matter for petitioning my return to law school. He then congratulated me on my persistence, making it clear that readmittance would mean repeating the first year. About two weeks later, I got the news that I would be readmitted. I wasn't thrilled about having to repeat the first year, although I vowed internally to make more of an effort to collaborate and socialize with the other students. The dean's kindness surprised me. I'd prepared for the worst, and he'd turned out to be so approachable.

I began my second year of law school as a full-time, first-year student. I kept a lid on my sexual orientation. I think the three women I carpooled with were the only peers who guessed I was gay. Every day at 7:00 a.m., I piled into a blue sedan with Marilyn, Sharon, and Kris. They talked about their husbands, but I never mentioned Kim, my current partner. I'd started seeing her several months after my breakup with MaryAnn. One Thursday in November, Sharon looked subdued as she squeezed into the back for the drive home from Tacoma. Straight-shooter Marilyn piped up, "What's up, Sharon?"

"Oh, I don't know. You think I would be used to it by now, but Gary Johnson said something to me."

"What? What?" we asked in unison.

"He asked me how long I'd been here."

"You mean, like how long you'd been here in the United States?" Marilyn said.

"Yes, yes. That's what he meant. I, of course, told him I'd been born here." Sharon looked down at the hands in her lap. She was Japanese-American.

I was stunned. *How stupid to ask somebody that, just because she wasn't white.* It was my first encounter with discrimination against someone besides me. It wouldn't be the last.

I knew Gary and didn't like him. He was in several of our classes, a Vietnam War vet who'd lost part of his arm. He wasn't shy about sharing his Christian conservatism. In fact, six weeks after Sharon's revelation, I liked him less when he wrote a letter to the editor of our school newspaper, the *Amicus.* A co-editor had written an editorial arguing for the banning of army recruiters from campus interviews because of the military's discrimination against gays—and Gary took the co-editor to task for it. The headline above Gary's letter read "Homosexuality is an Abomination to God."

"I have no tolerance for the attempt of homosexuals to insinuate themselves into American culture in the name of 'freedom' or 'tolerance,'" Gary wrote. He ended the letter, "I hold no ill will toward individual homosexuals, but I will do all in my power to prevent the sin of homosexuality."

I was furious—not only at Gary but with my classmates for not speaking out. If I wanted to stay in the closet, writing a response letter to the editor would likely knock down that closet door. I wanted to call Gary to task but feared for the invasion of my privacy. I believed that the right of homosexuals to exist in our culture superseded society's tolerance or sense of freedom. Gays existed regardless of their acceptance. I eventually decided to write the letter. I didn't want to join the army—I just wanted the army and the rest of society to stop treating gays differently. Just like I had been treated differently at my brother John's recent wedding. I'd been forbidden to bring my girlfriend. I'm sure my parents would have preferred I stay single forever than bring a girlfriend home. I could stay in the closet in Evanston, but not here, not in my newly claimed home.

So much for fitting in. The truth was, I itched to get out of that damned closet. But I was surrounded by too many Garys. This was the era of homophobe Anita Bryant, the once-adored "Sunshine Tree Girl" and former television advertising spokeswoman for Florida citrus, along with outspoken fundamentalist and televangelist Jerry Falwell. The two of them formed the infamous Moral Majority, a Christian far right organization that campaigned against homosexuality for fear it would destroy the sanctity of the American family.

In my letter, I addressed Gary directly. "Gays do not need to insinuate themselves into American culture. Gay men and women have been around for a long time—they are already a part of American and other cultures and will continue to be part of American and other cultures." Marilyn, Kris, and Sharon commended me on my letter, and I was relieved they still liked me. My letter otherwise caused few ripples at school. No one came up to me and said, "Oh, so you're gay." I held my head a little higher as I walked the halls at school. If asked, I wasn't going to hide who I was. But my law school experience turned out to be a rare reprieve. The homophobia of my parents and society in general would shadow me beyond those halls. *Why was my whole identity up for public consumption?* Perhaps that's why I so identified with Sharon.

CHAPTER TEN

THE WEDDING/ CHRISTINE

I WAS SITTING with my eighty-six-year-old grandmother, Fern, at one of the huge, round tables encircling the dance floor at the Crystal Lake Country Club, captive to an occasion I should have been happy about. But I was not happy. Far from it. It was October 1983. John had just gotten married. A partially full champagne glass sat in front of me. I was waiting for my brother to come ask me to dance. He and his new wife, Susan, had done their dance and he had danced with my mother. Now, John was dancing with mother-in-law Connie. I had made him promise to give his unmarried, twenty-eight-year-old sister one dance. I wondered if I might be waiting all night.

Grandmother started to get up and I asked her where she was going. "Mary Fern, I'm ready to go home," she said.

"Grandmother, I'm Jill, remember?" Her niece Mary Fern hadn't been able to make the trip up north from Bloomington, Illinois. I wasn't offended. Fern had dementia and I knew Mary Fern was one of her favorite people. At least she had mistaken me for someone she liked. Fern and I were sitting farthest from the dance floor, the better to stay hidden, I thought. I didn't feel part of this wedding at all. I'd been relegated to doing the guestbook, and now my duties were over. I had also taken it upon myself to act as Fern's minder, forestalling my parents' friends from coming over and asking me about a nonexistent boyfriend. Besides, I knew few people my age here.

Mom and Dad were happy to have me watching over Grandmother. They didn't want her wandering off and interrupting their gracious and happy moderations at the only wedding they would ever host. That thought—that membership in the gay community meant not only my parents writing off my future marriage but me giving up those hopes as well—had been on my mind the whole weekend. I desperately wanted to be happy for my brother, but I couldn't help thinking I would never get this opportunity. My parents' only daughter would never be the star and my mother would be robbed of planning that picture-perfect wedding.

C'mon, John, I thought, *come find me*. The dance floor was full of partygoers shaking their booties to Eurythmics' "Sweet Dreams (Are Made of This)." I couldn't distinguish my brother's familiar, sandy brown hair in the pulsing crowd. It was one of my favorite songs, but I refused to get up and dance alone. My lack of a male partner would be so obvious, and I worried the unwanted attention would detract from my family's happiness. Shame rooted me to my spot. *Come rescue me, John. Help me feel like I'm a part of this ritual that I myself will never get to enjoy.*

That gay people could even get married was such a remote and wacky idea; I was certain it would never happen. I had paid my dues as the sister of the groom. I did their token assignment in minding the guestbook. I smiled during the obligatory family wedding photos. Now I sat there watching my mother making the rounds, talking to guests, lapping up all the attention as mother of the groom. Her dress was an emerald green, its brocade fabric flowing from her waist; the top featured multicolored stripes with puffy sleeves gathered below her elbow. My father, in a traditional black tux, appeared in his element, grinning from ear to ear as the welcoming host. My mother too was smiling. But I couldn't sweep out the words from my head that she'd said two nights earlier.

We were in the family den, both of us sitting on the leather sofa. She had her legs tucked under her, a drink in one hand and a cigarette burning in the ashtray. Neither John nor my father were home. We had been discussing the wedding and talking about the rehearsal dinner, which was going to be the next night at Sunset Ridge Country Club. "What are the happy couple's plans after the wedding?" I asked, hoping my sarcasm wasn't evident. "Are they going to live in Evanston or what?"

I had asked because Susan was teaching elementary school in another suburb and that seemed like quite a commute from Evanston. And then, out of nowhere, she'd said, "You know, Jill, if John and Susan have children, they probably won't let you see them." I gasped involuntarily at her comment, but Mother didn't hear me. I didn't ask her to elaborate. But I had my suspicions about her reasoning: she considered my "life-style" a bad influence on her future grandchildren. And then, when she went on to ask me why I wore a ring on my wedding finger, I got up and left the room. I couldn't take any more of her hurt. She was angry with me. I knew that. She was angry at me for being gay, but this was a new low. I had not experienced my parents' intentional hurts while growing up. I wanted Kim.

I so wished Kim could have been there.

Kim and I had been living together for about two-and-a-half years. I'd met her about three months after my breakup with MaryAnn. A mutual friend had introduced us at a party and somehow I had invited Kim home with me. I badly needed her support at John's wedding, but she hadn't been invited. As far as my family was concerned, she didn't exist. They knew about her but when my mother called to tell me about the wedding, she had added no "be sure and bring Kim." I had wanted to see if she would suggest it, so I played passive-aggressive. And yet, it went without saying that Kim would be overlooked. I didn't even talk with Kim about it, except to tell her that I had to go to John's wedding. She didn't ask me if she could come. She had heard enough about my family and felt the brunt of my mother's inability to understand my life. Each time Kim answered the phone with my mother on the other end, she heard a cursory hello and then my mother asking right away if I was there.

I only wished I had been brave enough to bring her to the wedding in spite of everyone's wishes. The band was playing contemporary songs, the types of songs I danced to back in Seattle at Eastlake East or even the Crescent: two places in Seattle where I felt at home in my skin. I didn't feel "in my skin" at the wedding even when my friend Betsy, the sister of John's best man, came by, because we didn't have much in common anymore. We made small talk about our careers and the wedding and then she moved on. Finally, after several songs played, I saw my brother approach and I got my one dance. After that, I was ready to get on the flight back to Seattle.

Back home, I felt freer to be myself with Kim and my circle of friends. But at law school, I kept a lid on my sexual orientation. Even the letter to the editor I wrote about gays in the military didn't prompt me to tell other students I was a lesbian.

I still felt like I was fighting the battle for acceptance a year later while preparing to graduate. I said goodbye after a call from my parents and turned to Kim. "They're not coming to my graduation. I can't believe it, but they're not coming. After all my hard work, they're going to China instead." I hung up the yellow phone receiver attached to the wall in our kitchen apartment. It was part of a duplex on North Capitol Hill. Our living room windows provided a stunning, west-facing view of the Olympic Mountains. But right then, even that striking blue confluence of mountains and sky couldn't ease my distress.

Kim murmured sympathetic noises, but really, what could she say to make me feel better? She did say, "Never mind. I'll be there, and so will your aunt and uncle. We'll still celebrate." Her words didn't help much.

My mother had called to say they couldn't come to my law school graduation because their trip to China had been planned way back last fall. I might have given her the wrong date, but I know I wasn't that far off. She knew her daughter was graduating sometime that month. She could have double-checked.

"We're coming through Seattle on our way back from China and we'll see you then. We just won't be there for your graduation." Mom tried mollifying me.

"Mom, that's not the same thing and you know it," I retorted. "I've worked so hard and I want you there. It's important to me." But my pleas failed to rouse her. Probably one of the hardest things I'd ever done—law school—and they weren't even going to mark my success in person. I felt helpless, hurt, and angry. But, there was nothing I could do. I questioned if they wanted to be there at all. Throughout law school, I'd felt like my own island, emotionally. My parents had contributed financially, but that was it. After coming out, what little encouragement I'd previously received from them evaporated. Thank goodness for Kim. She was so supportive. Unlike my parents, who seemed ill at ease showing that kind of support.

When I questioned whether or not that emotional support had ever existed, I struggled to remember either my mother or father saying, "Gee, that must have been rough. How did that make you feel?" Or "I'm so sorry that happened to you."

My parents' lack of empathy was something I'd learned to live with. That didn't mean I was okay without it. I pined for understanding, and with each of life's milestones, I hoped for *their* "coming out," the day they would rally behind and cheer alongside me. But at each of these events, I was, in turn, disappointed. Opting out of my law school graduation was just another slight to be tucked into the vault, my mind's silent storage place. I'd stubbornly return to the vault and peer into it, again and again.

I looked over at Kim after hanging the phone in its cradle on the wall. "What is the fucking point? My parents care about certain things—such as my sexual orientation—but don't care about the things I want them to care about. I know they're proud of me for finishing law school. I know that on a visceral level. But I want them to show it." Kim didn't respond at first. What could she say? She'd never met my parents and only heard me grumble about our fraught relationship.

"Well, I'm very proud of you," Kim finally said and hugged me. In the end, graduation in the Exhibition Hall at the Tacoma Dome seemed like a non-event. I marched with my fellow grads across the platform. My aunt and uncle and Kim were sitting on their folding chairs. I heard them yell, "Yay, Jill," but their words fell flat. I stood tall on the stage like an adult, but I wanted my parents there.

After graduation, I faced little time for relaxing before studying for the bar exam. A law degree was insufficient for becoming a practicing attorney. I'd have to endure this crushing test of my ability to cram.

Washington's bar exam was a two-and-a-half-day test that occurred only twice a year at Seattle Center. Back then, it was all essay questions and issue-spotting. No notes. No books. Just me, the typewriter, and the test. I dragged the Smith Corona electric typewriter I'd received for my sixteenth birthday to Seattle Center to take the test. It got me through Whitman and law school. And, I was hoping it would get me through the exam.

I took Gay Pride Sunday off, though. It was always the last Sunday in June in Seattle when the gray skies finally allowed the sun to peek through. As usual, people packed along the sidewalk on Broadway dressed in short shorts and tank tops to enjoy those early summer rays. Couples walked arm in arm. Some even draped themselves over the other like partner accessories. I breathed in this day of energy and pride. This was back before corporate America co-opted the day as an excuse to wear rainbow colors and march en masse for the local bank or cell phone company. It was a celebration of gays for gays, and in my mind, our day to stick out our chests and proclaim who we were and feel good about it. Gay Pride took place on Capitol Hill: our hill, our hood. It was like a huge block party—one that always brought a tear to my eye, watching my AIDS crisis community come together in feathers and jockstraps and with dykes on bikes. Participants threw out free condoms. *This is what I am a part of. This is who I am*, I thought with pride. That event, that summer, was my only break from studying. My anxiety about taking the bar began to ramp up.

Kim surprised me amid my pre-exam jitters. "I think you need something special, something that will help when you take the bar."

"What on earth would that be?" *Oh, she's going to give me some good luck talisman*, I thought.

"Well, I had this idea of something that might help," she added, her words lifting me out of that horrible hole I'd been finding my way into too often of late.

"I'm willing to try anything," I said.

"There's this woman over at Unity Church, a lesbian therapist who does astral readings. I thought maybe she could get you out of your funk. I'd be happy to pay."

"What do I have to lose? That's so nice of you, Kim." And that's how I met Sam, a licensed therapist who would introduce me to new, albeit eclectic ideas. Sam would go on to be a significant part of my life—more or less—for the next seventeen years.

On a warm summer day in July 1984 I showed up in the cool basement of Unity Church near Denny Park to see what wisdom Sam could impart. *Boy, she's a young woman*, I thought when I sat across from her. *Not much older than me.*

I felt my skepticism rising like a snake that might choke out the hope of learning something from this woman. I shook it off. Sam began to talk about chakras and healing energies. *This is kind of woo-woo*, I thought. But Kim had paid for this session. Besides, I was curious. *Who knew? Maybe this woo-woo stuff worked.* I opened myself to Sam and soon she was talking about a blue light hovering and then surrounding me. The blue light signified the imminent arrival of a strong memory and sense of calm. She had me close my eyes and imagine that blue light. *Boy*, I thought, *this is kind of dumb*. All I could see was darkness. Then suddenly, with rising excitement, I saw the blue light. The light appeared in multiple shades of blue, melding into a single shade of cobalt. When I left Sam's office, I thought about the damn test and felt the calmest, most serene energy I'd experienced all summer. For the first time, I let go of despair. I thought that indeed, I might actually pass.

I'd felt open as I never had before—as though Sam had acquainted me with the power of the universe. I was so grateful for seeing something so positive within myself. At once, the experience hooked me onto the power of Sam.

After almost four years together, my relationship with Kim would ultimately fizzle, because I couldn't see the successful person she saw in me. When I first met Kim, she'd worked for the Fremont Public Association, a community-based organization providing employment and an emergency food bank for the economically disadvantaged. She then got a job as director of a University of Washington student advocacy program aimed at building healthy, sustainable futures. Kim had a vision for me. Under her progressive political lens, I would work as a progressive lawyer toward the betterment of society. While I liked that idea of myself—particularly in relation to causes affecting women—I wasn't sure I could pull it off. My academic performance in law school had been unremarkable, and studying took much of my time. But Kim saw me differently.

"Just think what you can do when you're a lawyer!" Kim said. She had a law student on her WashPIRG advocacy team fighting to rid 1950s nuclear waste from Washington's Hanford Site. WashPIRG was a nonprofit public interest advocacy group based on the University of Washington campus. Kim was its director. She was a strong believer in the Catholic slogan, "If you want peace, work for justice." She had even painted it on a canvas and framed it for me as inspiration. It's not that I didn't agree. I just found these aspirations lofty.

"I don't know, Kim, I'm no Clarence Darrow," I said. "You're not afraid of anything and your self-confidence far exceeds what I have."

"Don't say that, Jill. You have to believe in yourself more." She focused on my accomplishments and triumphs, believing me to be amazing. I thought myself an imposter. My parents' betterment campaign had sown seeds of doubt about my greatness. I felt pressure from Kim to be this progressive lawyer, while I'm sure my parents just wanted me to work for some prestigious law firm. Where Kim saw Lady Justice, I saw a law school grad crawling to an imaginary finish line. I did not see the young woman who persevered and got a special diploma, one that Dean Tausend explained in a private note had his middle initial C on it whereas all the others did not. This was to acknowledge my diligence. But Kim's and my opposing outlooks on my abilities weren't the primary reason our relationship failed. Our union lacked passion, and what's more, I had difficulty feeling Kim emotionally. Where Kim loved to talk about politics and ideas, I wanted to talk about feelings and I sought reassurances. I sometimes felt as though I were reaching out to her through clouds of cotton. I knew I was not in love with Kim. Perhaps I couldn't love anyone anymore, because I couldn't love myself. In the end—during the same summer I took the bar exam—my connection with Christine allowed me to sabotage my relationship with Kim.

Christine and I had met through mutual friends while I was in law school. She was an avid racquetball player. I too played racquetball. I'd picked up the sport at Whitman and played with a non-Tri Delt friend. I loved the fun, fast pace, and the workout.

"You could stop by my place in Federal Way and we could play a few games," Christine said one day. My interest was piqued. Kim and I hiked, but didn't really play any sports. I missed that. Federal Way was thirty miles from Kim and me and about halfway between Tacoma and Seattle.

The next week, I met Christine at her gym and we began to rally. She was really whacking the ball in our first warmup. I was hesitant when we began to rally, but the exertion of the game soon made my nervousness disappear. "That was fun," Christine said, as she beat me two out of three games. "Do you want a drink at my place? I'm just down the road in Redondo Beach."

"Yes," I said. I was curious about her place, which turned out to be a luxurious condo right on the water's edge. We sat in her elegant living room sipping lemonade and looking out at Puget Sound. It was a far cry from the overstuffed apartment full of used furniture I shared with Kim. Christine's furnishings gave the message of having arrived, of having money and being settled—all of the things I still longed for.

"What do you do?" I said after an awkward silence. I wanted to know how she could afford this place.

"I'm an only child and both my parents recently died. First my dad, and within a year, my mother," she said with some sadness. She was forty-one to my thirty, and the eleven-year difference gave her an air of maturity. She had been married and had two boys; she still shared custody with her ex-husband for one of them. I would soon learn that the sadness surrounding her came from the relative newness of a breakup: eleven years with another woman who had helped raise the two boys. She seemed to be trying to figure out where to go next.

With regard to her professional life, she said she was currently in massage school. *Wow*, I thought, *there's no way she can afford this condo if she's just in massage school.* That's when I figured she must have inherited some money, being an only child and all. *Hadn't she said her dad had been a banker or something?*

"What are you hoping to do with your law degree?" Christine said.

"At first, I wanted to be a public defender, but I just got this summer internship with the prosecutor's office," I said. "My dad's happy about that. He says it will give me more trial experience than working for a law firm."

"He's probably right," Christine said. "You know, Pam was a prosecutor and in trial all the time. That's how she met this woman she left me for." I couldn't imagine how anyone could leave Christine.

"Well, that's pretty rotten. But, it's her loss, really."

"I don't know about that, Jill. I really miss her. I thought our relationship would last forever," Christine then asked if I wanted to set up another racquetball date. I had to get going, anyways, to beat the rush hour traffic. We began to meet weekly for racquetball. It sure beat studying. It also created an outlet I didn't have with Kim. She was busy putting in long hours to create better environments for people to live in. I admired her passion and wished I had something to be equally passionate about in my life.

My friendship with Christine soon came with free massages as well as racquetball games. She said she needed so many practice hours to absorb her lessons and qualify for her license. I was a willing guinea pig. As her long, slender fingers moved down my spine and around my muscles, the stresses of law school melted away. Christine left me feeling cared for. To me, the feeling was not romantic or erotic.

No—Christine was friendly and safe, I told myself: she was recovering from her breakup, and I was in a long-term, committed relationship. Christine had a beguiling smile, coffee-colored eyes, and curly brown hair. I enjoyed her company. She talked about her teenage son who still lived with her part time. He was just learning to drive and she was nervous about it. She wasn't sure she could be in the car with him. I offered to take him out. She didn't say much about her former relationship but seemed to be trying to figure things out. With her massage practice, she was exploring new spiritual paths, featuring quartz crystals and meditative music in her massage room and attending a church of religious science. The New Age movement was in full swing, and after my recent session with Sam and the blue light, I was learning about a new realm of awareness. I started to embrace some of these new teachings because they brought new insights into how the world worked in a way that my God and Presbyterian background had not provided. Christine seemed to be further along her path of enlightenment. Heartfelt conversations and racquetball—that's all it was—until one weekend in early August after I took the bar exam.

Kim and I were standing in the kitchen after dinner one night when she announced that she was going to visit a "friend" in Montana, a former lover, in fact. I had some idea of what they'd likely be doing. Kim had been clear from the beginning that she wanted an "open" relationship. "What do you mean by open?" I had said. This was a new concept. *Weren't you just supposed to be with someone and not have sex with anybody else?* This is what I'd been taught about the coupling process and is what I believed to be true.

Kim said, "I mean, we can have sex with someone else when we're in a different state."

"Well, that works nicely for you," I said, telling her this approach was too one-sided. "The only other state I visit is Illinois and I'm certainly not going to have lesbian sex in my parents' home." But she was going to go with or without my approval.

To her credit, she was trying to be up front. "Go ahead and go and do whatever," I told her. "And don't think just because you told me it makes it any better."

With Kim off in Montana, I thought I'd like to go dancing and avoid spending the weekend alone. I immediately thought of Christine. We hadn't done anything besides racquetball and massage. I wondered if she'd be up for coming to Seattle. Kim and I rarely went out dancing and I hadn't gone to a gay bar in a long time. I wanted to get my groove on. I picked up the phone to dial and almost hung it up again. What if she said no or was going out tonight with someone? It could be risky. *Oh, Christ, Jill—it's just dancing. It doesn't mean anything.*

I hastily dialed before I lost my nerve. "I'd love to go. I haven't been dancing in a long time, either," Christine said.

"Come around eight and we'll go to Eastlake East."

She came to the house looking sharp. No blue jeans and T-shirt. She wore black jeans and an open-necked, rose-colored blouse with ballet shoes, earrings, and lipstick. None of my Crescent friends wore lipstick. Kim's friends tended to be progressive, radical women who didn't believe in makeup. Christine was softer than the dykes I knew from the Crescent days. Christine did not fit the classic dyke stereotype, or at least the one I had become familiar with. No one would have thought she was gay based on appearances.

She said she'd drive. She had this really sweet, black Oldsmobile Cutlass Supreme. It was the kind of car that grown-ups like my parents would drive, a far cry from my used VW wagon. When we first arrived, the club was kind of dead. But I knew pulsating music, neon laser lights, and the ubiquitous disco mirror-ball would soon jolt it back to life. I offered to get her a drink. Red wine for her and a beer for me. We made small talk, apparently waiting to dance once the crowd grew. More people started gathering and then Tina Turner's "What's Love Got to Do with It" came on and I grabbed Christine's hand. Tina's music had that effect on me. All I remember is that dancing with Christine brought a surge of energy I hadn't felt in a long time. I felt alive. We danced to one song after another. Boy, she could dance. When a slow song started, I waited for her to signal whether she wanted to slow dance or sit this one out.

When I didn't get a signal, I shuffled my feet and started to move away from the dance floor. She touched my arm. It felt like an electric charge and I turned toward her and said, "Do you want to dance to this one?"

She didn't hesitate. "Yes," she said, her face breaking into the most wonderful smile. Although we were close in height, I assumed the traditional male role and put my arm behind her back. I had already felt a spark between us even when we weren't dancing but being this close turned things up a notch. As we danced, our bodies touched and we drew closer together. Kenny Rogers sang "Lady," and I felt as if I was dancing with the lady Kenny was singing about. Her thigh pressed close to my crotch and I didn't want her to move it. Soon we were just swaying, no longer dancing, our bodies clasped together. The libido I thought had died somewhere between my law case studies and conversations with Kim poked her finger up and tapped me on the shoulder, reminding me there was more to life than reading Anais Nin in bed with Kim as a way to bring excitement into our lovemaking. I hoped the song would never end. The dance ended, and neither of us spoke, but my body was on fire. Did she feel the same way? She didn't say. We danced to more tunes and soon it was close to midnight. "I should probably go," she said, "before I'm too tired to drive back to Federal Way."

"Sure," I said. My insides were a mishmash of longing and confusion. She took me back to my house and I wanted to kiss her, but I was too scared. Perhaps I wanted time to be with the afterglow. "Thanks," she said. "That was so much fun." She left and I ran up the stairs to the home I shared with Kim and sat, savoring the evening.

The next morning, Christine called early and asked, "Did you feel what I did last night?" I had no question about what she meant.

"Oh, my God, yes," I said. I'm sure she could hear my barely disguised lust.

"Do you want to get together today?" she said.

It was a Saturday and I had the day free. I should have used it to study, but instead said, "That would be wonderful. I want to spend time with you." *Man, did I ever!*

We went to Richmond Beach. We walked and talked and poured out our feelings for each other. I was in such a state of limerence that when Christine asked if I wanted to come down to her place and spend the night I didn't hesitate. "That's an offer I can't refuse." Christine and I saw each other every night while Kim was out of town.

And then—Kim came home. I told her what had happened. After all, she was the one who wanted an open relationship, and whether it was in-state or out-of-state didn't seem to make much of a difference. I told her I wanted to continue both relationships. Kim's answer was an unequivocal no. She gave me a month to move. While looking for another place, I tried to spend as much time as I could with Christine or as much time as Christine would let me. It was becoming apparent that Christine had most of the power in the relationship. I couldn't have her come to the place I shared with Kim and didn't feel I could invite myself over.

Even after I moved, we seemed to spend most of our time at Christine's. Her place was nicer anyways, and it saved her the drive to and from Federal Way.

My infatuation with Christine kept me at her beck and call. She was that older woman with the beguiling smile and come-hither look. With just one glance at her alluring eyes, my heart dived to the pit of my stomach. That stomach flipped in anticipation of running my fingers through her thick, curly hair while we made love. In bed, my breath seemed to stop altogether. I had it bad for Christine. What I realized later was that all the women I fell in love with—Jude, Kim, and Christine—all seemed to exude the self-confidence I lacked. Had I thought they could somehow transfer it on to me?

But for Christine, love was not what our relationship was about. Little did I know, she was only toying with me. My fragile heart beat like a young puppy's. She was likely bemused. She would call at 8:30 p.m. and coyly ask if I wanted to come over. Never mind that it took thirty-five minutes down to her Redondo Beach condo. "Should I bring wine?" I would ask. Drinking wine was a prerequisite to our lovemaking. Later in our relationship, she would only say, "If you need it." Oh yes, I needed it. I needed to perform and felt bolstered by the wine's added courage. I was in awe of Christine. She lived a lifestyle I wanted, with a cleaning lady who came in weekly and even changed the sheets. She wasn't ostentatious, but her carefully chosen, modern furniture and paintings hadn't come from Goodwill. Her "classy lady" stature only heightened her appeal.

She lured me through her lovemaking, touching me in ways I hadn't been touched. Perhaps it was only the wine or my being crazy drunk in love with her, but often, when we made love, she cried. I'd never had someone cry during lovemaking. I hadn't known that lovemaking could cause that intense kind of release. Her tears felt like they came from a deep place, a place I did not feel I had access to. Something about the depth of what Christine was feeling told me that I couldn't even begin to access those sorrows within myself. But I made the mistake that Icarus had before he flew too close to the sun. I thought that if I could evoke that kind of release for Christine, I was the one who held that special power. I didn't know that at thirty, I was just a plaything. After two long-term relationships, she was sowing her oats. That's when Christine began telling me about another woman, Brenda.

"Oh, Brenda?" I said. "Was it fun?" I tried to hide the intensity of my dismay. But inwardly, I said, *nooo,* and cringed. *That's supposed to be me, only me.* If she was trying to make me jealous, it worked.

Through all of this love-induced, wine-drinking fog, I waited for my bar exam results. The problem with the bar exam—aside from the sheer range of topics I'd be hammered with—was the two-month wait until October for results. The wait was excruciating. I couldn't bear to fail and admit to being a further disappointment to my parents. But dating Christine typically took my mind off the waiting. Our affair seemed to be going so well.

And then I got the results of the bar exam. They arrived while Christine was at my newly rented half-duplex. My hands shook grasping the envelope. All those years of law school and then a long summer studying at UW's Gallagher Law Library. Now I held the future in my hands.

"Well, open it already," Christine urged. I did. My heart sank. I did not want to share the results and have her think less of me. I had passed the ethics part of the exam but not the substantive part. It meant taking another exam in February. I didn't want to study anymore. I was so tired of studying.

Suddenly, with Christine standing there in front of the window, her copper hair shining in the early afternoon sunlight, I threw the envelope with its damning results to the ground. I stamped both feet and raised my voice in one huge roar, "FUCK, NO. Fuck, no! Absolutely, fucking, no!"

Christine backed up. She had never seen me angry and I rarely used the word "fuck."

I'd scared myself too. I stood up with my feet on the envelope and my eyes wide toward the ceiling. My blood was pumping hard and my hands were turning into fists. I tried to breathe, but I couldn't.

Then I looked at Christine. I thought she would understand my pain.

"I have to go," she said quietly, like a child retreating from view. Avoiding eye contact, she gathered her coat and her purse and walked quickly, but softly, out the door.

I sat down on the floor and sobbed.

I thought she'd be back. The next day, at least. But apparently, I either terrified her or she used my sudden tantrum as an excuse to discontinue our relationship. I sunk into the aftermath of a broken relationship made worse because I'd been dumped. Rejection stings like an angry insect bite that you can't scratch enough. You're not supposed to scratch them, but I did. I sat in my lonely living room smoking cigarettes near the only open window in the room and ruminated and waited. I waited for her to call and explain. I waited a week, a month, and then two months before I realized she was not going to call or come back. I went to work, studied, and moped. Those three activities became my pattern over the next excruciating months. I became a lovesick teenager who hadn't had the opportunity to fall in love as a teenager with all of its wonderful and complicated feelings. Still grappling with my loneliness and homophobia, while struggling to find my way as a young professional, I had no life skills to deal with this outsized loss. My parents' reaction, I figured, would amount to an "I told you so," along with a firm suggestion I forgo my same-sex love interests and focus solely on my career. Without Christine, I needed someone to reassure me that my life was going to be worth living at all.

CHAPTER ELEVEN

THE POWER OF SAM

"HOW WOULD you kill yourself?" asked Sam. I had been formally seeing her as my therapist for a few months now. Breaking up with Kim, my all too brief, but intense relationship with Christine, and failing the bar had made me realize I needed help dealing with the sucker punches life was throwing at me. We met in the basement of Unity Church until she opened her own office in a different part of town. I had no qualms about going to therapy and Sam was easy to talk to.

"I think I would do it with a rope," I said.

"Tell me more about how, specifically."

"I think I would hang a rope from the light fixture in the living room ceiling."

"Do you have the items you need to do that?" she said.

"I have the rope in the back of my car."

"Can I have the rope?" Sam said. Such a simple solution. No hysteria from Sam about what we were discussing. Her tone, matter of fact, as though asking how my week had gone. I went out to my car to get the rope and hand it over. We then discussed my suicidal thoughts. I was so relieved that she had asked for the rope. Sure, I could buy another rope, but just her asking for it seemed to take the wind out of my thoughts and my intent to commit suicide.

I had been at the literal end of my own rope when I flunked the bar. What would I do with my life? My sexual orientation had been a huge disappointment for my parents, and I had thought by pursuing this profession, I could at least regain some of their love and approval. Not passing the bar was the final measure of my worth: a grade of zero. As the famous lesbian writer Rita Mae Brown said in her book *Venus Envy*, "The reward for conformity is that everyone likes you but yourself." I wanted some measure of conformity but didn't feel I was achieving it. *What the hell,* I thought, *I might as well end it.*

After I failed the bar and failed to keep Christine, I began to think *I* was the failure—that nothing would ever go my way. Christine represented my dream woman: easy on the eyes, sexy, independent, smart, and financially free so she wouldn't be dependent on me as other love interests had been. Years after the relationship ended, I referred to Christine as the "love of my life." She was the one who got away, the one I hadn't been able to keep. I had only felt that same intense, sexual energy with Leslie. My inability to keep either signified a dead end. I lacked the life experience to look ahead and see future romantic possibilities. I'd had my shot—and I blew it. It was my fault I couldn't hold a woman's interest for long, and worse, maybe I was just a bad person. I was inherently flawed; perhaps I was pathologically unlovable too.

I went to some pretty dark places looking for fault. I blamed my failure with Christine on the fact that I hadn't passed the bar, so I wasn't smart enough. I wasn't attractive enough because of my lip. I lived in a ratty apartment and couldn't wine and dine her as I wanted to. I just didn't have what it took to impress her. She had eleven years on me and had raised children already. I wasn't mature enough. Shame clung to me like the hot, humid days of my Chicago youth. I was still that naïve, insecure teenager when it came to dealing with rejection and disappointment. I had no deep reservoir of resilience to call upon. Any resilience I'd had had gone into surviving law school and my parents' rejection.

Because I didn't pass the bar, I lost an opportunity to become assistant city attorney for the City of Seattle and lost out on working as a King County prosecutor—employment opportunities I could have cinched if I had passed. As I pondered these losses, I realized I needed help with self-acceptance. Sam became my therapist. She and I began exploring why the pain of failure was so big for me. The weight of my failure and sadness seemed too much to bear, as though I was chained to a broken-down car and relying on my personal strength to pull it along. *Where was the repair shop? Why couldn't I just cut the chain?* By putting my vulnerable self entirely in the hands of a determined therapist, I thought I was asking her to fix me like the beaten-up wreck of a car and thereby set me free. It didn't occur to me that what I really needed was a road map toward self-acceptance in the here and now—that the car and the chain were one.

I began to question my previous perceptions of my parents and my "idyllic" childhood. I realized I had mistaken privileged for idyllic. Their rejection of my sexual identity and withdrawal of affections felt like a slap—and possibly one I deserved. Without a successful profession or relationship, I had no way to earn my way back into their good graces.

The depression that I brought into Sam's office had been seeping into my body, weighing me down in my claustrophobic apartment. I spent hours staring out the window at the gray gloom blanketing the mountains. I sat on the windowsill in my living room blowing smoke out the window into the dismal, ashen skies. I began thinking about ending my life because I couldn't let go of that weight, and I couldn't see a way forward. Who could I be in a society that refused to support gay people? My parents didn't want me, Christine didn't want me, and the legal profession didn't want me. *Without a profession, who exactly was I?* Where was the success I thought I'd been promised at birth? I was a *Vanneman* after all. *Weren't good things supposed to flow to me naturally because of that?* I never thought to ask why it wasn't enough for me to just be a human, taking up space like everyone else, allowed to be here like everyone else. It would take me years to discover that birthright wasn't enough. I had my own work to do, but I didn't know that yet.

My devastation over Christine and the bar exam results first led me to Sam's office, but the dangerous direction of my underlying thoughts spurred me to return. Sam was like Nancy Drew with a magnifying glass looking for clues to my profound distress. Perhaps she would help me uncover why I didn't merit occupancy on earth.

After the first few sessions, I came to rely on Sam as a weekly client. Anything she was into, I was into, even if her approach seemed a bit woo-woo. I got to pick a card from her box of "angel cards" at the end of each session. Each card contained one word that drew from the spiritual lessons from the book *A Course in Miracles*—words like "gratitude," "grace," and "forgiveness." The card was meant to resonate with you on the day you drew it. I always looked forward to that part of the session. The angel card words signaled hope.

As I studied to take the bar again, Sam became my lifeline. She kept my depression and thoughts of suicide at bay. I looked forward to seeing her each week. I truly believed she would find the answer as to why I was so miserable in my sparsely furnished, one-bedroom apartment, smoking cigarettes and drinking wine. The wine was my reward at the end of the day for studying property law about the rule against perpetuities and the theory of proximate cause in an accident, as well as lots of other legal minutiae that I was sure I would never use. But that was the problem. The bar exam covered everything one had learned in law school, and the test-taker had no idea what minutiae would be covered. I had to pass this time. I had to prove to my parents, the world, and to myself that I was "normal" and deserved to take a place in the society I grew up in.

When I entered Sam's office, I took a seat on the white, tufted couch and immediately grabbed one of the throw pillows. That was my custom—to grab the white-and-brown tweed throw pillow and hold it like a shield against my middle. Whether I clutched it to be defensive or protective, the poor pillow got a lot of love from me.

"Jill, let's start with you telling me about your family." I later found out Sam was digging into "family of origin" work. We spent a lot of time talking about my parents, and I extolled their virtues. I was blind to their reaction to my coming out: how it tainted the excellent work they had done in raising me. In particular, we spent a lot of time discussing my mother. Sam had me read Alice Miller's classic psychotherapy book,

The Drama of the Gifted Child, which I totally identified with. Through reading Miller's book, I saw the ways my parents might have just seen me as an extension of themselves, and not as an individual. The parts of me that didn't jibe with their vision remained unseen. I tussled with Sam, however, whenever she cast aspersions on my mother.

My mother thought I was overanalytical, I explained to Sam. My mom wanted me to be more competitive and was often uncomfortable with my adolescent musings. "She was my mom," I told Sam. "She was doing the best she could. I'm sure she did what she did because she wanted what was best for me."

"Really Jill?" Sam said. "Is that what you think she was doing when she threw you under the bus the day you came out to her and your dad?"

"She just thought I would live a life of loneliness," I protested.

"She wants you to be like her, Jill."

"What's wrong with that?"

"Why do you keep defending her, Jill?"

Then she asked, "Do you think your mother ever felt inadequate?"

"No," I said instantaneously. But then I remembered certain scenes from my childhood. The scenes were mere flashes.

I recalled several instances where she clashed with my grandparents, usually over politics at the dinner table. I knew it was politics, because my mother's roots were Democrat and blue collar. My strong, vocal, Republican-party-faithful grandparents were not shy about expressing their hostility toward the Democrats, especially when one was in the White House.

And, most likely they were discussing unions. The scene must have been from the tenure of Lyndon Baines Johnson, for I would have been old enough to register the importance and feel the tension as the barb was thrown and found its target in my mother. I saw the flash of anger register on her face as she quickly arose from the table on the pretext of getting something from the kitchen. I'm not sure she felt inadequate, but she surely felt the jab of her "fish out of water" existence, as it pointedly called out her roots and her marriage into a different tribe.

On another occasion, I recall an ordinary weeknight dinner in which my mother had tried a new recipe and spent longer in the kitchen before dinner was served. Dad had said some word I didn't know, and I asked what the word meant. As he often did when I asked, he said, "Go get the dictionary." Dinner would stop while I went to retrieve our Merriam-Webster, brought it to the table, and looked up the word. I don't remember the word I looked up, or what Mom served, but as soon as she did, John started to complain, "What is this? I don't want to eat this." I expected Dad to jump in and reprimand him, but he didn't. Instead, he said, "What is this, Shirli? It's a bit unusual."

I looked at Mom and her reddening face. I empathized with her hurt, because I knew how much time she had spent preparing the dish. I thought my brother and father were being mean. But, before I could say anything, Mom got up, left the table, and we heard the front door slam. My mother had never done this before. I briefly wondered if she had her cigarettes. It was dark out and cold.

"Aren't you going to go after her?" I asked my dad. "Someone should go after her. You hurt her feelings." None of us moved. After about half an hour, she came back. But we never discussed what happened. These occurrences were so rare, it was easy to think of my mother as super-confident, one-half of a power couple, and not as a woman with her own wounds.

I didn't want to discuss my mother with Sam. I preferred talking over the problems of the day and having Sam help me figure out a solution. *Why wasn't Christine calling me back? Why had Christine dumped me?* I wanted to feel soothed and relieved of my immediate burdens—not lured back into a vortex of complicated feelings toward my mother.

"My mother wasn't a beast," I told Sam. "Good grief! She didn't hit me or abuse me." I said these words after a recent trip home where my mother had criticized my unshaven legs and demanded to know why I wore a ring on my left ring finger. I wanted Sam to back off. I hugged the pillow tightly. Every time Sam would say something negative about my mother, I would swoop in to protect her. I'm not sure what I was afraid of. Perhaps I was afraid that if I did not protect my mother, she would disappear from my life forever.

Sam played a significant role in stopping me from committing suicide, but I was still depressed. And because I was depressed, I failed to fully appreciate Sam's intervention. At one Sam session, she asked me about my energy level, appetite, and zest for life. I had no idea why she was asking these questions, but when we were done she suggested I start seeing a nurse practitioner to obtain antidepressants. I had no idea that suicidal ideation was often a result of depression. From then on, we began to work in earnest on the despair that came from not being "good enough." This quest was the start of a seventeen-year therapy relationship with Sam. She also helped prepare me emotionally for taking the bar the second time—which I passed.

In addition to asking me to draw daily "angel cards," Sam was also into Reiki, a means of channeling spiritual energy through the hands of the Reiki practitioner, who places her hands at various places on the client's body. Sam was convinced she'd been able to use this technique once to help start her dishwasher. But I didn't want Reiki to start my dishwasher. My apartment didn't have a dishwasher. I just wanted to feel that energy. I liked this idea of being in tune with something outside my head. I soon found myself exploring many of the spiritual paths Sam seemed to be seeking, including Reiki training, neurolinguistic programming, astrology reading, and acupuncture, along with seeing Sam's gay male massage therapist and attending the same Unity church on Sundays. Anything she was into, I was into as well.

Sam also helped me face a grim reality I wasn't prepared for. Shortly after passing the bar, I went to a birthday lunch for Carol. She and Jude were still together. The lunch was in a private room at a local restaurant where I recognized some CC Grains womyn. About twenty of the womyn were there. I felt uncomfortable, especially now that Jude was with Carol, and ordered a glass of white wine. I didn't usually drink before dinner, but I wanted to straddle my social unease. Jude, who was sitting next to me, said, "Jill, do you see anyone else ordering wine with lunch?"

"Why do you need that? Do you see anyone else drinking?" she said. I guessed Jude was trying to warn me; both she and Carol had recently quit drinking. But then she hissed at me over the loud table chatter, "You have a problem Jill. When are you going to stop?" To spite her and to bolster my self-defense, I ordered another one. I needed to show her who was in charge of my life.

After that lunch, I drove to a subsequent appointment with Sam. On the way there, I struggled to gauge the distance between my car and the cars in front of me, all distorted angles and blurred edges, as though I was looking through a funhouse mirror. I began to realize my drinking was affecting my depth perception. I made it safely to Sam's office, but blurted out my consternation over Jude's comments at lunch. Rather than reassure me, Sam announced, "Jill, I can't see you anymore." I felt my heart clench. Sam was my life raft. She couldn't fire me as a patient. She was the one keeping me sane. *What will I do without her to guide me*?

She continued. "I can't see you unless you agree to quit drinking. I want you to go get an alcohol assessment."

"What? You think I have a drinking problem?" I knew what an assessment was. I had worked as a baby prosecutor the previous summer during my internship in the King County prosecutor's office. I'd seen the paperwork for the many drunk driving cases I'd prosecuted. Probation usually used these assessments in the sentencing phase.

I'm not one of them, I angrily said in my head. I was scared and I felt shamed, my defensiveness rising. But I did go for the evaluation. It came back that I had a "borderline problem," suggesting my habits needed changing, lest my "problem" grow bigger. I resented the hell out of this diagnosis. Having two glasses of wine every night wasn't alcoholism, was it? I could manage my job, but I didn't want to lose Sam. I quit drinking and started going to a gay Alcoholics Anonymous on the weekends and one for professionals in the mornings on my way to work. My double life had tripled—hiding my sexual orientation and alcoholism while appearing perfectly capable in court. I recoiled from the horrors I heard around the AA table. I was not blacking out, I was not hiding bottles, and I had not hit some proverbial bottom. Instead, my therapist decided my proverbial bottom. I heard one gay man admit during a meeting that he had killed someone. I did not belong with these people. I avoided working the steps or finding a sponsor and, consequently, started drinking again about a year later. I knew I wasn't an alcoholic. Of course, I did not disclose my conclusions—or my renewed drinking—to Sam.

In the meantime, Sam seemed to want to get at the root of why I didn't feel worthy of love from anyone. What I didn't realize then was that I had picked the perfect therapist to help further my parents' betterment campaign. It was as if my parents had said to Sam, *We've done what we can. Now, you fix her.* Sam's pathological approach was perfect: we moved from causality to causality. I bought into the idea that something, one thing, had to explain why I was different and didn't fit in. I was looking for the answer to why nobody seemed to love me. I felt like I had gone through so many abandonments and betrayals: Leslie, my parents, Jude, and now, Christine. I just didn't understand my own anguish. I felt crippled by it. Why did I feel so ashamed of who I was? The pain of feeling like I had no control over my life was unbearable. I had been psychically knocked to the floor and could not get back up—as though my bones had given out. One day I arrived at therapy and settled into the couch, adjusting the pillow security blanket, and Sam asked the oddest question. "Do you think you've ever been sexually abused?"

"Not that I am aware of," I responded immediately. I had heard of repressed memories—particularly as they applied to incidents of incest or sexual abuse—but felt certain they didn't apply to me. That's when my therapy with Sam began turning bizarre. During our next appointment, she coached me to close my eyes and go within for deeper messages from my subconsciousness. I envisioned one childhood neighbor, Paul, a rather crude man whose daughter was a friend of mine—someone who might fit the bill of a child molester. Paul was a physician, the son of a small-town Oregon drunk who was literally referred to as the town drunk. I had thought that this was a character name only found in novels. Paul had risen above his roots and had gone to Harvard undergrad and then to its medical school. He liked to tease and flirt with me and his daughter's other friends. I conjured up my memory of the bedroom he shared with his wife. I had spent enough time in their house to know this bedroom was right across from my friend's bedroom where we'd spent a lot of time. He'd said suggestive things about his wife and verbally abused her in front of others. I wasn't afraid of him, but he'd definitely made me feel uncomfortable.

In subsequent sessions, Sam worked harder at helping me discover my so-called repressed memories. I could see the image of my former neighbor in my mind's eye, but then the edges would get fuzzy. Sam kept pushing, "Go deeper, Jill." I thought, *what the hell*: if I couldn't remember, I couldn't remember. However, I liked to please others and I wanted to please Sam, so I offered Paul's name. "Well, maybe—I don't know. I don't have any clear recollection."

When I came back the next week Sam pushed more and wanted to know the specifics, but I couldn't think of any and said so. Sam wouldn't let it go. It was like she was onto something, like this affliction *had* to be the reason I was so messed up. She had me read *The Courage to Heal*, but I didn't get very far into the exercises. The theory just didn't fit. I kept telling Sam that Paul hadn't molested me.

We continued to explore this topic regardless, with her coaxing me to go inside myself, and on one occasion, I started to make up shit. I knew it was made up when I said it. Stuff like being taken to some bonfire in Olympia where sheriff's deputies made women strip and suck the guy off. I don't know where the hell that story came from, though I vaguely recalled hearing some news story about a similar scenario. Another time, I was in the Jacksons' kitchen watching men other than Paul tie a woman up and have her perform sex acts on the men. Most of these offerings had to do with men assuming power over women while I simply observed. Sam didn't say anything and I didn't tell her I was making these stories up—no matter how lurid or fantastical. She kept pushing for more. Each time I came away uncomfortable, wondering why she didn't stop me.

I had given Sam so much power that when she suggested I join a group she had started for sex abuse survivor clients, I started going. I kept thinking Sam must be right, that repressed incidents of sexual abuse were at the root of my problems and all I had to do was magically remember them. At the same time, I began dreading these sessions. "I don't think this is it," I eventually blurted. I wanted this line of exploration to stop. Still, Sam never questioned if or why I'd made up these stories.

We just moved on to other possible reasons for my lack of self-acceptance, this time concerning my cleft lip.

Sam began asking me questions about the length of my hospital stay after I was born and had facial surgery. I told her about my earliest memory. "I don't know how young I was, but I remember lying in a crib looking out the slats. Sunlight was pouring in from a large window and I noticed I was not in my own room but a bigger room. I had no fear, only curiosity. I remember someone walking by, her long, black robe brushing against the crib. I couldn't see her hair; she wore some kind of hood. Years later, I decided that I was recalling being in the Catholic hospital nursery where I'd had these surgeries." Sam's only response was an "Ah." And off we went on another deep dive into yet another cause for my psychic anguish.

Not long after broaching the subject of my surgeries, my parents came to town and I thought to ask my mother Sam's question about whether I had been left in the hospital after my birth for surgery to close the hole in my palate. My mother and my aunt had their cigarettes going. The three of us were sitting in my aunt and uncle's living room in their tiny West Seattle home. It was a summer day and my mother, dad, and uncle had just returned from a day of golf. I sat on a chair across from my mother and everybody seemed to be relaxed and enjoying each other's company. My dad and uncle were out on the deck a few feet away. We had been talking about my mother's Seattle-area relatives, the Johnsons, when I asked, "Mom, how long did I have to stay in the hospital after I was born?" It seemed like a question any child with a similar disability might ask a parent. But my mother stood up abruptly. Her hazel-brown eyes pierced me with laser-like intensity.

"Why are you asking me this? We of course brought you home right away. Why would you think any differently?" It was as if I were challenging her in some way. She appeared shocked—speechless.

"I . . . I only wondered . . ." but I couldn't continue and petered off. The subject was closed. What I didn't understand was why my mother seemed so rattled and hurt by this question. I wasn't questioning her parenting. I was just asking a question. She made it clear, though, that the conversation was closed: we would never discuss this topic again.

I went back to Sam's the next week and dutifully reported the conversation. As I repeated the story, Sam sat up straighter and her face broadened into a smile as if to say, *Aha, I knew it.* I asked her why she thought my mother had responded this way. "Don't you think she was overreacting, Sam?"

She nodded. "I think we're on to something here. Don't you see? You were probably left in the hospital for days, cut off from your mother at a very young age when those bonds are forged." Contrary to my mother's denial, Sam seemed to think that I had been abandoned. I seemed to have no way of confirming Sam's theory, but somehow, it felt right: the answer to what was wrong with me—why I was filled with shame and self-loathing and was considering ending my life—perhaps it had something to do with my lip. I was desperate for one answer to why I didn't fit in and why my inner critic was so tough on me. It would take years to figure out that there wasn't just one easy answer, but I persisted in the belief that there was one cause and if we got to the root of it, I would be healed.

I received confirmation of this belief several weeks later when I went to a Siddha Yoga retreat in Vancouver, British

Columbia. Sam was there as I knew she would be. This retreat was a big deal, since Gurumayi—the spiritual head of Siddha Yoga—would be there. The guru herself was offering personal blessings if you persisted long enough to grab her attention after standing patiently in a long line. Your wait would be rewarded when she looked into your eyes, smiled, and waved a peacock feather over you. What a thrill! The devotees called it being "bopped."

But that's not where I received my deep revelation that weekend. It arrived during the second day's long meditation session. We had sat in the auditorium chanting for about half an hour. I found great comfort in singing praises to any higher being, whether it be a Christian God or the Hindu version of God or a spiritual leader. I'd worked myself into a trancelike state and I could feel Sam's presence nearby. She was serving as an usher and was the person who had seated me.

The devotees such as myself would usually chant the same phrase over and over for anywhere from half an hour to an hour or more and it was hypnotic. After this particularly intensive chanting session, I found myself floating in a blue space that seemed tinged with otherworldly light. In that light I saw my face in a way I had never seen it.

I didn't usually look at my face. I don't hate it, but I am aware that it looks different from others'. But in that moment my face hovered there, suspended in space, and I became overwhelmed with such love for myself. It was as if I were seeing myself for the first time. Tears began to flow freely down my face as if a dam had broken.

I understood in that moment that I was not my lip. This one little difference lost its power to set me apart.

After that day, I would no longer dwell on the particulars of my cleft correction surgery, and eventually, I would give up encouraging Sam to "fix me." I stopped envisioning committing suicide and eventually stopped seeing Sam for therapy. But the message she'd reinforced that I still needed fixing—accompanied by inexplicable shame—still lurked somewhere below the surface.

Sam and I had talked about shame and the power it held over me and through *A Course in Miracles* I had learned about having compassion for myself, but the core belief that there was something wrong with me was like bedrock.

CHAPTER TWELVE

GUILTY AS CHARGED

"MADAME PROSECUTOR?" Judge Evans said. I turned around. Was he talking to me? He couldn't be. But I was the only one in the courtroom who fit that description. "What are we doing with this case?" the judge continued.

"It's a DUI, your honor. But we have an agreed recommendation to reduce the charge to reckless driving and include attendance at AIS (Alcohol Information School)." Todd, the public defender, nodded in agreement. I was glad to see that his other partner, Dave K., wasn't with him. Whenever we were in the courtroom together, Dave seemed to fight me on everything, and I was sure he took advantage of my newness. A veteran lawyer, Dave would always explain in laborious detail the weaknesses of my case, or—worse yet—that I had no case at all.

It was the spring of 1986. I had passed the bar in February 1985 and it had taken me a year to get this full-time job. When I hadn't at first passed the bar, the King County prosecutor's office had thrown me a bone and offered me a job as a paralegal. I'd hated that job, thinking I was overqualified for it and resenting having to unofficially train the baby prosecutors when I should have been one of them.

But now, I was a prosecutor, the only prosecutor for the City of Kent. I wore suits with skirts and jackets, which had big, padded shoulders. I even started wearing makeup and high heels. At five-foot-eight, I towered over some defense attorneys, or could at least look them directly in the eye when they tried to weasel a plea bargain their client didn't deserve or told me their client was a good guy and didn't really deserve a year in jail. Defense counsel would insist that, "No, what he needed was a treatment program to address his alcoholism," even though he'd already been through three different programs. When I had to say no, the heels helped a lot.

I sat at the counsel table and defense attorneys would wait their turns to come speak to me about their client, whether they were going to trial or tossing out a plea negotiation they hoped I would agree with or presenting me with an iron-clad defense. I was terrified of my sudden power. I didn't know what to do with it or even if I deserved it. What if I made the wrong decision? What if I let the guilty go free or the innocent pay an unwarranted price? That's why I never wanted to prosecute felonies: too much was at stake. I feared the weight of my responsibilities, my novice claim to stature in the courtroom. I'd grown a lot since my suicidal days, but my self-esteem was still on shaky ground.

I tried to hide my stage fright as each defense attorney came to my table and I sorted through what to accept. Ken F., a well-known and highly regarded attorney, walked into the courtroom in suits with bolo ties and expensive cowboy boots.

He was known for his rigorous, legal attacks on testifying police officers and their reliance on Breathalyzer machines. Whenever he wanted to go to trial, I would panic and then pull a deep breath. Rather than trying to get a conviction, I almost always wanted to plea-bargain to spare myself Ken's excellent litigation skills.

Something like twenty-five cases would appear on the morning docket that needed to be plea-bargained or tried. Often, I didn't have much time to prepare the cases, especially those cases tried as bench trials before the judge. While I had final say over a case going to trial, I often anguished over internal second-guessing. One day, the local public defender, Todd, came up to me. "I don't get it, Jill." I sensed but couldn't understand his exasperation with me.

I invited him to sit down next to me. And then he said, "What is your theory about justice?"

"Theory . . ." I pondered aloud. Inwardly, I thought, *I'm just trying to keep my head above water here, that's my theory*. I didn't add, *That's what I've been trying to do my whole life: keep myself together as a functioning, rational human*. Some days, I was more successful than others. To Todd I said, "I'm just a gatekeeper, trying to move the cases along, the winnower of justice." Todd rolled his eyes and walked away.

Regardless of what Todd thought of my approach to lawyering, my parents were finally proud of me. They didn't exactly say those words, but I sensed that I had at least arrived professionally in their eyes. My father was particularly pleased, and often asked about my cases. At thirty-two, I was finally financially independent. We just veered away from talking about my personal life—an arena I got the feeling they were still loath to explore.

As a newbie prosecutor, I also had to learn how to get along with the cops. I needed their knowledge and they often knew the case law better than I did. They respected me, but I couldn't determine if they were my friends or just my coworkers. A part of my training at this new job required going on a ride-along. One night, I settled into the front passenger seat with officer Pat Lowery. I listened to calls coming in over the police radio with operators reciting strange number codes. The radio would hiss and crackle: "There's a one-o-two-one-o over on the Kent-Kangley, officer needs assistance" or "Burglary on Smith." Pat picked up the extension mic and told them we were closest to the location, so he'd take the call. Without bothering to turn on the siren, he sped us quickly to the location and parked a few addresses down. He grabbed the shotgun anchored in place between us, turned to me, and said, "Do you know how to shoot?" I barely sputtered a reply, my adrenaline coursing up to the base of my throat. "No," I croaked. But then he said, "Come on, let's go." I looked at him as if he'd lost his mind.

"You want me to go with you?"

"Yes, I might need backup." We clambered out of the black-and-white cruiser, my heart clunking around like old boots on concrete, and with Pat leading the way, we snuck up the side path. My pulse was now racing at all the things that could go wrong, my mind wondering how in the world I could be of assistance. But the house sat quiet. Pat left me to go around to the back and I really began to shake. Then he reappeared just as quickly. "Nothing's happening. Let's go." Pat must have caught the look of relief on my face. He chuckled. "Wasn't that fun?" I couldn't believe he was making light of this situation. Was this all a joke or was the dispatcher number code for something like "Time to mess with the new female prosecutor"? I knew that the cops liked to play practical jokes on one another, but I didn't know how to relax in their presence or take things in stride. I was also worried they would find out I was gay. I'd heard them make mean-spirited jokes about gays. When I wasn't in the courtroom, I kept my distance from the cops. Safer to protect my private life and otherwise keep my distance, I thought.

Not that the police officers were knocking at my door to have lunch and if they had, I'm not sure what I would have talked to them about. I certainly wasn't going to offer up what my girlfriend and I did over the weekend. I would hear the guys talking in the courtroom hallway about social events they were going to with girlfriends or wives. What would I have to contribute to this hetero conversation?

But the cops weren't the only ones who I felt uncomfortable with. I didn't feel like I had much in common with most of the straight office women I worked with, either. Morning court often pushed up against my one-hour lunch, and I had to be back at one to talk to witnesses and prepare afternoon cases. To address the pain of not having lunchmates, I decided to take up running during lunch. I would drive to the local athletic club to change my clothes and then pound the pavement. Sometimes a cruiser might slow down and honk at me in recognition. Running was a good way to let off the stress of being in court six hours a day. I was also running because even with all the power and apparent respect I got from those I worked with, I still didn't feel good enough to be a prosecutor or even to lunch with the others.

While I remained terrified of making mistakes in my first real job, sometimes I felt like a star. I hadn't expected to feel this way. I wasn't used to power or sudden popularity. People talked to me: they included me in conversations and seemed to like me; I could feel it. Linda, especially, made me feel this way. She was the telephone receptionist who sat outside my office. She had nicely coiffed, short, black hair and a professional demeanor. She seemed to enjoy her job. When I returned from court, she always had a smile for me. She'd be clutching a sheaf of pink message slips and hand them to me, saying, "I don't know how you do it, Jill. All day in court and then all these phone calls you have to return when you get back." I felt respected. I felt seen. Something I hadn't felt in a long time.

Just one thing niggled at me. One tiny thing. I was hiding the fact that I was gay. I worked with cops and at times heard mean-spirited jokes about gays. AIDS was in the news. Headlines about the "homosexual disease" and the government's clear abhorrence and lack of concern for this population set the tone for society, which included our law office. I kept my distance from the cops by going straight from court to the gym to change into my running gear: to get out of my suit and heels, if only for an hour. I packed yogurt for lunch every day to allow most of my lunch hour to run. The minute I picked up my pace, I could feel that day's defense attorney and his caustic remarks about the weakness of my case sliding off my back, and the judge's bored expression soon left me as well. None of the police officers were knocking at my door to go for lunch and I didn't know what to talk about with them if they had been. I don't know why I thought cops and prosecutors should be best pals. Perhaps I'd absorbed the literal picture of that scenario from a hit TV show during the '80s, *Hill Street Blues*, that featured Captain Frank Furillo often in bed with public defender Joyce Davenport, discussing their daily triumphs and frustrations within the legal system. In reality, the cops I knew viewed the world in black and white. Some were even Christian. Christian cops . . . They might shun me if they knew I was gay. Why risk that pain? I'd been there before and had no desire to face that rejection again.

During my lunchtime runs, I kept seeing this woman around the small campus that included city hall and the other city departments. She looked fit and attractive, with gray-streaked, black, curly hair and a ready smile. She looked as if she could be a kindred spirit. I made some discreet inquiries and learned her name was Cheryl and that she worked for what was then called the "special populations" section of the parks department. I was intrigued.

One day I saw Cheryl in the lobby of Kent's city hall and I casually walked out of the building with her and into the spring air. When I was sure no one was around us, I said, "Hey, this may be a weird question, but are you gay?" She looked at me as if she'd been struck, her eyes radiating fear. "Shhh," she cautioned me. She continued walking and I followed along toward her office building. It turned out that she was about my age and worked with disabled youth in the parks program. I told her how I had come to notice her and she admitted that she too had wondered about me. I was starting to learn about this strange sense of mutual recognition gay women acquire whenever they're around each other. Cheryl was equally closeted in her workplace and we talked about the worry that our respective coworkers could nonetheless tell that we were gay. You just didn't know who you could trust. We could be fired for being gay. Kent was not Seattle, where employees were protected. Since 1973, Seattle had declared it illegal to discriminate in the workplace based on sexual orientation. Small town Kent was not that progressive.

I had been the City of Kent prosecutor for a few months when my boss, city attorney Steve, had approached me. I liked Steve. He was easygoing, but also decisive and helpful when I came to him with a question. I was even more impressed with the fact that he was willing to come to court and get his hands dirty—to actually prosecute. It was a job well beneath his title, but he told me he liked keeping in touch with the judges.

At midafternoon on a summer Friday, I was wearing my freshly ironed, navy-blue khaki slacks and a pale pink polo shirt. I didn't have court that day, but a mound of pink paper slips with phone numbers awaited my response: messages from cops, witnesses, and others. A thick pile of case files spilled across my desk. The sun poured in through the partially open blinds in my little office. I needed to take a break and stretch. I ran into Steve just outside my office. He smiled, looked at me pleasantly, and then frowned. "I need to talk to you," he said.

Uh oh, I thought, pondering the millions of mistakes I might have made or which judge I had pissed off. I swallowed the lump in my throat before following him back to his office.

"Jill, the outfit you're wearing just isn't appropriate," Steve said, when he turned to face me. I peered down at my clothes right away, because I couldn't remember what I'd put on that morning that could be so offensive. In 1986, women wore slacks. I blushed. "Can you tell me what's wrong with what I'm wearing?"

"It's just too casual and sets a wrong image," Steve replied.

I was relieved I hadn't screwed up in court but I was taken aback. Steve wore khaki slacks and a polo shirt. *What the hell*, I thought. *I look exactly like you.* But what was the point in arguing? He was the boss, and while it was okay to argue in court, one didn't argue with the boss. Besides, I liked Steve and was willing to tolerate his opinions. I reminded myself that even though we'd "come a long way baby"—as the television ad for Virginia Slims cigarettes cajoled women of our era—the double standard spoke up louder and clearer in our day-to-day realities.

The next day, I switched back to wearing dresses and pantsuits and waited for the rest of the world to catch up. *How mortified my parents would have been*, I thought, *by my boss needing to comment on my attire*. But they didn't need to know that little detail now that I was in their good graces: slotted into a profession that fit what they'd wanted for me.

The glow of being a star for my parents faded, however, each time I returned home to my bleak, one-bedroom apartment on Capitol Hill. A furnished apartment seemed like a deal, but it was oddly shaped and the bedroom seemed like an afterthought: a cramped space containing a double bed where the owner had installed French doors to suggest a room. The carpet throughout was vomit brown. I hadn't decorated or placed art on the walls. I hadn't given it a thought. Perhaps I knew the move would only be temporary—one of many in my ever-growing list of serial relationships. After Kim and I split up and I'd graduated from law school a year ago, I had gladly latched onto this parental apartment. It was only right that I left the duplex we'd shared. I'd been the cause of the breakup because of my infatuation with Christine. While the apartment was great for its proximity to restaurants on Broadway and for mixing with other gay people, it felt empty. Even when the sun shone, the light didn't penetrate the walls. When it rained, sitting inside on a weeknight or weekend could be downright depressing.

The apartment contained the ghost of my sorrows. Christine had witnessed my devastating first bar results here. As a way to distract myself, I picked up extracurricular activities like soccer and running and working out with a trainer at a nearby gym. My new girlfriend, a woman named Carroll, lived in Olympia, meaning most of my weekends involved driving south on the I-5. Nonetheless, the apartment contained my landline phone, and when I was home, it became the source of ongoing, unhappy conversations with my mother, the most recent of those being about weight.

"Happy Mother's Day! Did you get my card?" I said during her call shortly before Mother's Day.

"Yes," she replied. "Nice sentiment. What's new?" I wanted to talk about Carroll, my new girlfriend, but I knew she didn't want to go there. The permafrost on my private life had morphed into a thick layer of ice. I felt the constant disapproval over my "lifestyle," the unspoken sentiment that I'd failed the betterment campaign. This failure seemed to be mine alone, but in combination with society's censure, I felt obliged to hide my true self from view. "Your dad and I played bridge with the Roths the other night and they asked about you," my mother ventured over the phone. I wondered what my parents had told the Roths about me—probably something about my great job. I mumbled in reply.

Then my mother jumped in with: "How's the weight?" Instant outrage clamped me around the throat.

"For Christ's sake, Mom. Drop it," I said. "I am a grown woman and you don't get to ask me about that anymore. Get it? That topic is off limits." The heat rose to my face. I had allowed her to ask this question for far too long. I ran or went to the nearby gym to work out at lunch, and I was in the best shape I'd ever been. I was running five- and ten-K races several times a year. Physically, I felt on top of the world. Other than the infamous moment in the car when I came out to my parents or when I'd stood up to Mom after she'd called Jude a bull dyke, this was the first time I'd truly spoken back to her. But as I hung up the phone, I wondered if the criticisms would ever stop. My mother had offered no response to my lashing out. We never discussed my weight again. Perhaps she had heard what I said. Yet in the years of family visits following our conversation, I felt the question about weight dangling over me as she took me in with her eyes, assessing in silence whether or not I'd gained or lost a few precious pounds.

I felt momentarily vindicated by taking a stand against my mother, but I knew our relationship would continue to be one of small talk and polite conversations. We had no connection. It was like someone had left the phone off the hook so long it began droning on—loud and persistent—waiting in vain for someone to offer closure by finally cutting off the line. *I'll never get a chance to tell Mom how I really feel,* I thought.

CHAPTER THIRTEEN

KATHRYN

I DECIDED I'D simply view the ride-along experience with officer Pat Lowery as a way of stepping into my new female prosecutor identity—me. The men and women of the Kent Police Department were a great bunch to work with. So what if I didn't get invited to their parties? I was at least beginning to feel a moderate sense of belonging, even if it were contingent on the position I held. Besides, I lived in Seattle and had this whole other life with my girlfriend. Everything was going so great. I had a girlfriend, a good-paying, professional job, and had kept in good graces with my parents—sort of. I had this job that they valued and wanted me to have. There remained the problem of the absent, ideal male partner. But, as long as we didn't talk about my personal preferences or my new girlfriends, I was on safe ground.

And then Steve dropped his bombshell. I'd only been there six months and he was leaving to join a top-tier firm in downtown Seattle. I was devastated, losing the guy I'd thought would be my mentor and show me the ropes in local government. My world felt wobbly. How would a new boss fulfill this role? Would they help me as much as Steve? I was still trying to navigate my way through untested territory as a closeted gay career woman. Somebody new would be hired and I would have to win them over. Steve kept me feeling secure: he'd had my back.

Kathryn, the new boss, was a statuesque six feet tall with sandy-brown curly hair and a big smile. I was attracted to her even though I knew she was straight. Her friends called her Kathy, but to me, she was Kathryn: an enigma. She showed little interest in criminal law although her closest friend and ally appeared to be the chief of police. She made it clear that land use law and personnel legal issues were her areas of expertise. These were areas of expertise she had cultivated while working as legal counsel for a local school district. I think she felt criminal misdemeanor law was beneath her and she didn't want to have too much to do with it. It made me feel insignificant and I worried who I would now go to with legal questions about my cases.

Her rule was law, yet she told me she would never prosecute or pitch in for me at court if I had a doctor's appointment, or God forbid, a vacation. Conversely, I got the impression her lack of criminal law experience made her afraid of trying a case in court. I figured our paths would only cross if she had a meeting with the judges. *Thank goodness I wouldn't run into her often and embarrass myself.* I was smitten with her, only six years my senior and so poised and confident in herself. *What would it be like to date her? What could I do to win her over?* But let's face it, she was straight.

Kathryn sure gave off mixed signals, though. On various occasions over the next five years, the legal office would go to lunch to celebrate a birthday or Christmas holiday. I carefully watched how she interacted with men. She gave off a sense of personal power that I found particularly attractive. Here was a woman in charge who knew how to deal with equally powerful men. Way cool, I thought. I wanted that—that sense of security in who I was. I wanted to know how she pulled it off. I also wanted her to mentor me. But she made it clear she was not going to do that. I hardly saw myself prosecuting misdemeanors forever. But she seemed to think the criminal side had its own niche, and that one could not jump to the civil side as I wanted to do.

One day, Kathryn called me into her office, saying she wanted to get to know me.

"So tell me a little bit about yourself," she started off. "What do you do for fun?"

"*Go to AA meetings*," I wanted to say. But I couldn't say that. I didn't want her thinking I was *one of those people*. She didn't strike me as someone who would applaud someone trying to recover. Although months later I did tell her because there was a morning meeting I wanted to attend before I came into work.

So instead I said, "I'm taking the Forum. It's the new Werner Erhard training program."

She didn't have much to say about that, ignoring the topic, and asked, "What part of town do you live in?"

"Capitol Hill." I said. *Oh dear, does she know that a lot of gay people live in that part of town and think I'm gay?* I thought.

And then suddenly I just blurted out, "I'm gay." I had told no one else in the office this information. Who knows, maybe I wanted a reaction—to see how she took my words. Or maybe

I was testing her to see if she might reveal she was also gay.

She looked at me, smiling with all her teeth, and said, "How interesting. I've never known anyone personally who was gay." She said it as though I might be a lab specimen, like she wanted to get to know this species of woman. I was confused. *Was she saying she didn't consider herself gay, but might be open to exploring the possibility? Or was this just more of my wishful thinking?* These questions would only get more confusing.

It began with Kathryn's obsession with Starbucks coffee. Starbucks was just starting to be the "it coffee," its franchises popping up on Seattle street corners and beyond. I loved coffee, and I too drank Starbucks, but Kathryn concocted her special blend using the iconic brown-and-white, twelve-pound coffee bags, and an eighty/twenty blend of Yukon and Viennese. In truth, I thought her something of a coffee snob for this. But—devoted acolyte that I was—I started drinking her blend at home. The fact that I remembered Kathryn's peccadillos enough to copy them spoke volumes about my longing to be her friend. I even thought drinking her coffee would make me cool too. If Kathryn accepted me, perhaps I could accept myself.

My fascination with Kathryn spilled over into a discovery that we shared musical preferences, despite her being older than me. The next day, she brought me a mixtape. I was delighted but befuddled. The giving of a mixtape—a compilation of favorite songs recorded then on a cassette tape—meant something special. It usually signified a romantic interest. Lovers made mixtapes for each other. Friends rarely did. And certainly, casual coworkers did not.

What was she trying to communicate with this gift?

I thought about the "gift" while playing it in my new Toyota Tercel station wagon during the thirty-minute commute to Kent and back every day. Finally, I decided I would ask Kathryn to go to a movie. That would let me gauge whether I'd read her "friend" message correctly. One Saturday, after several hours of agonizing, I nervously dialed the Seattle home number she'd given me in case I needed to call in sick.

"Hi Kathryn," I said, and then my heart skipped a couple of beats. "This is Jill. I . . . I . . . was wondering if perhaps you wanted to go see *Steel Magnolias*? It's playing at the Varsity." A long, pregnant pause ensued on her end, which I took to mean she was either surprised or trying to decide how to answer this request from a work subordinate.

"Well, Jill, I wish I could, but I already have plans tonight," she finally answered, crushing my fantasy. *Probably a date with some guy*, I thought mournfully. I nearly hung up on the spot from embarrassment. Before she'd even closed the conversation—"Okay, bye now"—I was already beating myself up. *What had I done? Did people do that, ask their bosses to go to a movie? What would she think of me? Would she think I was trying to hit on her?* I hung up the phone thinking I could not bear to go back to work Monday. I didn't want to face the awkwardness I'd surely created between us.

Monday—like Mondays do—came, and I dragged myself to my Tercel wagon to make the trek to Kent. When I got there and saw Kathryn in the hallway, there was nothing. No "sorry I couldn't make it." No acknowledgment. Our phone conversation had just been a blip on her radar. Soon forgotten.

Another old deposition file headed for the shredder.

But still, whenever we found ourselves in her office alone, she kept asking me questions about gay women. What did I do on the weekends? Where did gay women go dancing? Again, I was thrown into turmoil. *Could she be toying with me? Or worse, was she one of those straight women who flirt with a fantasy of themselves as gay?* I hadn't experienced these advances but had heard from gay friends who'd had the misfortune of being on the receiving end—only to be left sad and alone. Some women just liked to flirt and it didn't matter whom it was with. Who knew? Maybe she'd even had a same-sex relationship in college or law school and didn't want me to know. Perhaps it was all subterfuge: Kathryn hiding her feelings for other women. I would never find out. That did not stop me from trying. I told her about starting to play soccer with a women's team in Kent. I had never played soccer, but I was lonely and looking for a place to belong. A sports team seemed like a good place to start. All the other women were seasoned players and straight, while I had never passed or dribbled a soccer ball in my life. After all, soccer wasn't really on the women's roster in the Midwest in the 1960s.

During one game, I burst out from the goal against an incoming striker and our legs got tangled. I suffered a common female soccer injury, a partially torn ACL and torn meniscus. Kathryn lived in Seattle. I needed a ride to and from work and Kathryn volunteered even though I lived well out of her commuting drive. This forced intimacy provided the cold facts: Kathryn was straight. I asked about the prominent Auburn male criminal defense attorney I'd seen waiting outside her office at lunchtime after watching them leave together. Yes, indeed, she was dating this guy. This tall, straight guy who tromped into court in shiny gray suits, bolo string ties, and cowboy boots. The obvious was brutally clear. Kathryn was no prospect for me, and pursuing her had only deepened the shame I felt for being different. Not only was I sure that Kathryn could tell I was taken with her but I had bared my soul to her. Would she use that information against me? I was overly worried about what she thought of me. I had not read the room very well, and I was embarrassed.

CHAPTER FOURTEEN

DEBRA

WHILE MY career seemed to have taken off, my love life had ground to a halt. Since Christine had ended our relationship, I had dived into a four-year relationship and two other, shorter ones. I wanted to get off this merry-go-round of short-term relationships. *Where was Ms. Right?* What I didn't know at thirty-six was how insidiously my parents' betterment campaign had seeped into my being.

Friends had introduced Debra to me at a poker party. Mutual friends thought we might have things in common, aside from being single. Debra and I happened to be the only two single guests at this party. I knew how to play poker, but I didn't know how to bet. Soon I ran out of my allotted money for the game and was forced to watch. Debra seemed even more inexperienced and soon she too was out of the game. Then she announced that she needed to get back to her studies for her master's in teaching. She was a year younger and I was still working as the prosecutor for the City of Kent.

When Debra said she needed to leave, I saw my chance to leave as well. It would otherwise be a long night watching other people win and lose money, and I would be stuck waiting for our mutual friends to drive me back. "I need a ride home," I said to the group playing poker. Unlike me, Debra knew everyone there.

"I'll take you," Debra said.

I slid into Debra's tiny red Honda Civic that carried a definitive odor of wet dog. The interior was messy. She brushed a textbook off my seat before I sat. Papers were strewn among dog toys and a jacket in the back seat. It was a cold October night, and it took a while for the little car heater to start working. An awkward silence hung over us.

"So how do you know these women?" I finally broke the silence.

"I know Jeanne, one of the party hostesses, because I was involved with her for a year," Debra said.

"How long ago was that?" I said, surprised she was still on such good terms with her ex and her ex's new partner.

"Oh, we broke up about five years ago," Debra said. "They took care of my dog last year while I was in the Philippines working with Laotians and Cambodians at a refugee camp. It was really hard to leave Kol with them. I wasn't sure I could do it, but I hated what I was doing here, working as an economist for a bank in Bellevue. I needed a break."

This dog seemed to be a major player in Debra's life. Kol, a clever play on coal, was a black cockapoo and Debra continued to talk about Kol in great detail—what they did together (seemingly everything), his antics, and her love for him. I kept waiting for her to take a photo of him out of her wallet to show me. If I was going to get involved with this woman, I hoped her dog was at least cute and lovable.

Debra's thick, shiny, espresso-colored hair was so voluminous she seemed to have trouble keeping it contained on her head. The other thing I liked was her thin, fit body. I especially liked that she was thin. I knew this sentiment was uncool: politically incorrect and anti-feminist. But my parents' obsession with my body seemed to have nurtured the neural pathways that dictated my own taste in body types.

The other thing I learned about Debra was her love of cross-country skiing. I knew only how to downhill ski. The drive home took about thirty minutes, so I didn't learn much else that night. Debra asked little about me. Her disinterest seemed to pique my curiosity. As I turned the key in my door, I thought, *hmm, she might be interesting to get to know*. But I did nothing to make that happen until several months later. She seemed busy with school and her dog. I had my prosecutor job and I had begun to work out. I had recently signed up to be a Big Sister in the Big/Little Sister program, which occupied my weekends. I was lonely, nonetheless.

I did a few other social events with the group from the poker party. They asked me if I wanted to go to a k.d. lang concert, Seattle's first time hosting the Canadian lesbian who sang pop and country music and would later pack huge venues. I didn't know if Debra was coming, but the seat next to mine was empty. Debra arrived about fifteen minutes after the concert began. She seemed distracted and left immediately. *Well*, I thought, *she obviously has no interest in me*.

The group's next invitation involved ice skating at an indoor rink in North Seattle. I shied away from asking if Debra was coming but kept scanning the rink to see if she'd made an appearance. I had a vague desire to know her better, even though the feelings didn't appear mutual. I never stopped to wonder why I felt drawn to her disinterest. I told myself I loved to ice skate and could have a good time whether Debra showed up or not. Debra arrived late again and in baggy red sweatpants and an oversized red sweatshirt. She skated haltingly around the rink but refrained from holding on to the edge. I warmed to her apparent vulnerability. She didn't stay long and we exchanged no more than a few words.

Two months later, Debra hosted a New Year's Eve party and I was invited. *Oh happy day!* I felt optimistic about this invitation, and this time I arrived late, so as not to appear overly eager. At the party, Debra and I seemed to circle each other all evening as though lacking the courage to connect. When midnight came, everyone was kissing. Debra and I stood in close proximity. Our eyes locked and slid away. *Maybe*, I thought, *but no*. I left with hope in my heart just the same. Shortly after New Year's Eve, I phoned Debra to see if she was finally interested in me. *Would she never pick up?* The ringing went on forever before I heard a receiver lifting. "Hi," I stammered, blurting out my name. "Are you free on Sunday to go to the matinee for *My Left Foot*?"

"I've been invited to watch the Super Bowl game at Claudia's," she said.

"Oh, I got invited too. But I'm not really into football."

Her reply surprised me. "I'm not really, either, and I did want to see that movie. What time does it start?"

I held my breath. *Was she going to say yes?* I told her the start time.

"Well, we could go watch the game and then use the movie as an excuse to leave," she suggested. I let out my breath and we both started to laugh. I thought it was a date. I really didn't know how she felt, but she had said yes. A good sign?

After the movie, Debra invited me back to her house. She busied herself making tea and then she asked me if I knew who the pre-Raphaelite painters were. "The PRB," I said. "Sure, I studied them in college. I had a minor in art history." She brought out a treasured book about their paintings and I thought, *wow, look at this, we have something in common*. I took it as a sign that this relationship would be different. One where we would share our interests and enjoy long, meaningful conversations.

We talked some more about our backgrounds and then she decided to have some fun with me after I complimented her on the stylish, faded, rust-colored overalls she was wearing. Well—stylish if they weren't so baggy. "Oh, I had these when I was pregnant," she said. I didn't know what to say and hoped that my face didn't show my inner turmoil. It took a few minutes—long minutes—before she burst out laughing. Her pregnancy was a ruse to shock me. That was my first taste of Debra's quirky sense of humor and love of pulling my leg.

Before I met Debra, I had begun to despair over ever finding Ms. Right. Since coming out ten years earlier, I'd grown tired of serial, monogamous relationships. Many of my high school and college friends had been married for years and were raising children. I had thought about children, and talked about it with my last partner. She had already raised a son and was not interested in co-parenting. She was done. Eventually the relationship foundered and I called things off. I wanted to settle down and share a home with someone forever.

Although I'd only known Debra a couple of months, I felt a certain pull toward her. She ticked off a lot of boxes for me. She was physically attractive, enjoyed the outdoors, had the same level of education, and a similar background. I thought we might share similar values. My previous girlfriends had dissimilar backgrounds and I'd been thinking that factor posed a problem for my parents. Despite being semi-estranged from my parents, I was still trying to win their approval in my mid-thirties. Maybe if I aligned myself with someone in sync with their values—someone who hadn't grown up impoverished, whose parents weren't divorced, who'd achieved a high level of education and a high-status profession—they might overlook or put less emphasis on that someone being a woman. I could hope, couldn't I?

I was similarly drawn to the vulnerability I had witnessed in Debra when we went ice skating, and the fact that she seemed as nervous and awkward as I was. But really, she had captured my heart that day at the ice-skating rink when she skated haltingly around in her oversized sweatshirt and sweatpants. I can't explain it. It just touched my heart. Her aloofness and seeming disinterest also lured me in. *What was that about?* I wondered. Once I had decided that Debra was the one, I seemed to lose any remaining sense of perspective or rationality.

My distorted judgment seems ever so clear to me when I look back on February 1990 and the start of my relationship with Debra. I went on the cross-country skiing trip in the Methow Valley in Eastern Washington I had signed up for before meeting Debra. I longed for this vacation. The grind of being a prosecutor and in court seven hours a day was taking its toll. I wanted to learn how to cross-country ski and recalled that this was a passion of Debra's. In the beautiful, peaceful, and frigid Methow Valley, she was all I could think about.

The cold crispness seemed a perfect foil to the white-heat of my obsession. In the peaceful schuss of my skis through the carefully groomed tracks, my mind was free to wander and ponder the possibilities. After working up a sweat, I went so far as to buy her an expensive jacket while poking around the small town's sports store.

When I returned and presented Debra the gift, she seemed overwhelmed by my outsized gesture. I'm sure she wasn't expecting something this big at this point in our relationship, which was only just beginning, but in my mind loomed so large. Debra's reaction to the gift and to me seemed to match that particularly cold February. "This isn't the best time for me to get involved with someone" she said. "I'm trying to finish this master's program and student teach. I'm also trying to end a relationship." I remembered her mentioning Sue that evening we went to the movies where she gave me the impression that their relationship had run its course.

"I thought you said that it was over," I said.

"Well, it is over as far as I am concerned. But the timing is off. I wish you and I had met at a different time." Of course, Debra's ambivalence only heightened my attraction.

I wasn't going to take no for an answer, so I persisted in asking her out and she agreed. I was going to persuade her—timing be damned—that I was good for her and that she needed me in her life. And, she did need me. She needed to see the alternative to the sick, manipulative relationship she'd been in or still was in with this "Sue woman."

Debra had blown into my life like a scent that one whiffs briefly but whose memory lingers long. Part of the obsession came from her wanting to put the brakes on my desire to rush forward. She wanted to take her time getting to know me. But I was impatient, and I sensed she wasn't exactly saying no. Several weeks went by, and after a few phone calls, she asked me if I wanted to go cross-country skiing.

Debra knew of a good trail up near Stevens Pass, and as she drove us there, she chattered about aquaculture and fish farming. I was impressed. She held a wide range of eclectic knowledge and could talk about things I had never heard of. From her knowledge of the pre-Raphaelite brotherhood to English Tudor history to fish farming. On this trip, I was the one without the right clothes. I sported a pair of corduroy ski knickers I'd found at Goodwill. It was snowing and I got soaked falling on the ungroomed tracks. I didn't mind. Being in the outdoors and sharing a new passion with the woman I loved made it all worthwhile. Even the wet wool and wet dog smell permeating her Honda on the drive home couldn't dent my enthusiasm.

On another outing, Debra wanted us to go to the Viet-Wah Asian Food Market at 12th and Jackson and visit her favorite pho place. I had never smelled or seen the products sold in this market, like durian, the fruit that smelled like garbage, and Thai basil and lemongrass. I appreciated Debra introducing me to Southeast Asian food and this new, exotic market. I began thinking of the nearby, hole-in-the-wall pho eatery as "our place." The owners soon nodded and smiled at us whenever we were there, which was often. Debra liked to go to the market and have pho, because it reminded her of her year working in the Philippines with the refugees. Debra's adventures overseas enveloped me like perfume. I had wanted to work in the Peace Corps and I envied her nerve to do something equally daring. Never mind that she took this trip partly to call an end to a murky relationship with Marcia, her girlfriend of two years. She told me stories about playing basketball with the refugees, teaching them English, and living with sudden, intermittent shutdowns of water and electricity. I gushed over her adventurous spirit.

I soon discovered that Debra possessed another, slipperier side. She seemed to be afraid of caring and sharing her affection. Whenever I pressed for more of a commitment, she kept telling me to "go with the flow" and see where life took us. I was learning that liking and even being smitten with someone isn't necessarily enough. Those feelings need to be reciprocated. Even though Debra said she was interested, and she acted interested, she kept repeating the mantra that "our timing was off."

One evening at her house, the subject of Sue came up. Debra was now student teaching at the same middle school where Sue taught, meaning they would run into each other, especially since they both worked with kids with disabilities. I couldn't believe it. *With so many middle schools in Seattle, how could they end up at the very same one?* I groused inwardly.

"So, do you two still do things together outside of teaching?" I said.

We were sitting on Debra's sofa and she flicked her gaze away from me when she said, "Well . . . well . . . yes. She's kind of hard to avoid, Jill."

"What do you mean? Can't you just say it's over?"

"She's pretty persistent, Jill. And it's just not that easy."

"But you're not having sex, right?" Debra began twisting the knot in her overalls and avoiding my eyes completely. By this point, Debra and I had had sex a few times. I could hardly contemplate her still having sex with Sue.

A long silence descended before Debra spoke. "Yes, when I said we weren't together anymore, that's what I meant, that we weren't having sex anymore," she stammered. Using sex to define a relationship seemed like a hairline distinction. Debra had led me to believe that the relationship was truly over. Either Debra wasn't really through with it or Sue wasn't ready to let go. Her relationship with Sue would complicate our first year together in many ways. Sue's pull on Debra was strong. Since Sue's name rarely came up, I felt at times like I was competing with a phantom. I almost wondered if my presence in Debra's life preempted her from dealing with the "Sue issue." Debra may have been done, but Sue wasn't, and she went to great pains to indicate those feelings to Debra. Debra said she was trying to break it off while still being friends with Sue. "She needs me, Jill," Debra explained. Those words threw me back to my unhealthy relationship in college with pitiable Leslie.

Leslie and Sue appeared to have trained at the same school of interpersonal dynamics. When I first met Debra, Sue lived on Capitol Hill. Within three months of my dating Debra, Sue bought a house a block down the street from Debra's. I wondered at the coincidence. Debra, however, did not seem to know how to end relationships. She could not or would not be direct when she perceived her behavior would cause discomfort or conflict.

Although we'd had sex twice, Debra felt pressured. One night about four months into what I considered "our relationship," Debra wouldn't look at me and kept shifting about on the sofa while she fussed with a frayed hole in her jeans.

"Why?" she said. "Why are you so anxious to have sex so soon?" Never mind that neither of us had mentioned the word "love" in any real, palpable way.

"Why do we need to wait some magic number of months?" I said. My libido was in overdrive and the waiting seemed intolerable. The target date of six months or even a year seemed arbitrary. "Isn't making love what two people do when they have feelings for each other?" I said.

"I just don't want to be rushed, Jill," Debra said. She wouldn't confirm or deny any feelings for me. I knew I was aggravating Debra, and I also knew if this relationship had any hope of developing further I was just going to have to wait. The waiting nagged at me, though. One weekend I tried calling Debra several times, each time getting her answering machine.

"Where were you last weekend ?" I said when she finally called back.

"I . . . I . . . was out of town," she finally sputtered. "I just needed to get out of town."

"Did you go by yourself ?"

"Yes, just me and Kol." I fumed inwardly that she loved that dog more than she would ever love another human being. Later, she admitted that Sue had begged her to come to her family's Orcas Island cabin. "I couldn't refuse her, Jill," Debra said.

"What do you mean, 'you couldn't refuse her'?" I challenged.

"You don't get it. I just can't," she replied. I didn't know what to do with this non-answer. "Stop pressuring me, Jill."

And then she stood up, making a fist and turning toward the wall, and I thought, *Oh my God, I've gone too far. She's going to punch a hole in that wall.* Her anger scared me. Clearly, she felt cornered, but she never told me to go away.

Another weekend, Debra was more up front, telling me outright that she was going to Port Townsend with Sue. I just didn't get how going on trips with someone meant ending a relationship. When Debra returned, I asked her the question plaguing me for two days.

"So . . . did you like, sleep together? Or what?"

I sat through a long pause on the telephone until Debra piped up. "I slept in my sleeping bag on the floor."

"Oh, really?" I retorted. This scenario seemed preposterous to me.

But other times, Debra would call out of the blue and invite me to go hiking or would volunteer to come over and help me plant bulbs. Enough of these times were good and I stuck around. The more I tried to divert Debra from my thoughts the more she dominated them, like some perverse parasite feeding on your insides. I tried to put my frustrations about Debra at bay by running and lifting weights until I fell into bed at night, exhausted. I felt like I was a yoyo, though, and my infatuation with Debra—or the idea of Debra—skittered out in ugly ways.

One night I called, and unlike other nights where she didn't pick up, this time she did. "Where were you when I called last night?" I demanded.

"I don't know. I was here all night. Maybe you called when I was taking the garbage out."

"Well, how come you didn't call me back?"

"I didn't know you'd called until this morning when I heard the clicks on the phone and listened to your message."

"I called a couple of times, Debra."

"I took a shower too."

"Look," I said, "if you don't want to tell me, that's your business. But just don't flat out lie to me."

"I'm telling you I was home. I just didn't get your message. Haven't you sometimes not noticed messages until the next day? What's the matter with you? You're acting like you think I would lie to you."

"I called you several times," I repeated.

"Oh, come on. Now you're acting like a jealous lover and we haven't even known each other that long," Debra said.

I could just picture Sue being there listening to our conversation and rolling her eyes. Sue was probably smiling a knowing, Cheshire cat smile. *Sue and Debra had heard the phone ring repeatedly and ignored it.*

"Are you still there, Debra? Are you listening to me? Do you understand what you're doing to me?"

"Look." Debra sighed. "I was here last night, okay? Just let it alone. I'll see you later. We're still going to the Huskies basketball game, aren't we?" Debra's denials were so cheap they made bad cologne smell good.

Here I go again. So many times in my life I had wanted something so badly—like a certain guy to like me or an invitation to prom—and my wants just wouldn't pan out. It seemed the more I wanted something, the less likely I was to get it. My willingness to accept little was at the root of my problematic relationship. Debra had all the power. Did she know she did? She must have. Was she blind to her own cruelty? I often assumed she was with Sue even while she denied it. Sue was just a friend and blah, blah, blah. Sue needed her. Sue was going through a bad patch. *I was going through a bad patch too*, I wanted to scream.

During a rare day when Debra asked me over, I decided to blurt out the source of my suffering. "Have you told Sue about us?"

Again, Debra's murky brown eyes shifted to the left, then up to the ceiling, "W-w-well no . . . no, I haven't."

I clenched my jaw. "What do you mean, you haven't told her? Why?" I fumed.

"I have my reasons," Debra said. But she wouldn't tell me what those reasons were. I suspected she was afraid of Sue—of what Sue might do. Debra had confided earlier that her high school friend had committed suicide while she was in medical school. Her phone had rung at 2:00 a.m. one night, but she didn't want to get up and go all the way downstairs to get it. She'd hoped it was a wrong number. Even now, she was second-guessing herself about whether the caller had indeed been her suicidal friend. Similarly, Debra continued to be half in, half out of our relationship, as though looking for reasons not to be with me.

Then, out of the blue toward my birthday at the end of December, I received a call from the phantom herself. I got rattled when I heard Sue's voice. "I know my call is a surprise," she said, "but I just wanted to tell you that Debra and I have been having sex off and on the whole time you've been involved." Short and to the point. By this time, I had been dating Debra for about ten months. Later, I confronted Debra at her house about what Sue had told me. "No, no, that's not true," she said—words I knew were a lie. She added a caveat. "It's only been since August."

"That's supposed to make me feel better?" I retorted. "I'm leaving. I can't do this anymore. No, I won't do this anymore. Trust and honesty are the foundation on which relationships are built. We don't have that; we've never had it." I stopped my speech. That's what it felt like. I had practiced my lines in the car on the way over to her house. I had never yet been this honest about my feelings with Debra.

"No," Debra cried, then her voice became a whimper. "I don't blame you. If I were in your shoes, I'd do exactly the same thing." Her eyes widened and I saw her fear, her desperation. I was numb. I hadn't expected her to agree with me. I couldn't seem to make my feet move. Debra stepped in front of me and tugged at the lapels of the beautiful, black leather bomber jacket she'd given me for Christmas. "I didn't mean to," she mumbled. "Don't hate me. Please don't hate me. I'm bad. I've been bad, but please don't hate me."

My heart hardened. In truth, I felt nauseated. I took the key to Debra's house off my key ring, removed the watch I had borrowed as recently as last week, and headed to Debra's closet. The closet was in complete disarray—much like Debra's life at the moment. I rifled through the clothing on the top shelf. I wanted my T-shirt back, the one from the Cascade run-off, a big race for me: the first I'd ever done. I lifted my belongings from the piles of clothing. I don't know why I wanted the T-shirt right then, except that sorting through clothes distracted me from having to look at Debra. I hadn't expected her to care this much. I hadn't ever seen Debra cry that first year. I didn't know what to do with her tears.

My hardened heart began loosening as I picked up the T-shirt in the closet and turned toward her. I needed to get out before I changed my mind. It had taken all my willpower to make this decision. I didn't think I could afford to change my mind. I didn't change my mind easily, after all. I pondered things and then I made a decision, though the pondering could take a while. In my relationship with Debra, it would take years. But here in this moment during our first year, I was definitive.

I walked to the front door and Kol followed me. But Debra did not, and I left.

The holidays passed slowly that year, and ringing in 1990 alone and broken hearted was excruciatingly slow. While I had ended relationships before, this one with Debra was especially hard. I'd really wanted this relationship to work and had spent many weeks crying. When she hadn't been distracted by Sue and her full gaze was upon me I had dared to hope that she was the one: my forever girl, the one I would grow old with. A week into the new year, I got a contrite call from her. When I first picked up the phone, I heard only silence, and then: "I-I-I want to try again, Jill. I promise I'll ease Sue out of my life. She's now seeing a psychologist three times a week."

"Really? She's going three times a week?" Inwardly, I thought, *Oh, good*. Debra no longer needed to be her listening post, attending to her every need. Still—this pronouncement was a crumb. Little for me to go on, but I jumped on Debra's weak commitment to get Sue out of her life and mine. I had not asked Debra to choose between the two of us. All I needed was a meager sign she wanted me in her life. Apparently, she did.

Debra grew more willing to make the drive from her house in North Seattle to mine in South Seattle. We did more activities together and more lovemaking. We took our dogs to the beach and went running together and spent more of the weekends together. Her spending more time with me signified she cared and could be trusted. But then a call came that disrupted this idyllic time.

"Jill, Sue has cancer," Debra said.

"W-w-what? What kind of cancer?" I asked.

"I don't know, Jill."

"You didn't ask her?" I paused. "Does that mean something for us?" I asked about our relationship, because I had no concern for Sue. Sue represented an obstacle. Cancer made her even more of one. I knew by now that Sue's illness was just another way for her to hold on to Debra. I knew this translated to me taking even more of a back seat. Debra, after all, needed to be needed—an all-too-familiar-sounding trait, given Leslie's primary hold on me fifteen years earlier at Whitman. I continued to hear about Sue's "cancer." She had to go to San Francisco for "unspecified" treatments. I asked Debra if she knew where Sue was being seen locally and learned she was going to Swedish Hospital. By now, I was fed up with Sue's shenanigans.

I asked Debra for Sue's birthdate. Then, I went to work and ran Sue's name through the licensing department database to get her social security number. This was back in the days when those numbers appeared on driver's licenses. With that information, I called Swedish Hospital. I needed tangible proof to convince Debra she was being duped. I wanted to show her that Sue would fabricate as much as she could to manipulate Debra into staying in Sue's orbit.

"Yes, this is Swedish medical records," a female voice answered. My hands were sweaty as I questioned whether my ploy would work.

"Yes," I said. "I'm Sue Donaldson and I just wanted to check on a bill I owe."

"What is your social security number?" I rattled it off.

"I'm sorry. There must be some mistake, because we don't have anyone by that name in our system," the voice replied. I thanked her and hung up. I now had the goods to bring to Debra. "Look," I told Debra. "Sue may be sick, but what proof do you actually have that she has cancer? Swedish has never heard of her." Debra thought the evidence I provided was telling but insufficient. Then I learned that Sue had embellished her lie.

"So now she's telling you she's going to San Francisco this weekend for cancer treatments," I said. "What doctor sees patients on Saturdays?" Debra looked pensive. She was probably regretting telling me this latest piece of information about Sue.

Eventually, I outlasted Sue. In response to Sue's increasingly weird behavior, I convinced Debra to take away Sue's key to her house. Sue then frightened Debra by sending her a weird videotape talking about her sexual fantasies. I didn't see the tape, but I was there in Debra's basement when she took a screwdriver and hammer to that fucking tape and destroyed it. Surely Debra would now see that I was the saner one, the safer bet for a long-time relationship?

Or did she? She repeatedly rebuffed any suggestion of moving in together, even now it no longer made sense to drive thirty minutes back and forth to see each other or manage two separate households. We were spending more time together and Sue was in the background, though I got irritated every time I had to drive by Sue's house while driving up Debra's street.

Even though the presence of Sue in our relationship presented obstacles, I thought we could and should be together. This was further cemented the one and only time Debra met my mother. That occurred when she came to Seattle during my hysterectomy. The visit was early in our dating days and Debra's mother, Martha, was coincidentally visiting while I had the surgery. Debra and Martha both came up to the hospital and met my mother. I had shared with my mother that Debra and I were dating and offered a quick sketch of Debra's career and background. I could tell my mother liked Debra as a person. Debra had a master's in economics and was working on her MA in teaching. Her parents were still married to each other—a plus in my parents' eyes that included Debra's previous employment as a banker. What upper-middle-class parent wouldn't like those bona fides, even if the object of her daughter's affections happened to be the same sex? Debra was the first person I'd dated who checked off as many boxes for my parents.

Debra and I completed several couples counseling sessions and I thought we'd arrived in a good place—so good, in fact, that our therapist described our relationship like a "comfortable couch." Nonetheless, Debra and I puzzled over that phrase. *How could that be bad?* we wondered. It would take years to figure out exactly what those words meant and why they were not necessarily a good omen. I moved into Debra's house a year after my hysterectomy. Several months later I learned my mother had lung cancer and would have surgery to remove the tumors. She didn't tell me how long she'd been dealing with this diagnosis before she told me.

All that damned smoking my mother had so righteously done ever since college had caught up to her.

The doctors said they would operate, because they thought they could contain it. She would follow up with radiation. I'd talked to Mom shortly after the surgery at a pay phone on Highway 2. Debra and I had stopped on our way to a hiking trail specifically so I could make the call that day in July. Dad told me that I didn't need to come for the surgery, so I stayed home and took the trip to Evanston later.

In the hospital Mom had sounded winded, and I could tell she was struggling to talk, but she reassured me that everything was fine and that the doctors had gotten all the cancer. I went home at Christmas without Debra to reassure myself that she was okay.

The house exuded a surreal, mysterious glow. My mother had gone all out in decorating and in making sure we did all the usual Christmas traditions. We had the neighbors over for a Christmas Eve open house and my mother had served her traditional, homemade Baked Alaska for Christmas Eve dinner. She always busied herself in the kitchen while Dad, John, and my grandparents gathered around the piano and I played Christmas carols. We all sang as Mom created her specialty alone in the kitchen. Tradition usually involved her smoking while baking, but that Christmas it did not. She had finally quit.

CHAPTER FIFTEEN

FORGIVENESS

OVER THE next few months I heard from my mom about different ailments—her diminished hearing, pains in her legs, and the doctor prescribing quinine, which came with other, troublesome side effects. My parents didn't share much and I thought she was on the mend. Still, I worried about the side effects. "Your dad called," Debra said.

"Did you talk to him?" I said.

"No, he left a message on the answering machine." She gestured toward the machine with the cassette tape.

"He did?" I was surprised. Dad rarely called. It was mostly my mother who called, and she would put him on the phone if he was home in Evanston. He would go to the upstairs phone so the three of us could talk at the same time.

Debra, my partner of a year, looked at me straight on, moving her slight body to the left to stand in front of me, as though needing my full attention.

"He said," she paused and then continued, "he said, you'd better come now."

"What?" I looked at her in disbelief. "No, no, really, that's what he said?" I asked. "He didn't say anything else?"

I was still in my heels and suit, just having come home to our house in Phinney Ridge from my second week at a new job with the City of Everett, a town north of Seattle and larger than Kent. I was Everett's new city prosecutor and police legal adviser. It was late May of 1992 and I was thirty-nine. We were just about to head off on our planned, three-week trip to Thailand—a project we would end up postponing for a year. Debra pointed to the machine and urged me to go listen. She was right. The message was short and to the point. My dad's usually ebullient voice sounded flat. He offered no explanation, just that I should come.

My father's summons in May would end up doing me in. I felt untethered. My father would never summon me unless it meant, unless . . . well, unless it meant Mom was dying. My Dad said that I should make a reservation for the next flight to Evanston and to tell my new boss that I needed two weeks. I would end up staying more than five weeks.

As I finalized my reservations, I recalled the Christmas Eve we spent together five months earlier. I'd caught myself looking at her all dressed up in her favorite black sweater and tweed-checked skirt. She even wore her favorite necklace, a sterling silver choker with a large, polished stone my father had given her. Just five of us gathered around the table, including my ninety-year-old grandmother with dementia. Grandfather had already died. But gazing at my mother from across the room on Christmas Eve, I saw her smiling as if she didn't have a care in the world—although she probably knew that her days were numbered. But there she sat bathing in a glow—an aura around her—and in that moment I knew she was dying.

It was the strangest thing: I just knew, though I couldn't have known when her final days would be.

That Christmas I heard no personal criticisms. A first for me. I think Mom and I were both really trying to have a good Christmas. In truth, the appraisals had lessened over the past few years, perhaps in response to my father's urging or her own desire to make peace—I don't know. I was just happy to be away from the lens.

Days after my father's cryptic phone call, my plane landed in Chicago and I went straight to Evanston hospital. It was just up the street from where my family lived, a short, five-minute walk. I spent two weeks going to and from my mother's bedside. During these visits, my mother was lucid and lively and at times I felt surprised my father had called me. I would visit, go home, and the next day start the cycle over again.

My mother complained about my bad breath every time I bent to kiss her, even though I brushed my teeth and gargled with mouthwash before I walked up the street to visit. Someone suggested that dying people possess a heightened sense of smell. Outwardly, Mom seemed fine, except that she was in a hospital. We played gin rummy and my father and I took turns keeping her company. John drove up from Indiana for a few days. But by the third week, she was talking little and sleeping a lot. My brother wanted me to pluck her chin hairs in the manner we had seen her do weekly over the years. I don't know why she didn't realize that the more you plucked, the more bristly those pesky hairs became. I brought the tweezers once and tried to do it, but she jerked after I did one and I couldn't continue. I didn't want to cause her pain.

One day, after sitting by her bed, I got up to leave. She appeared to be in her final days. I'd been there probably an hour and she hadn't said a word. Perhaps she didn't even know I'd been there. I'd never watched anyone die, and I didn't want her to die. Truthfully, I was torn. I felt relieved, but also guilty that I would no longer have to worry what criticism she might pull out of the air to assault me with. As I got ready to go, I recalled a time she had come to visit Seattle with my dad. He'd had business with a marine company and Mom said she would find things to do. I was working but decided I would take an afternoon off and throw a party when my friends were done with work for the day. About six of my friends came over for wine and appetizers. I wanted her to see that lesbians were normal people who had regular jobs and looked like regular people. Afterwards, I recall Mom saying, "Why did you do that? Why did you throw a party for me?" She seemed surprised, almost in awe.

"Because I wanted you to meet my friends and I thought my friends might enjoy meeting my mother," I said. I had been nervous, wondering how she would react to having so many lesbians in a room together—knowing her daughter was one of them. But she seemed touched. I was frankly surprised at how touched she was. That party had only been two years ago, and I remember thinking, *maybe now we can turn a corner and have the mother-daughter relationship I've dreamed of having.* Maybe now I could openly and honestly talk about that part of my life she disliked so much.

Now, in her hospital room, I tiptoed toward the door. I didn't want to disturb her. I grabbed the door handle to leave her room and heard her speak. "Do you forgive me?" The words were spoken to my back. I froze, my hand stuck to the door handle. I had to answer her. But I didn't know what to say. I wondered what she meant, specifically, in asking me to forgive her. Was she talking about the vile and hateful words she had said in the car when I came out to her? Those words so devoid of compassion and understanding. Was she talking about something even earlier? Perhaps she was sorry she'd had so much shame about having a daughter with a cleft lip or what she perceived as her failure in creating a lesbian daughter. Because I remembered her asking so plaintively in the car all those years ago: had she done something wrong? I had assumed she'd meant in creating a lesbian daughter.

A few times, she had revealed her struggles to mix in with the Evanston upper-middle-class, Republican milieu she had married into. I suppose she did not want me to be different, either. She had moved across the country from Washington State, a place where people still thought lumberjacks prevailed and culture was only a passing thought. She had been raised in a working-class, union, blue Democrat family. Her relatives were Swedes and Welshmen, more recently arrived than my father's relatives. She never forgot her roots, even if her current life bore little resemblance.

My mother was not morose, but at times she let slip her perceptions about not fitting in, and I think she carried that belief all her living days, despite evidence to the contrary. I remember overhearing her comment to my father about friends of theirs having made some ignorant comments about Seattle. She'd said, "All they think that's out there in Seattle are trees and lumberjacks. They think I don't belong." Dad made some reassuring remark. I believed she did not want that for me either, to be treated differently.

I wanted to say, "No, I do not forgive you." I wanted her to own up to all the hateful things she had said to me since that fateful car ride. That was my initial reaction. Even though our relationship was starting to mend, I was angry and still hurting. Now I was angry she was dying by her selfish choice to smoke herself to death. She was going to deny me, my brother and his three children, and my father the benefit of many more years but for this self-centered desire to smoke. I so longed for my mother's unconditional love that I couldn't dare criticize her for her own choices. I couldn't have the last words between us be ones of condemnation. What if these were the last words she and I would speak? It had been days since she had spoken and her breathing had become more labored.

I also wanted to believe—like a child who believes in Santa Claus long past the age one should—that we could have some sort of closure. I was seemingly unable to pull the door open to exit the room, because I so badly hoped for more. I was unable to ask for more because I didn't think she was capable of more. She'd had years to ask for my forgiveness but she couldn't ask before. She didn't know how. Somehow she had gathered her courage at this last moment with the clock ticking on her life to ask me for forgiveness. But no more words came from my dying mother.

What would happen if I just continued to walk through the door and pretended I haven't heard her? Doing so seemed cruel. My parents had raised me to be a dutiful daughter. And that is the woman who showed up that day, the girl my mother wanted. I couldn't continue through that door. The "betterment campaign" demanded that I answer her question. I had to give her the answer I thought she wanted to the question she was asking.

"Yes, I forgive you."

She said nothing in return, but I'm sure she heard me. My heart felt heavy with the untruth of what I had just said. Did she believe me? Did she know—sense—that I didn't really forgive her? She probably did, but I'll never know. I ambled along the block to her house, the one that no longer contained the smell of long-ago smoked cigarettes, and cried in my childhood bedroom with the Laura Ashley floral-patterned wallpaper my mother and I had picked out. I cried because I was losing my mother when it felt like we were just beginning to heal and could no longer have that dreamed-of mother-daughter relationship. I cried for the stubbornness of a woman so addicted to nicotine that she'd caused her own death. I cried because I was losing my mother. The three of us continued our vigil. I do not know if she spoke again to either my father or brother. She did not speak again to me and died two days later.

When I share this story, people tell me my last words to my mother displayed kindness. But I don't know about that. Is it right for me to say I forgave her when I didn't, really? Forgiveness is something I'm still working on. My longtime partner once told me that I hold onto grudges. And she's not wrong about that. But I wouldn't call my response to my mother's rejection a grudge. It was a life-changing moment when she reacted to my coming out with those words: "Why would you do this when we tried to make you so perfect?"

Why would anyone want to be perfect, after all, if doing so required pretending to be someone else? It seemed like so much work with so little satisfaction for either of us at the end. My mother set us both up for an impossible task.

Still, over the years I wondered what my mother was thinking when she asked me for my forgiveness. And why had she put the onus for forgiveness on me? Over time, I realized that my mother could easily have said, "I'm sorry for the hurtful things I've said about your gayness and how I ruined any chance of a real, mother-daughter relationship when I rejected you that day in the car in 1981." But that's not what she said. She didn't say any of that, never had, and never would. My parents' reaction to my gayness was harsh, but my mother was the one who made me believe something was deeply wrong with me—from my cleft lip to my coming out. She was the primary bearer of hurtful words. She had created and carried out the daily betterment campaign of making me the person she thought I should be. After I came out, though, her bitterness over her lack of success in that campaign made her mean. Before coming out, I had not experienced that side of my mother.

Recently, I subscribed to a monthly newsletter called *The Monastic Way* by Sister Joan Chittister, a Benedictine nun. She says that, "Forgiveness occurs when we don't need to hold a grudge anymore. When we are strong enough to be independent of whatever, whoever it was that so ruthlessly uncovered the need in us. Forgiveness is not the problem; it's living until it comes that takes all the strength we have." Sister Chittister also advises watching out for premature forgiveness. "Examine what the bitterness is saying to your own soul about your own needs and expectations."

Now my mother has been dead thirty-three years and I am still working on forgiveness. Until recently, I hadn't even realized this bitterness was there. When I came out, and during the intervening years, anger arose in waves, but I stuffed down that anger because I didn't know what to do with it. Historically, even primally, my family dealt with anger by ignoring it. I was taught that. Hence, when I forgave my mother, I'd yet to toil long enough in that hardscrabble earth of forgiveness, digging toward the root of my bitterness. No, back then in the hospital room at thirty-nine, the only anger I felt was at her dying.

What I didn't know at thirty-nine was how deeply bitterness was buried in me, hidden from the light. I didn't know the cost. The cost of excusing my parents' reactions and treatment of me. I told myself that they had done the best they could, that they loved me and wanted the best for me. I told myself it was a different time and certainly my parents had grown up in a different world. For a long time, I made excuses for them, because to do otherwise would mean breaking free from the vise of their disapproval. And, what is disapproval but shame? Shame is the coat that came out of the closet all of those years ago, the shell I've donned since then.

What does that coat look like? It looks like the time my father wanted to watch me in court, but I said no, because I was afraid he would see me mess up. It looks like my fear of letting anyone know me at work because they would find out I was gay or find out something even more horrible, like the fact that I was imperfect. It looks like me giving up prosecuting because of fear of failure. It looks like me switching careers entirely and staying in a job for twenty years that paid less and required less accountability. I mitigated the cost of my mistakes by avoiding being responsible for people's lives—for my own life, for that matter.

"Shame is the caution light of the heart. It stops us from giving ourselves over to what we do not want to become but now realize we are more than capable of being," writes Sister Chittister. I wish I could say my mother's death freed me from shame. It did not, but I've begun to think about the difference between guidelines and expectations. My parents' betterment campaign was all about expectations. All my life I'd been looking for what would tell me how to live my life. What my parents gave me was not their wisdom—only their expectations. Because clearly I surmised I was doing something wrong. Relationships failed, job satisfaction wore off quickly, and the only solace and hope I found was in nature. The ocean and the mountains did not judge me or expect anything from me. They existed as they had for thousands of years. Ironically, my parents provided for that love of nature. My father loved nature. As a child, I received five wonderful, six-week summers at a Colorado camp reveling in the outdoors. My parents gave me that life-changing experience, but not their unconditional love.

In wanting that elusive guidebook that offered formulas for various situations that I might encounter, I was looking for unconditional love. Guidelines are predictable and offer parameters for you to exist within and where you can be free "inside the lines." A guidebook helps us wrestle with difficult situations and delves further into who we are and how we might interpret society's rules—even which ones to break as we see fit. With unconditional love, I could have learned to become more myself. This is what my parents could have provided.

In their own way, I suppose, my parents loved me, and a legacy of shame was not all my mother bestowed. Where to begin to describe this complicated relationship, a relationship so central to my all-too-brief, first thirty-nine years? So central, but like a hot ember, one I hovered around anxiously and feared to touch. My memories of Mom bring up feelings of not measuring up. A hint of maternal nurturing came through at times, but not often enough.

I most felt her nurturing when we were discussing or rather communing in silence as her blue pencil raced across a page of a school paper I was writing. She seemed to care about these moments. These moments contradicted her attempts to help me with the math assignments I hated and didn't understand. I would take out my frustration on her and angrily rebuff those attempts. But with the writing, I sensed a connection.

I would bring the rough draft of the paper downstairs hot off my typewriter or from my hot, "creative" hands—or so I thought—until she picked up her blue pencil. I would approach her hesitantly, sensing a long editing session ahead. She sat in her green chair, the one in front of the built-in bookcases lined with my father's law books, novels, and a copy of Dr. Spock's book on parenting. She almost always had a cigarette in hand and a cup of long-cold coffee on the side table. *How could she drink coffee at night?* I now marvel. She always kept a pencil nearby so she could do the daily crossword puzzles from the *Chicago Tribune* or the *Chicago Daily News*. I sat on the carpet with my knees tucked under me as I watched her pencil flutter across the page, inserting the necessary semicolons, periods, or capital letters. She didn't bother to read the piece straight through before her pencil started going. The pencil, often her blue, special one for crossing out words, making her little caret copyediting marks for an insertion of a word that would make my paper better. All of her marks were copyediting marks: marks she had picked up while she was in her graduate journalism program at Northwestern in the mid-1940s. There wasn't much talking. But sometimes, there was.

"Why does he do this in this section here? I don't understand this," she would say. And then I would try to explain why this Civil War soldier in my story was talking about his dog back home and why it was important. I would tell her this and her pencil would magically turn my thoughts into a coherent sentence. Not writing, exactly, but using caret marks to insert words and making periods using an "x" with a circle around it. Or perhaps she would say, "I don't think this part is that important," and would cross out my carefully chosen words. I would feel my creativity spark snuffed out with one strong pinch of her wet fingers. It's how she put out the dinner candles.

Her pencil would move again. Kneeling by her chair, watching her, I waited for the pencil to stop. I waited for the praise I wanted to hear. But it didn't come. She would hand me back the paper and I would go back to my room and dutifully type in the edits. We both waited for the grade. I knew she wanted to know how well she had done as much as I longed for that red "A." These moments didn't happen with all of my papers, but the few she helped me shape left an indelible mark on me. These moments by her chair late in the evening to me were a shared, joint effort. They created some sort of intimacy that I longed for and hoped would seep into the rest of our lives together as grown women, still mother and daughter.

CHAPTER SIXTEEN

ADOPTION DAY

PRIOR TO MY mother's death Debra suggested going to Thailand for three weeks in the summer. I was intrigued. Along with her belief that one shouldn't have sex with a new partner before you'd been dating three months and that you should date a year before moving in together, she'd thought that traveling was a good test for a relationship. My mother's death coincided with that trip, which caused us to postpone for a year.

Other than a trip to France in high school and family vacations that were within the United States, I mostly traveled through reading books, my favorite kind of escape. As a kid I could sit in our living room reading and tune out WBBM news radio invariably playing in the background as well as the drone of my mother on the phone. What I recall most were books my mother had given me throughout grade school and middle school. They tended to be mostly Newbery Medal winners. *A Wrinkle in Time*, *Island of the Blue Dolphins*, *The Witch of Blackbird Pond*, among others. These were books that took me to different places and historical times.

By now, Debra and I had been living together in her house in the Green Lake neighborhood of north Seattle for about a year. Debra had been to Thailand twice before as part of her work in a Vietnamese refugee camp in the Philippines. She was passionate about its wonders, which included the food, the street markets with cheap knockoffs, and the warm, friendly people. If I was ambivalent about going to Thailand, it was because I'd never thought about going to Southeast Asia. I had just started a demanding new job with the City of Everett and wasn't sure I was eligible for three weeks' vacation. We kept talking about the trip, although we made no reservations or looked at any guidebooks. I was going to put all of my trust in her to get us there, get us around, and get us back. For some reason I had no doubt that she would be able to do this. Before we left, Debra waxed almost poetically about Thailand's quaint guesthouses, the delicious food, and the great deals to be had. Eventually, I was all in.

When we arrived in Bangkok after the long flight the taxi dumped us on the side of a very busy, noisy street. Horns beeped from every direction while Debra and I ventured cautiously along streets owned by motorbikes, cars, taxis, and bicycles and offering no distinguishable traffic lanes or crosswalks for pedestrians. I walked past barefoot construction workers framing buildings with large sticks of bamboo. It was 11:00 p.m., but the hustle and bustle resembled rush hour in Chicago. Throngs of people hugged the sides of the busy roadway as I staggered, jetlagged, behind Debra toward our first night's lodging. She had wisely counseled that we confine the next day's sightseeing to certain areas of the city to allow for horrendous traffic.

I would soon discover that the food, as Debra had promised, was outstanding. Too nervous to order directly from street vendors, we approached a collection of vendors gathered near buildings and feasted on steaming bowls of noodle soup and som tum thai: papaya salad with huge, grated green papayas drizzled in a salty hot sauce and tiny, dried shrimp mixed with the tasty-but-ubiquitous Asian fish sauce. But the best part about the street food was the wonderful "sticky rice" used to sop up soups or whatever else you were eating—perfect for balling up in the palm of your hand.

We traveled with our backpacks by train to the northern province of Chiang Mai. The heat was stifling and I sweated profusely, unused to the humidity that dampened our shirts with the least amount of exertion. I got drenched in my first downpour, weightier than any rainfall I had ever experienced in Chicago or the Pacific Northwest. We glimpsed solemn, orange-robed monks ranging from age five to ancient. And we saw dogs. Lots of dogs—licking their balls and rear ends. In Thailand, dogs were sacred and welcomed at Buddhist monasteries. Debra started taking photographs of these dogs and we jokingly talked about her soon-to-be published book, *The Dogs of Thailand.*

She wanted to do a trek. These hikes for tourists up to see the settlements of local hill tribes were heavily promoted. I remained unconvinced that traveling by elephant and sleeping on floor mats in the native huts on stilts was going to be the penultimate experience. It might have been for Debra, but not me. What's more, I found the heat and humidity daunting. Perhaps Debra sensed this, and she compromised more easily than I thought she would. This sort of test would come to define many of our outdoor adventures in the years to come. Debra lived for the outdoors. Her sense of well-being so depended on outdoor hikes and outdoor activities it seemed like an addiction. After our trip to Thailand, she wouldn't give in so easily. Or perhaps I just stopped trying to compromise. I initially relished her pushing me out of my comfort zone, but soon came to resent it. But in Thailand, she settled on the two of us renting a jeep for a guided day trip to the hill people. I was glad we did the jeep, but then Debra went on to exclaim repeatedly how great it would be to take a year off and live in Thailand. I countered with a tentative, "How about three months?"

At this point in our relationship, I realized that living in Thailand was just another of Debra's enthusiasms. Other enthusiasms included living in a cooperative housing situation, building a cabin, and going back to the Philippines. I was neither opposed to these plans, nor did I hanker to live in Thailand with a language seemingly impossible to learn and a climate unfavorable to light-skinned, northern Europeans. I learned to nod at these ideas and wait to see how far and how long she would dwell on them. Me, I just wanted to settle down, prosecute, and enjoy Seattle and Debra. I had fought hard for her.

One idea that I shared Debra's enthusiasm for was possibly adopting a child. Three years after our Thailand trip that dream became a reality and we were on our way to China to do that.

The pilot announced we would soon be landing in Chengdu, China. Immediately, all of the Chinese passengers stood up while we were airborne and started retrieving their belongings from the overhead bins. The flight from Hong Kong wasn't even close to touching down, but neither the pilot nor the attendants were urging passengers to sit back down. Debra and I stayed in our seats until everyone deplaned. It was October 1995 and we were on our way to pick up our first child from China. Neither of us had wanted to do artificial insemination, and because we both had hysterectomies, neither of us could carry a baby, anyway. We had just spent a week in Hong Kong sightseeing and acclimating ourselves to a different culture. We thought we were as ready as we could be to have a child. What foolish new parent hasn't thought this very thought? One can never be ready and if anyone says she is, then she is lying.

Our adventure had begun the year before when we decided to adopt from China. But really it began before that when we first began talking about children. We were unaware of Cheri Pies's groundbreaking book from 1978, *Considering Parenthood: A Workbook for Lesbians*. But we were part of what a 1996 *Newsweek* article called "the gayby boom." Our closest friends had just had a baby girl through artificial insemination. Neither Debra nor I had ever wanted to go that route. We looked at adoption through foster care and domestic open adoptions. We then started looking at international adoptions. China had a surplus of female infants and was one of few countries open to single-parent adoptions, since we obviously couldn't legally adopt as a lesbian couple at that time in the US.

We wanted as close to a newborn child as we could get, and Chinese adoptions had begun taking off in 1991 when China's one-child policy began. We worked with an agency that knew we were a lesbian couple. But that didn't bother them. We just had to find a friendly social worker who might "wink, wink, look the other way." Nonetheless, when the social worker came for the home visit, we had gone to the trouble of making the guest bedroom appear as if it were where I always slept. The Chinese government had decreed that it would not let same-sex parents adopt, and it went so far as to say that if they found out, they would come take the baby away. This terrified us and heightened our anxiety about the trip.

About six months earlier, the adoption agency faxed us ten passport-sized photos of ten female infants we could potentially adopt. The photos reminded me of those thin strips of tiny black-and-white images spat out by a photo booth. Debra and I pored over the small, grainy, faxed prints trying to make this wonderful but horrible decision. Wonderful, because the adoption was really happening, and horrible, because we wanted to adopt them all. We chose the girl who would become Ren because we wanted a young baby, and she was four-and-a-half months. We met her as Zhu Yun Xia, the name the orphanage gave her. Her name meant "beautiful sunset cloud" in Chinese. How could any parent choose based on a faxed, two-by-two-inch photo? But that is how we did it. We received no information about her, except that she had been left at a train station and taken to the local police station, and then to the Chengdu orphanage. This was the custom during China's thirty-year, one-child policy. Mothers would leave the child—almost always a girl, because of the importance of boy children in China—in a place where she knew the baby would be found.

Once we deplaned in Chengdu, we found few people at the airport, barring a Chinese gentleman holding up a sign that read, "Arlene & Linda." We turned to each other and wondered who those obviously English or American women were. I looked at Debra and she looked at me and our shoulders sagged. We had come so far, and no one appeared to speak English. We saw no one holding up signs for us and we weren't sure what to do. But then the Chinese man with the sign came over to us, and through the use of pantomime and a mention of Doctor Chen, whom we were working with in Chengdu, we all managed to figure out that he was our driver and that he was indeed there for us. Months later, we would learn that Linda and Arlene were the women coming two months later to adopt their child through the same Chengdu doctor and the same agency in Seattle.

The man told us he would take us to the orphanage right away. Oh my gosh! We were excited beyond words to soon be holding our chosen child. Our trip fatigue seemed to vanish, and we began chattering to each other in excitement. We hadn't expected to get our new child the moment we arrived. "Are we ready?" I said to Debra during our babbling in the back of the car. Debra's nerves had been on edge since we'd left Seattle: she was the one we'd agreed would play adopting parent. I was just a friend along to help. Her name appeared on the bulk of the paperwork and the stress seemed to have almost done her in. She turned to me with worried eyes—holding worst-case scenarios. These fears had erupted in hives on her arms during the weeks before we left.

It had been my job to keep those worries tolerable as opposed to catastrophic. I had assisted in scouring the numerous forms, which included financial disclosure forms, credit history, medical information, and other legal and personal forms—so many forms. We also had to seek letters of recommendation from three people and agonized over which of our friends could most impress the Chinese government. We each had to go to the police station to be fingerprinted and undergo a criminal history background check. We also had to provide family histories and current photos of what our family enjoyed doing. In short, we had to prove we were—well, really Debra had to prove she was—worthy of being a parent. Debra earned adopting parent status, we figured, because she was a teacher and I was a lowly attorney. After all, the Chinese revered teachers more than lawyers.

And then, after all of that work, we endured months of hearing nothing from the agency or the Chinese government. Would we be approved? Would the Chinese see Debra as worthy? It did not escape us that every day, straight parents were creating babies with nary a thought, never having to go through this labyrinthian deluge of paperwork—along with a measure of deceit—for the privilege of parenthood.

But now the weight of all those steps was materializing and I knew I was unprepared. The desire to have children was there, but the confidence that I knew anything at all about being a parent was missing. Good thing, I thought, that we had each other. I don't know how garden-variety single parents do it. I had yet to read the words of NPR host Scott Simon, the author of *Baby, We Were Meant for Each Other*: "That every adoption is, more or less, a success because every child who is adopted embodies a fresh new chance for the world." All I could hold in that moment was fear, excitement, anticipation, and sleep deprivation as we drove through rice paddies to the center of Chengdu, a city housing four million back in 1995.

As I looked out the car window, I remembered our trip to Thailand and felt a surge of gratitude that Debra had suggested that trip three years earlier. In a way, it prepared me for the potent non-Western smells and seemingly chaotic bustle of China. I saw bicycles and streets full of every type of vehicle, but mostly bicycles laden with piles of merchandise or produce, as well as pedestrians, all walking briskly. The air was gray and heavy with coal dust, the leavings of the city's major heat source. Suddenly, we veered off the busy, wide streets, rounded the corner, and stopped. The driver had pulled us up beside the orphanage. I squeezed Debra's hand before we got out. The driver deposited our large backpack and even larger, stuffed duffel bag as we grabbed our smaller backpacks and the video camera. The duffel bag was packed with some of our belongings, but much of it contained the gifts we were told to bring for the orphanage: books, crayons, coloring books, and clothing, as well as gifts for the women assigned to care for the babies.

We hurried toward the orphanage by way of a covered courtyard five stories high, but no one was there. We waited and waited some more, and then a young woman strolled out to greet us. She looked fifteen or sixteen. She had limited English and we only knew thank you and hello in Chinese; we struggled to make ourselves understood. We were clearly unexpected. It was a Sunday and minimal staff were on hand. We finally learned that Ren was not living at the orphanage. What we would discover is that prospective adoptees were sent to live away from the orphanage and temporarily receive better care at a foster mom's house. I looked up and realized that an array of children were now watching us from the balconies on each floor. We were offered seats and asked if Ren should be fetched from her foster mom's house. Little did we know that the wait would be two hours. The waiting was interminable. Debra and I barely spoke, awash in fatigue and spent anxiety. *Were we really getting our daughter right now?*

Then the young woman came back and motioned for us to follow her. I turned to Debra and said, "They're offering us a tour of the orphanage?"

Debra looked surprised. "I thought they tried to prevent foreigners from seeing the living conditions of the orphans."

We were taken to rooms where the older children were kept and then to one room of six bassinets that appeared to keep infants needing special care. Several infants had huge holes in their faces where the cleft from their nose to their lip didn't close properly, and my heart naturally went out to these children. I knew the repairs for this defect could be addressed affordably in the States, but the Chinese government did not consider fixing this kind of birth defect a priority for female orphans. Debra looked at me to see how I was taking this in because of my own cleft palate. I struggled to stay in the room. In one hallway, we saw toddlers tied by the waist to some sort of toilet. We had been told we might see this. We had no idea whether the infants had been left untended for minutes or an hour, but either way, the sight was unnerving.

And then we came to a large room of infants in bamboo bassinets lined up on either side of the room. The room probably held ten infants, but we already knew our Ren would not be among them. We were then escorted back to the waiting area on the first floor with no update about when Ren would arrive. The children were clean, as were the rooms. Aside from too few staff and the infants on toilets we saw nothing to warrant the bad press these orphanages had received. I had expected worse.

The afternoon heat bore down on us. We were tired and not much conversation passed between us, but I do remember one thing Debra said. "Now remember, Jill, when Ren arrives, we can't both go up and greet her and hold her. You'll have to wait, because otherwise they might get suspicious." My jaw dropped. I felt like a scolded child—for I had forgotten in my excitement that Debra was the adopting parent. Or at least, that's what we'd told the Chinese government.

"Do you think we'll get to take her with us? Are we actually getting her now?" I said to Debra.

"I don't know. I don't know if I'm ready."

"I don't think I'm ready, either," I replied. And then I started to worry about that very thing: our readiness. About a year prior, we'd babysat our friends' infant daughter and I put her diaper on backwards. I think I now had the mechanics of diapering down after we took several required classes with the wife of the couple facilitating our adoption. We'd received a practical six weeks of instructions on taking care of an infant. That part of parenting I felt more prepared for, but the emotional and responsibility part were questionable.

Just when my patience had about run its course, a woman walked into the courtyard steering her bicycle by the handlebars with an older girl astride them. Strapped onto the woman's back, papoose-style, was an infant. It was Ren. Debra immediately jumped up: she'd recognized Ren from the fax photo, whereas it took me a moment or two to do the same. The foster mom placed her into Debra's arms and I—the good friend—took a photograph and then tried to operate the new video camera I'd had little experience with. I so wished I could hold Ren, but I knew I'd have years ahead to do that. Still, restraining myself from touching her was immeasurably hard. The foster mom and the girl we'd learn was her older daughter explained that they called Ren "Hei Mei," which meant "dark sister." Ren's complexion was darker, in keeping with those who come from northern China. We would learn that skin shades were just as important for the Chinese as for Blacks in the United States. A lighter complexion was favored, allegedly signifying a life not spent toiling in the fields. After Debra held Ren, we prepared to take her and then received the cruelest news of all. No, we could not take Ren, because we needed to deal with paperwork and the authorities before the official handover. I was crushed but relieved. I needed breathing room. We reluctantly said goodbye to Ren, not really knowing when we would see her next. Would it be tomorrow or in several days?

It would, in fact, be several days more before I got to hold Ren for the first time in the privacy of our hotel room. As I cradled the slight heft of her tiny, five-month-old body, I also felt for the first time the weight of this new responsibility. I was happy beyond measure and felt that Debra and I were up to it, but when a frightened, crying Ren gave us a subsequent night of little sleep, I wasn't so sure. Poor Ren, alone with these two women who looked nothing like her and bumbled their way through soothing her cries. It was then that I remembered what my mother had told me many years ago, long before I even thought about mothering. She said it during a conversation when I'd first started babysitting for a neighbor with three children, one of whom was an infant. I'd had little experience with infants, and I expressed my concern to my mother. I have no idea what my mother felt about mothering, but she did provide this tidbit: "When I first held you, I was terrified. I remember asking my father what to do." Papa T.—for my mother's maiden name, Thomas—told my mother, "Just love her." That sounded like good advice in caring for Ren, but was it enough? What did "just loving a child" look like? As a mother, I marveled at the importance of this question. This memory of my mother sharing her feeling of unpreparedness about raising a child hit me as I first held Ren.

Love showed up in a different way on our first night alone as new parents. It was also that first night in the hotel room with our new baby that allowed us to discover a unique, previously undisclosed feature about her. When we unwrapped her many layers of clothing, we found out that Ren had a lucky toe. The fourth and fifth toe on her right foot were webbed together. I immediately thought of my special feature and prayed that this "lucky toe," as Debra dubbed it, would not prove detrimental to Ren's health or self-esteem in the way my lip had affected me. At that moment of discovery, I vowed that Ren's lucky toe would be something we all talked about and didn't hide away as my parents had done with my lip. I believe my parents tried to protect me out of love, but by never talking about my cleft palate, I received the message that it was something to be ashamed of. These feelings only multiplied when I came out in the car with my parents and heard my mother's anguished cry, "But we tried to make you so perfect." I assumed these words reflected more than just a general statement; they contained a veiled reference to my "imperfection."

When Debra and I made this discovery about Ren in the hotel room, we didn't know her unique feature would be of little consequence in her ability to walk, her overall health, or her sense of self. This discovery did prompt me to reflect on my parents' perception—at the tail end of 1953—when their daughter arrived with her "unique feature." The difference being that in the 1950s, a cleft lip or cleft palate was relatively common rather than unique, and instead of being described affectionately as a "feature," it was seen as a birth defect. After all, the post-World War II era gave rise to the "can-do generation," proffering a period of great growth and the promise of a better tomorrow. The 1950s was the wealthiest decade in American history, a miracle time to those who had survived the Depression. I'm sure my parents were concerned about whether and what they could do to make this promise come true for their "less-than-perfect" daughter. They were going to do everything in their power to pave that way forward for me, and by extension, all four of us.

The next day, after a night of minimal sleep, Debra, Ren, and I ventured out in public for the first time as a family. We needed supplies. We stopped at a local department store and were the only Caucasians in the place. Me at five-foot-eight and Debra lugging a Chinese infant in a pouch were magnets for clusters of Chinese "aunties" and mothers, who surrounded us and often stopped us in our tracks. They chatted amiably at us in Chinese. One woman had no compunction about reaching out and pinching Ren's plump cheeks. Others communicated their dissatisfaction about Ren's moderately warm clothing through clucking sounds and finger-pointing. We had removed Ren's previous layers of Chinese clothing and dressed her American-style in a fleece jacket, thick socks, and a wraparound blanket. This outfit was obviously not the norm, but the women were kind enough to offer only mild scoldings. "Lucky baby," one woman remarked to us in English and the other women clucked and smiled. Both Debra and I responded, "No, we are the lucky ones." We purchased one of the towering, stainless steel thermoses commonly seen in China, used all day to replenish hot water for tea carried around in glass jars. One thermos had previously stood on a chair on our hotel floor by the elevators and we'd needed to make frequent trips there to make formula for Ren's bottle. We wanted our own to keep in our room and as a souvenir of our trip.

In the evening, we headed out to a restaurant that served hot pot, one of the culinary treats of the Sichuan province. Dr. Chen, the kindly doctor who had facilitated Ren's adoption, had arranged this outing for us from afar. We knew the food would be good, better than we'd had in previous restaurants offering ambiguous or incorrect English translations of Chinese menu items. One night, I had tried something labeled as "mixed meats," which I later believed contained snake, based on the live animals in cages kept at the front of the restaurant to advertise the freshness of their meat. This time we felt more at ease about the offerings and were eager to taste this highly recommended hot pot specialty, a promised highlight. No sooner had the food arrived than Ren began to wail. Debra retrieved the bottle with formula, but Ren refused it, and the more Debra tried with the bottle, the more Ren fussed. Soon we'd become the center of attention in the restaurant, equally flustered by our loud, miserable baby. Several female diners came over and tried to offer suggestions, but nothing worked. We tried pacing up and down with her beside the table, and eventually, Debra stepped outside to ease the distraction.

We tried calling Dr. Chen on the restaurant phone. After what seemed like hours, he appeared and immediately sized up the problem: the new American nipple we'd used to replace the worn, bedraggled nipple on Ren's original baby bottle. Ren was unused to the stiff nipples and preferred the looser, secondhand ones used in the orphanage. What's more, the orphanage nipples had larger holes, allowing infants to ingest their rice-with-milk mixture. No one had informed us about the nipples; Dr. Chen dashed off to find a local one. He reappeared and quieted Ren down, but by then, all we wanted was to get back to the privacy of our room. It had been a harrowing dinner, reinforcing that fear of not knowing what the hell we were doing. Poor Debra was only able to eat one bite of the special hot pot before all the commotion began.

The rest of our time went quickly and more easily as Ren and her two moms grew more accustomed to the other. We took a five-hour flight south to Guangzhou, staying at the wonderful, continental White Swan Hotel—the site of all adopting European and American parents waiting for American embassy appointments granting reentry onto American soil. Dr. Chen's portion of the trip had been solely about helping us navigate Chengdu. But here in Guangzhou, Debra and I would truly be on our own. We landed in the city and found a sea of signs written in Chinese characters and no one who spoke English. We had no idea where to pick up our luggage. I pulled out my huge, Chinese-English paperback dictionary and tried to communicate by pointing at words, but most people waved us off. One person finally gestured in a vague direction and we found our luggage in a completely different building from the one where we had arrived. The next challenge was finding a taxi to take us to the White Swan Hotel. Arriving at the White Swan was a delight. It was a Western-style luxury hotel with many other Western families with Chinese infants. Most of the staff spoke English and the atmosphere felt both regal and familiar. After a few days of sightseeing and enjoying the comforts of an upscale hotel, we finally got our embassy appointment. Our lavish surroundings seemed to have lulled us into believing we'd earned a smooth and speedy trip home. We hadn't anticipated how the bumps in our journey might mirror the complications that come with parenthood, not to mention adopting babies from a foreign country.

We had air tickets to fly home that October, but only via Hong Kong and then Taipei, since Red China was not allowing direct flights to the US from the mainland. We had delayed booking our flight to Hong Kong while waiting for clearance from Guangzhou. What we didn't know was that Guangzhou was hosting a huge trade fair. Every form of travel to and from the city—flights, trains, and bus trips—was fully booked. A Guangzhou travel agency finally told us about an overnight ferry option to Hong Kong, about 106 miles from Guangzhou, otherwise known as the "slow boat to China." The barge-like ferry trip took about nine hours.

We'd chosen one of the cheaper accommodation options. Our little cabin held a bunk bed with thin mattresses and a murky mirror. We took turns walking up on deck all night with infant Ren to induce sleep but mostly to entertain her in shifts. The treasured hot water thermos we had purchased in Chengdu was a godsend for tea, Ren's bottles, and washing. None of us slept well. The sunrise and overcast skies of Hong Kong were a welcome sight for our weary bodies. We were almost home. We spent a day in Hong Kong. Only twenty-four hours more. The flight from Hong Kong to Taipei took an hour and a half, followed by a six-hour layover in Taipei, and then a ten-hour flight to Seattle. Our baby girl was safe on home turf before the real adventure of parenthood would begin.

Five years later, we found ourselves flying back to China to adopt again. As older parents, Debra and I realized Ren could live a good portion of her adult life without any family. When we adopted Ren, I was forty-one and Debra was forty. We wanted a companion for Ren: someone with whom she could share early childhood memories or commiserate with or joke with about her crazy parents.

Sara came into our lives through serendipity. A year earlier while we were pursuing a second adoption, and shortly after an innocuous family outing with members of a group called Families with Children from China. We had joined the local chapter when we returned with Ren as a way to reinforce her Chinese heritage. The group held events throughout the year celebrating different Chinese holidays, such as the Harvest Moon in October and the Lunar New Year and other social get-togethers. Ren, now four, Debra, and I went with this group and their children to a summer weekend gathering on nearby Whidbey Island. We joined other families in games, songs, meals, and good family time. We knew some of the other families similarly led by two moms. Several days after we got home, we received an anonymous, typewritten letter with no return address. The letter threatened to report our adoption agency to the Chinese government if we tried to adopt a second child. Such an action would endanger the agency's license.

We had been working with the same agency that helped with Ren's adoption and had already gone through six months of paperwork. "Why . . . why would somebody do this to us?" we wondered aloud. But no one came forward. It was one of the few times I felt targeted as a gay woman—and also the scariest. To be denied the child we wanted and could easily nurture and provide for—something we had as much right to as a straight couple—was beyond comprehension. To be that reviled for doing something that only felt like a win-win for Ren and our family shook me deeply. Backed against a wall and unwilling to endanger the agency, we told them we couldn't work with them any further.

This devastating news meant restarting the whole process with a different agency and waiting even longer for a child. The anonymous letter's intent was never clear. We questioned whether the writer was against gay adoptions or whether the letter's author felt we were jeopardizing adoptions for everyone else. At the very least, the author's actions seemed mean-spirited. They fractured whatever confidence we'd gained in raising a child in an all-female family.

After a year, we'd gained some perspective on this incident and were ready to go back to China. Between 1995 and 2000, adoptions from China had doubled. We undertook no painful selection process from grainy, faxed photos. This time, the government went ahead and selected the child for us. Our chosen daughter was Tai Chunjing, roughly nine months old. We received a picture of a pretty-but-unsmiling, bald-headed baby propped in a bamboo chair. Unlike Ren, this baby had not been sent to a foster mom but was waiting in the orphanage. Debra and I wanted to go as soon as possible to limit her stay. This time, we took maximum precautions, inviting Martha and Debra's Aunt Nan to go with us to better disguise our lesbianism. My designated role on this trip was to entertain and take care of Ren while the others went to the orphanage and filled out paperwork. This trip would be a different one in so many ways: all the other couples accompanying us were straight and showed little interest in sightseeing around Nanjing. They seemed more inclined to pick up their child and hightail it back to the United States.

Sara's orphanage was about three hours north of Nanjing in the town of Taizhou, situated on the north bank of the Yangtze River. We arrived during a bitterly cold January. I keep a photo of the five of us standing in front of the Great Wall before we picked up Sara. There we were, bundled up beyond recognition, nobody else braving the cold to go sightseeing. Ren stayed toasty in her snowsuit while the rest of us couldn't pile on enough layers. The temperature seemed to warm only another ten degrees in Nanjing.

Eight days after we'd arrived in China, we were told that caretakers would bring our babies to our hotel in Nanjing via four-hour van ride. We ate dinner early. Then we heard slow murmurings among the diners, many of them waiting parents.

Our translator, Amy, suddenly appeared at our table. "The babies are here! The babies are here!" she said. All the diners jumped up and followed her to a room full of babies with their Chinese nannies. We recognized Sara right away. She was red-faced, no doubt overheated from her three layers of clothing. She also looked petrified.

This was only a first meeting. It took another two days—after Debra, Nan, and Martha went to Taizhou to do paperwork—before they got to carry Sara away in their arms. By staying behind with Ren, I felt distanced from Sara's adoption process. Having Martha and Nan along was helpful, but once we got Sara, they too couldn't wait to hold her. Again, I told myself I would get my holding time back in Seattle. They got to give Sara her first bath in the hotel sink, which she cried through. I wondered then how Sara would know who to bond with: so many friendly, white, adult females rocking and chattering to her, heaping upon her endless love and adoration.

The first two days—no matter how many goofy faces and sounds we made—Sara refused to smile. It was Ren who broke first ground. She'd decided it was fun to jump between the two double beds in the room, twirling her new pink Chinese umbrella, and for whatever reason—perhaps because of Ren's pure, childlike joy—these antics brought a look of delight to Sara's face. I think Ren was worried about her sad, unsmiling, little sister—unleashing an older sibling's sense of protectiveness that would characterize her relationship with Sara thereafter. On our plane trip back to Seattle, unlike Ren who hadn't slept at all on our first trip, our second child slept the whole way.

I continue to treasure the adoption processes of our two girls, not only for the priceless gift of their presence in my life, but also because of these adventures to China and jumping through so much angst, and Herculean bureaucratic hills Debra and I did together. It bonded us as new parents and a family, and would allow us to rise above our many challenges ahead.

CHAPTER SEVENTEEN

PARENTING FOR BEGINNERS

BEFORE I became a parent, I thought the hardest thing I'd ever done was finish law school and take the bar exam twice. Parenting would humble me to the core, but also be the best thing I'd ever done. Folding children into my life caused me to think about—and deeply question—the assumptions I had about my own parents and how I was raised. I hadn't expected our styles to be so different, but Debra took to parenting more fiercely than I did from the get-go. Ren became the center of our lives, but more so, the center of Debra's life.

I instinctively knew I could not be a stay-at-home mom, while Debra embraced this traditional role. Because of that, Ren's attachment seemed stronger with Debra. The first year of Ren's life with us, we both worked away from home, but Debra desperately wanted to quit her teaching job and stay full-time with Ren. I knew I couldn't take such drastic action—one of us had to work, after all—although we talked about both of us working part-time later in life to gain better quality time first with Ren, and then with Sara. At the time, I figured that staying at home would suffocate me. I had gone to law school because I wanted a career—and professional stimulation. We had been privy to much discussion about raising children in the lesbian community and the roles each woman would assume. Feminists felt that a woman should be in the workplace. Never mind the fact that she earned fifty-nine cents an hour to a man's dollar. It was only by being in the workplace, they said, that men would recognize our equality. I wanted it all, though—to be a mother and a breadwinner. But, how does that work with two women as parents? In our case, the relationship defaulted to the heterosexual model. I was the "father" and Debra was the "mother." And yet, if we could have managed it financially—and Debra were willing—I would have loved to balance part-time work with being a mom.

Although Debra and I never discussed it, we both came from middle-class or upper-middle-class backgrounds. We wanted our children to enjoy the same perks we'd had as children. This meant piano lessons, ski trips, and vacations—all of which came with a price tag. One of us had to work full time to afford these bourgeois trappings. That had to be me: my ego was wrapped up in bringing home the bacon for my family. This didn't mean our vacations had to be at the Ritz, though. Vacations often meant camping together as a family, which would inadvertently add stress to our union rather than take away from it.

Debra and I both loved the outdoors. Why stop just because we had children? I would carry Ren in a backpack on day hikes, and then it was Sara's turn. At first, these trips were delightful and became some of my best memories, either tagging along with other families or the two of us traipsing with the girls to Holden Village, a Lutheran community up on Lake Chelan. Debra and I particularly loved to go there—where meals were cooked for us and activities provided for the kids—a vacation away from the sometime drudgery of parenting. We also purchased a cabin in the North Cascades with another family and spent holidays and summers exploring Lost Creek, horseback riding, mountain biking, hiking, and just hanging out at a spot along Lost River playing in the water and building forts out of sticks.

This arrangement of Debra taking care of the girls at home and me immersed in a law office worked at first, but then became a competition about who was working harder. Heated conversations about parenting inequities ensued. Society didn't make it any easier for us. In the 1990s, few families featured two moms or two dads at the helm. The majority of those who weighed in on same-sex families felt that children would suffer from not having a mom and a dad. Research has since disproven this theory, with studies showing that children of lesbian moms are no more or less well-adjusted from the lack of a father figure. It wasn't until Ren was fifteen when a *Time* article presented a California study that not only disproved this theory but found kids from lesbian homes faring better than those from straight homes. Still, prevailing attitudes did little to support our fledgling union—one that ironically fell back on trying to replace a "real" mom and dad.

During Ren's tenure at the local elementary school, Debra and I knew of only one other lesbian parent-couple who were younger than we were. This was typical: we were ten years older than most parents because of our late start.

Debra and I worried about how having two moms would affect Ren. Would she feel different? How would others' judgments play out in her social development? Would other parents discriminate against us, and by extension, Ren? All of Ren's teachers knew that she had two moms and to our delight made sure that Ren got extra time to create two sets of Valentine's Day and Mother's Day cards. My father had died in 2000, so a Father's Day card went out to her one surviving grandfather—Debra's dad. With no gay or straight male friends, we also worried about the lack of male influences in Ren's life. This changed as soon as Ren started school. Ren made friends easily and we became friends with the straight parents whose homes Ren went to for play dates and vice versa. It didn't matter that we were gay or that we were older than the other parents. Our children were the main focus, and as long as they were happy, we were happy.

Debra and I discovered differences in how we parented. Debra believed our family should be child-centered and I did not share that belief. I certainly had not been raised that way. Often, I would come home from work and find Debra and Ren playing together on the living room floor under tents made out of sheets and chairs. While Ren would often rush out to greet me, I felt superfluous in these moments. Debra believed our roles were to entertain the child. My parents had not entertained me. Certainly, beyond the age of three, my mother never got on her hands and knees and played at being unicorns. Our different styles of parenting were neither right nor wrong, but we didn't talk about those differences, and our lack of communication would ultimately diminish the health of our relationship.

I had a much harder time entertaining Ren. I could take her to the playground and swing with her or chase her and later her sister around the jungle gym. I could play sports with her, such as taking them ice skating and skiing. Those were things my father had done with John and me, but I faced a steeper learning curve around putting up my short hair with barrettes and rubber bands when we played beauty salon. All I could sometimes see was the mess being created or the productive minutes I was being deprived of, minutes I could have spent cooking, shopping, cleaning, paying the bills, or even stealing a few minutes alone with a cup of coffee and a book. As all parents know but seldom realize is that parenting is a lifetime commitment. Even once the kids are out of the house, those minutes you gave up working or resting to play beauty shop will never come again.

In addition to battling over parenting roles and styles, Debra and I had many conversations about a last name for our children. "We could do Olmsted-Vanneman," Debra suggested. Then, perhaps realizing I might take offense, she quickly suggested "Vanneman-Olmsted."

"I don't know. Mary Ren Xia Olmsted-Vanneman seems like quite a mouthful to me," I said.

We went on like this for weeks, tossing out possibilities. We even thought of making up a whole new last name like friends of ours had done, changing their Anglo-Saxon last names to "Liu" in order to offer their child a Chinese last name. We weren't sure Debra's southern Baptist Oklahoma parents would cotton on to that idea. Finally, one of us came up with shortening my last name to "Van," and using the last name of "Van Olmsted." That name held a certain appeal and we played around with it for a few more weeks. But in the end, I didn't want my daughter to have a last name that didn't really belong to either of her parents. "I don't really care if they have my last name. Let's just go with Olmsted," I told Debra. And, that's what we did. On occasion, the fact that the girls didn't share my last name presented a problem—but not that often.

Later, I wondered why I didn't care. Why I didn't ponder the significance of trading away this element of my identity—a last name I felt proud of. I think I believed that we were a family now—and we would be a family forever—so what difference did it really make? Debra's parents were much more involved in Ren's life, after all, and my mother had already died and my father had died when Ren was three, so Ren and Sara became Olmsteds. But I knew and felt the girls were equally mine, even if they didn't share my last name.

What's in a name? I thought. *My love is enough.*

When I was in my thirties, I'd never thought that my parents wouldn't last forever. In theory, by the time Debra and I adopted our kids, my parents would have been older grandparents. I never dreamed they wouldn't be around to enjoy my children. But that's what happened, and in a weird way, the history of my shrinking family repeated itself. My maternal grandmother died while Mom was carrying me, so I lost the opportunity to meet her, and my mother's father died when I was three. I never really knew my mother's extended family in Seattle and my Illinois-born-and-raised father was an only child. I was raised with one set of devoted grandparents, and my children would have that same experience with Debra's parents, who were about ten years younger than mine. My children vaguely knew their uncle much in the way that I'd known my Seattle uncle—not well, but certainly my girls knew their Uncle John. They would never really know my parents.

Seeing this parallel helped me develop compassion toward my mother, who left her family behind when she came to Northwestern and became a Vanneman. She must have felt somewhat consumed by the Vannemans, much as I often felt the Olmsteds consumed me. I vividly remembered one occasion when I had grabbed an old photo album of my mother's and attempted to ask her about the people in the photos. "Why are you looking at that?" she replied. "Why would you care?" I was baffled by her response. Later, I thought she might have felt that the Thomas side had been so wiped out that of course no one would care. But I cared. By then I was living in Seattle and had heard my uncle talk about relatives that I had no images for. I did not want the same thing to happen to me. I attempted to incorporate Vanneman traditions into my new family, such as baking the coveted "Vanneman cake" for birthdays, an angel food cake with mocha whipped cream frosting. This was just one way I increasingly saw the Vanneman side of me come out, demanding attention for my half of the family tree.

While I saw my role in marriage as the breadwinner, occasionally a fierce, Mama Bear part of me would come roaring out. In third grade, Ren had an experience at school that shook me to the core. I happened to be home early one day, because Debra had asked me to be home so she could go to an appointment. Ren was already home from school when I arrived, and I asked her about her day.

"Mom," she said. "Ms. Carrington threw something away that I gave her today." I could tell that Ren was troubled. "It was a note that somebody put in my cubby that said they would hurt me."

"What did you do?' I said.

"I took it up to Ms. Carrington and she said not to worry about it, and she wadded it up and put it in the trash."

I glanced up at the clock and noted that it was almost four in the afternoon. Ren looked upset and I asked her if she thought the note might still be in the trash. I was busy speculating as to whether or not the custodian had gotten around to making his classroom rounds and asked Ren if she thought he had. "Probably," Ren told me. I then got down in a squat and looked Ren in the eye. "Do you want me to go see if it's still there?" A huge flood of relief washed over her face and she nodded. I drove Ren back to school, and we went directly to her classroom. Ren pointed out the trash can.

I started pulling out the wadded pieces of paper with penciled, big-lettered print and smoothed them out. The incriminating document in a third grader's penmanship soon appeared. "I have a knife," the note said. "You better watch out." Shock and outrage pulsed through my body. *How could the teacher have been so cavalier?* Ren would go on to receive more of these threatening notes, which we told her to bring home to us. The culprit was eventually discovered. This incident became a huge ordeal for Debra and me as the school seemed ill-equipped to handle the situation, and district personnel joined in. After three long, agonizing weeks, school administrators discovered the author of the note. A friend of Ren's was deep into the *Boxcar Children* mystery series, and for some reason thought she would make up her own version and send Ren these disturbing notes. The school ended up removing this child from the classroom and Ren didn't suffer any long-term trauma. I was just so glad that I had been home to respond to this situation, and more so, that Ren was able to move past it.

But for the most part, parenting didn't come naturally to me. I did enjoy taking the children to the library. I had loved to read as a child, and I wanted my children to have that same love. Books had offered an escape and taught me about the world beyond my sheltered suburban home and environment. I relished reading to them, although I eventually wearied of countless readings of *Don't Let the Pigeon Drive the Bus!* I particularly loved turning the pages of wordless, beautifully illustrated, big picture books with Sara so that both she and I could make up the words as we went along.

I also enjoyed singing to the girls to get them to sleep. While the attempt seldom worked, they delighted in the singing, and "Kumbaya" and "All My Trials" soon became favorites. Sara particularly enjoyed the singing. The other activity Sara particularly enjoyed was helping me make coffee in the morning. It became our ritual. I would pick her up, seat her on the counter, and give her the coffee spoon. Together, we would count out the tablespoons that went into the magic machine to make Mommy's favorite beverage.

But sometimes issues arose that made me feel inept. Ren would try to read aloud the books we had from the library, but she often stumbled over this task. In second grade, it was Debra who said, "This isn't right."

"What do you mean?" I said.

"Ren should be able to read, but she's struggling so with the letters. She's a smart little girl and she's not getting it."

I protested. "I just think it's taking her longer. Not everyone learns to read at the same pace."

But I was wrong. Debra with her teacher background and mother's love picked up what the school had not. Ren had a learning disability that prevented her from recognizing and sounding out the letters on the page. Who knows when the school would have picked up on it? With a "pull-out class," after-school, private tutoring, the help of a speech pathologist, and then a reading specialist, Ren was reading at grade level by the end of fifth grade. My appreciation for Debra's knowledge about learning disabilities and her willingness to do all the driving back and forth to these special lessons probably went unsaid. But I was grateful. It wouldn't have occurred to me then that I played my part by providing the resources that allowed us to help Ren.

I was desperately relieved when the lucky toe of Ren's that we first discovered in China turned out to be a non-issue. Addressing it was one of the first things we did when we returned. After consulting with our pediatrician, we took Ren to a specialist at Seattle Children's Hospital. He said what we so anxiously hoped to hear—that the toe wouldn't interfere with Ren's ability to walk, and it didn't. Contrary to my experience with my cleft lip, Ren's self-esteem never suffered because of that so-called "birth defect," either.

It was a delight, and yet, a chore to put the children to bed. Both girls struggled monumentally with sleep. But it was the act of helping them sleep that, more than anything, provided insight. I needed alone time. I craved at least one hour to myself each day to take care of my needs. Thus, I would not go to sleep when I lay down with Sara or Ren, because I knew that if I stayed awake, I could find that hour to myself, even if it was just to clear away the dishes or pay a bill. Debra protested that

I got all sorts of alone time at work, but of course, perpetual work tasks and performing in court gobbled up any sensation of enjoying my own company. Yes, I didn't have children grabbing at me, begging for my attention, but the gravitas of working as a prosecutor rarely allowed me to stop, breathe, and "be in the moment" with myself.

Our mutual love of outdoor activity did not stop when we had the girls—even on the days I would have liked to "press pause." I carried Ren first in the kid backpack on my back and then Sara for our hikes. While these backpacking and hiking trips tended to take all day, they were shorter than they'd been before kids, and sometimes Debra bribed the girls with Skittles candy, piece by piece, to convince them to hike one more step.

The girls both learned how to ski before they were five, something both Debra and I wished we had done as children; they also both learned how to swim at roughly the same ages. Debra's love for the outdoors knew no limits, however. I began to chafe at the almost weekly ritual of going for a hike or camping amid the escalating demands of housework, paying bills, and my need for downtime on the weekends. I prayed it would rain or I stalled getting ready for the day's outing, and yet, I could not communicate the underlying reasons for my discontent. I would look up the weather report for Snoqualmie Pass, where we often went for hikes, hoping the pass would be closed or complain about the rain in Seattle and mention it didn't look like a good day for a hike or I just procrastinated in my preparation. Instead, I ruminated in silence over all the tasks that needed doing at home. And rather than expressing these frustrations, I told myself there was no point: I would simply lose the argument. That's when my passive-aggressiveness began. I worried about having to put chains on the car when we went skiing. I further griped about returning late on a Sunday evening when I knew I'd be robbed of the last precious moments of a weekend to read my new book.

While I have many fond memories of these trips, I am plagued by the unpleasantness: the frequent effort required to get us all ready and the worry about leaving any crucial piece of equipment or sustenance behind. When outdoor activities had featured just the two of us, I could cope. But the extra stress of parental responsibility and perpetual organizing required for these weekends became more than I could handle. Debra and I began fighting—frequently. Yet these activities continued, regardless. I slowly gave in. I shrank back from voicing my preferences, and in the process, I began to realize that these weekends were nonnegotiable. At these times I wished I was still seeing Sam or even a therapist of some kind. I'd stopped seeing Sam when she had requested that I start seeing her three times a week without explaining why. I couldn't take that much time off work and I realized our seventeen-year therapeutic relationship had run its course.

Other warning signs cropped up that I should have paid attention to. Ren was in fifth grade and Debra and I decided she would gain a better education by going to a private middle school rather than attending the sprawling public middle school. We didn't want to deter Ren's reading progress. We began researching and touring various middle schools in the area, perusing the benefits and drawbacks of each one. The open houses were always on a school night, which meant hiring a babysitter, rustling together a quick dinner for the girls, and then hustling out the door. On the way across town one night, I told Debra that I was tired and didn't want to stay too long after the event: socializing after our previous open houses had made these evenings run on too late. The girls would never go to sleep with a babysitter. They might be in their beds, but we would have to finish up the job by reading to them and laying down with them after that. We needed to get home to allow everyone their rest, including me—I needed to be up early for work.

The ride over to the school delayed us. We needed to drive across town at dinnertime and Seattle's rush hour had yet to die down. We arrived late. We listened to the school's head teacher talk about their programs and school culture, and then a handful of current students stood up to talk about the joys of all-girls middle school. The girls seemed engaged and their talk, unrehearsed. *This place might be a good fit for Ren*, I mused. We milled around afterwards, and then—the moment I'd been fearing most happened right in front of me. Debra saw someone she knew from God-knows-where. I thought she might be one of Debra's former teaching colleagues. They chattered away face-to-face, deep in conversation. But after about ten minutes, I began tapping my foot and checking my watch. It was already eight-thirty. Debra and the woman had yet to break eye contact. I knew Debra missed having this kind of adult exchange, so I tried to remain equanimous for a few more minutes. But the ache of fatigue began rising up from the bones in my feet. I tried to catch Debra's eye, but she seemed to be avoiding my gaze. I then pointed to my watch, which was rude. I knew I was being rude, but I had warned Debra earlier that I wanted to get home early to get the girls to bed. She glowered at me and continued talking, apparently refusing to call me over to introduce me to her colleague. I stood alone in the same spot and continued waiting and fuming.

"That was so rude, Jill!" Debra said once we finally had gotten to the car. "I can't believe you would do that."

"Why do you always do this, Debra? You hang around and socialize and talk on and on when we have so many things to get done before we can even think about going to bed," I said. "It's not the first time, either."

"Why do you always want to pick a fight?" she said. "What do you want from me? I feel so unappreciated. You try carting around kids all day who are whining or don't want to be taken to wherever it is we're going."

"I'm not trying to pick a fight. I'm just trying to get us home at a reasonable hour so we can put the kids to bed. Geez, Debra, you just seem so unhappy. Are you sure you want to do this, continue to stay at home full time with the girls?"

"You won't even allow me a minute of social time," Debra said.

My voice softened at this accusation. I knew Debra had been feeling fragile of late. "You're at a really low point," I told her, "especially since your mom's just left. You always get like this after she leaves."

"Well, you think like she does," Debra jabbed back. "Nothing's ever good enough—it's just the same with you, only you don't express your thoughts, so I have to try to read your mind. I need to know what I'm dealing with."

I didn't know what to tell Debra. *What was she dealing with?* The bigger question haunting me was this: in trying but always failing to keep Debra happy—what was *I* dealing with?

We'd had this conversation so many times and I just wanted it to end. I'd been rude, yes, but I thought I had a point. Yet somehow my concerns had fallen into the ether and Debra wouldn't stop expressing hers. She continued to browbeat me about how wrong I'd been and how selfish I was about not giving her enough time. As always, she went on and on while I retreated into my thoughts and refused to engage with her. I recalled the remark from our former couples therapist about our relationship being like a "comfortable couch." We were fine as long as I didn't press too hard for my needs. Our efforts to have honest, difficult conversations never worked.

"I'm sorry," I said. I usually tried to make peace by just giving in to whatever Debra was saying. It had become a familiar pattern—and one I hated—both of us invariably walking away with mutinous looks on our faces. Nothing resolved, and no end in sight. Much later I realized that our relationship parallelled what psychologist Dr. Ruth L. Schwartz suggests is a common power struggle in lesbian relationships: that someone in the couple is always trying to make connection (Debra) and the other (me) is constantly afraid of losing oneself.

The arguments at home were worse. They usually concerned something I did or didn't do and in order to protect the girls from our battles, Debra would ask me to follow her down to the laundry room, where my imperfection was laid out like a loose thread or splotch of bleach on the towels. Or she would try to persuade me to change somehow—appear cheerier or attend more dinner parties or talk about wanting more sex—all of which I had less and less enthusiasm for. But I had given up. I couldn't have an effective disagreement with her. I had to agree with her, so I did. My head would flood and all I wanted was for the badgering and the criticisms to stop. I would try to stop a burgeoning disagreement or head it off at the pass, but she just never seemed to quit. I gave in and I kept giving in, thinking if I just agreed with everything, she said we'd all be happy, and these horrible disagreements would end. My faulty logic and willingness to subsume myself had never worked with my parents, either, so why would it work with Debra? Eventually, I stopped trying altogether. My parents had never modeled how to work out disagreements. They just didn't seem to have any or they were worked out away from children's ears.

The litany continued: squabbles about who was doing more work or should pay the bills or do the incessant tidying and sorting of the children's playthings brought back out of the toy box as soon as they were put in. As our children's needs became foremost, our moments of intimacy were frequently relegated to whenever we lay down at the end of our workdays. But now that we were falling asleep at different times, that last shred of closeness and affection seemed to dissolve.

One particular domestic scene remains seared in my memory—another instance of our seeming inability to glean joy from the everyday at home. The clothes for our household lay strewn on the sofa in the downstairs family room that Thursday evening. Debra's and my jeans, my Ralph Lauren tailored shirts for work, the girls' pants and T-shirts, sizes 6x and 8, were in there, at least I thought I'd seen Ren's purple-with-white-polka-dot pants sticking out. The clothes had been washed and pulled fresh from the dryer and placed upon the back of the sofa a couple of days ago. The intent was to keep them fresh until we or one of us could fold them neatly and put them away. I say that putting away the clothes was the intent. But with one of us working full time and the other a full-time mom and our two active kids under ten, that chore never happened as quickly as either of us would have liked—and unfolded laundry heaped up on our downstairs couch became a common sight.

Debra and I had agreed that tonight was the night. The girls were watching some Disney princess movie, giving us uninterrupted time to complete this task.

"So, you said you saw Lisa when you were picking up the girls today. What's new with them?" I said.

"Well, they're going to Whistler over midwinter break to go skiing," Debra said.

"Hmm, that's nice," I said as I tried to find Sara's other sock, the blue one dotted with fire trucks. I smiled inwardly at the thought of Sara's love for fire trucks, and at the same time, as I responded to Debra, my mind flashed on a memory of a ski trip the four of us had taken two years earlier to Big White with two other families. We'd all shared responsibility for the kids, playing games, cooking together as a group, and of course, skiing en masse. It had been such a wonderful time away.

But Debra was already talking again. This time she chattered away about some class on biodiversity she wanted to take the following semester. We both reached in unison for a T-shirt that said, "Life is Good," Debra almost tugging it out of my hands as I touched it. "I'll fold that," she said in a warm tone. I wasn't sure if the warmth was directed at me or toward some memory connected with the T-shirt. It was one I'd gotten her and had an image of a dog printed on the front.

I picked up Debra's red, baggy sweatpants, the ones that had made me fall in love with her and her vulnerability eight years earlier—a lifetime ago.

"I'm just going to run upstairs for a minute to check on the girls," she said.

"We can hear them if they need anything," I said. "We'll never get this done." We had each folded three items at this point and the pile didn't look any smaller. "I'm trying to make this quick so everyone can get to bed early for a change."

"It would help if you could get home earlier," she said. I'd heard this comment before, and it always amazed me. Debra knew my working hours and how long it took to ride the bus home from downtown Seattle. But this time, I decided to let it go. *Why start something now?* I thought. I found the other fire truck sock and folded the two of them into a ball.

By the time Debra got back from checking on the girls, I had at least five of Ren's T-shirts folded and stacked on one side of the sofa. "What were you doing for so long? I said. She protested that she hadn't been gone that long, even though her absence had seemed much longer than usual.

"Well, come on. Let's do the sheets then," I coaxed. I hated folding sheets, especially the bottom fitted sheets with no square corners. Apparently neither of us had ever learned how to do this correctly. But then I heard the telltale buzz of a text coming through on her cell phone.

I could tell she was fighting the Pavlovian urge to look at it, and the next thing I knew, it appeared on her palm. Her face lit up and lost its bored look. Her eyes flitted over the text with newfound energy. "Who would have thought that folding wrinkled clothes could be so much fun?" I interjected in what I thought was a jovial, jokey voice, but she wasn't fooled. Worried about the contents of the mysterious text, I'd reverted once again to being passive-aggressive. I hated when that side of me came out.

"Well, they wouldn't have gotten so wrinkled if you helped more around the house," Debra said, and then she wandered off. *Probably to respond to that text*, I thought. *Okey-dokey, the sheets can wait.* I grabbed another T-shirt and shook it with greater force than intended as Debra reappeared. She appeared shocked by my gesture.

"What are you doing!?" she said.

"I'm just folding clothes," I replied as my jaws clenched tight. "Why do you keep leaving?" I said, a question she didn't bother to answer.

The truth was, though, that we were both leaving, bit by bit. We just expressed our departures in different ways.

CHAPTER EIGHTEEN

MOTHERHOOD

TWO YEARS after Ren entered private middle school, I felt a surge of clarity: I needed to get out of my relationship with Debra. Years of couples therapy were not helping our ability to communicate. Our discussions were either so sparse or so heated that I needed to enlist a couples therapist to act as my advocate. I had become afraid to open my mouth and share my innermost feelings and decided I could only do so with a therapist present. Only in that way did I feel protected. I was withdrawing more and more into myself. I had thought by loving Debra I would finally find a way to love myself. But that hadn't happened. Along the way, I had lost who I was and what I wanted. Living in this state of misery wasn't fair to me, the girls, or Debra.

During these lost years, I would often find myself in the house on the weekends, standing and gawking at the kitchen we had remodeled nine years earlier. I would wonder what to do next. The kitchen remodel was just part of a larger project to open the living room, change the stairwell to the downstairs living space, and brighten and improve our living space in general. The project had been a huge undertaking and represented a fracturing of our relationship. Unbeknownst to both of us, remodeling would require the homeowner to take on the role of project manager. While I was at work, not only was Debra dealing with a small child, but often having to run to Home Depot or the lighting store to buy missing items or significant new fixtures. She was making decisions, hard decisions, that in hindsight I should have shared. We spent many of our weekends looking at granite countertops or paint samples or bathroom lights. Our frequent arguments and my strained silences often leaked out from our relationship. I had hoped Ren was oblivious to our challenges, but in retrospect, who can know what a four-year-old soaks up from a toxic environment?

To deal with the stress at home, I was soaking up wine. Wine had become an almost constant companion in my daily routine. I wasn't an all-day drinker; I preferred to drink at dinner—usually half a bottle by myself, and on occasion, the whole bottle. Enough to take the edge off. Ren would sit in her toddler seat at the kitchen table beside Debra against the backdrop of our deconstructed kitchen and bare-studded walls. I would join them with my chilled white wine. I tried to hide my obsession behind the pursuit of a self-improvement campaign to learn about different wine varieties. You know, the more sophisticated ones. I didn't particularly like hard alcohol, so I threw myself into becoming a wine snob: no official courses on becoming a sommelier, just a knowledgeable drinker obliged to experiment. Debra preferred the heavier red wines like Cabernet and didn't share my passion for finding the perfect wine to accompany dinner.

One solo wine-tasting evening stays branded in my memory. I tugged open the fridge to take out the nice, cold bottle of Johannisberg Riesling, barely pausing to consider the other two bottles on the shelf, the Ste. Michelle Gewürztraminer and the Indian Wells Chardonnay. Yes, I wanted something sweet that night, something to take the bitter taste from my tongue amid the chaos of this remodeling project.

"Really?" Debra said in a disgusted voice. "Again? Must you have it every night?"

The answer to that question was yes, I did need wine every night. And if we went out to someone's house for dinner, I always took a bottle of wine in case the host did not have the type I wanted. I had quit my prosecutor job with the City of Everett—I was sick of my boss harassing me and police officers treating me like a pariah because of my sexual orientation. My administrative assistant had voiced her concerns when I placed the photo of Debra and me on my desk, asking if I was sure I wanted to do that. "Yes, I'm ready to out myself," I told her. "I know many of the police officers already know. I'm tired of living in the closet. Not that many officers come and see me here, anyway."

Then I discovered that the city manager was telling select people that if they wanted to move up, they needed to live in Everett. They didn't want Seattle commuters like me. Debra had encouraged me to quit after the fourth time my boss had barged into my office unannounced and berated me for some perceived error in my legal abilities. I'd come home in tears.

"Jill, what's it going to take for you to quit that job?" Debra had said. It was a good question.

Without missing a beat, I said, "I suppose it would take him sexually assaulting me." My reaction might have reflected my growing paranoia. My boss wasn't coming on to me, just making my life miserable because he wanted me to quit. He had no viable reason to fire me. I was doing my job. But managers for the City of Everett were insular and provincial. They didn't want Seattle outsiders working in their government, and they certainly didn't want a gay woman acting as the face of police advisement and criminal prosecution. A few weeks after my conversation with Debra, I quit.

I would go on to work as a consultant to the City of Mountlake Terrace, the only one of us providing an income. We had been living off of and financing the remodeling using the money I had inherited from my grandmother. My consultancy job would be a step down in pay but give me something to do and continue my self-created myth that I was actually working and providing for my family. In truth, my grandmother's money was doing that.

But that night at the dinner table, Debra didn't stop with that one question. She continued her mantra: "You need to stop." I can't remember if Debra actually posed these words as an ultimatum, but that's how I heard them. And I, as if in some bad movie, lifted up my partially filled wine glass in protest. I briefly debated whether or not I would waste the contents, then—checking to see where both Debra and Ren were sitting—I hurled the beloved liquid directly between the two of them and watched it splash down the kitchen window. I had wanted to throw the glass and its contents at Debra but changed my mind at the last minute. The glass stayed in my hand and my eyes locked with Debra's. For once, she was speechless. The shock registered on her face like a beam of red light. I heard its warning signal: I'd crossed the line and I felt my throat tighten over the fact of my child bearing witness, the new low I'd reached through my depression and alcohol consumption. Debra was right. I was a high-functioning alcoholic. I didn't even know how long I had been drinking at this level, probably four years. It didn't matter. I knew I had a problem and I started AA the following week and began working with a sponsor.

Now, eight years later and sober, I was standing once again in the kitchen, the finished, remodeled version, its cheerful, newer coat of cream paint staring back at me. It was the weekend and Debra was off on some errand. I found myself wondering what she would want me to do next. When this thought popped into my head, I vaguely concluded something was wrong with me—how could I even think like this? But I brushed it off. I was so used to viewing the world through Debra's lens. I thought of other times when I would find myself waiting for her to come home and tell me what to do. Never mind what I wanted to do. I couldn't even figure that out. How had I lost my own agency?

Staring through the kitchen window, I studied the tall Japanese maples we had planted as seedlings for each of the girls out front. I thought of the recent trip to Italy we'd had to postpone twice, the one that almost never happened. Debra and I were a year apart and had come up with this grand plan to celebrate each of our fiftieth birthdays in Cinque Terre and Florence. Her parents had promised to come from Oklahoma to watch the girls. In the days before our dream trip, I was moving through the world in a fragile haze, tranquilized by a cocktail of prescribed antidepressants and anti-anxiety meds that didn't seem to be working as intended. I could hardly function in my job at the City of Seattle's department of Land Use and Construction, and at home, I was mostly numb and noncommunicative.

"I just don't think we should go, Jill," Debra had said.

"No, this is a once in a lifetime opportunity. If we don't go now, it won't ever happen." I'd banked on this trip revitalizing our dormant relationship and perhaps snapping me out of my depressed state.

"Jill, you can barely go to work. How will it be in a foreign country?"

"I'll manage. You'll see. I really think we should go. We've got your parents lined up and the reservations made. This is our chance. A new adventure is just what we need." I eventually wore her down.

But just as predicted, I was anxious the whole trip. I found myself following Debra around in my too-large travel pants owing to weight loss from anxiety. I often refused to accompany Debra on any of her suggested side trips, which further escalated the friction between us. Debra seemed constantly on her phone talking to a friend about how bad it was to travel around with a shell of a person. She wasn't wrong. My body had arrived in Italy to take in the sights and the good food, but for everything else, Debra acted as caretaker.

After a dinner she had cooked in our Airbnb during which we exchanged few words, I changed tactics. In my desperation to please her and get our relationship back on track, I asked if she wanted to make love. She looked at me with disdain. "No," she simply said. I guess that's when I knew our relationship would never get back on track.

I moved into an apartment soon after we returned. It was the most gut-wrenching thing I'd ever done. Ren was thirteen and Sara was eight. Although Debra and I had finally separated, we continued our roles as parents. I saw the girls about twice a week and usually on the weekends. I thought of all the relationships I'd had and left behind. This one, though, this one I had thought of as my forever relationship. Now I had the concrete ideals of children and a house and my idea of "forever" was demolished. I had lost my way. Separating seemed the only way to find my way back to me. I did not want to leave the girls or the family unit, but I knew that Debra and I could not go on in the poisoned air we had both created.

After we split up, our focus shifted even more toward the girls. Both of us were solid in setting aside our own differences so that we could parent the girls as seamlessly as possible. My parenting style had to shift: when I had the girls, I was on my own, requiring me to become a more engaged and attentive parent—the parent I hadn't been. I wanted to do better by Ren and Sara. When the four of us had all been together, I guess I had assumed the traditional, postwar-era-father role, going to work and playing with the girls at night and on weekends. Debra had executed the majority of our meals, and because she had been at home devoting her time to them, she knew them better. At least that was how I felt. I believed I was more affectionate with them than my parents had been with me, but the separation made me take a closer look. I didn't particularly like what I saw. While I was lonely without my children and looked forward to my time with them, I now realized that when they were with me, I would be responsible for everything. If a homework assignment had to be completed, I had to be the one to help. I had to cook dinner, a task made more difficult while working full time. I had to make sure I had the groceries on hand to make a quick meal, and one that they would eat. This amped up the stress on school evenings as we packed in all the activities a few hours before bedtime.

Our separation was hard on the girls. I don't think they particularly liked being shuttled back and forth, and they still considered Debra's house their home base. As much as I tried to turn my newly purchased townhouse into a home, from the girls' perspective, my place was just a stopover to see their other parent. They seemed okay with our visits, and I had hoped they might come around to wanting to see me more than twelve days out of the month. But over time it seemed they were eager to get back to the place where "they lived."

I broached the idea of spending more time with the girls one day when Ren was in the car beside me. I was driving her to high school that morning. "What would you think? You know, like one more night with me or Debra doing one week, and me, the other?"

"No, Mom," she said. "It would be too hard." She added: "It's not that easy to schlepp our stuff back and forth." I was hurt and I felt rejected as a parent. But I didn't push the point. I didn't ask Sara. I knew that Ren, as the oldest, was speaking for both. I felt I had failed, and Ren was saying no to me as a parent. With the vantage of twenty intervening years, I would later realize that Ren wasn't necessarily sending me a hurtful message. She was just being practical.

I already felt inept as a parent. I loved them fiercely, and while I was doing my best, my connection with them seemed weak from so little time spent together. At this age, their days were filled with school or on the weekends, soccer or ultimate frisbee games. Much of our schedules revolved around Ren's life, often leaving Sara resentful about being dragged to yet another soccer match or having to go in the car while we dropped Ren off at a friend's house. I wanted my house to feel like a place where they could bring their friends but that didn't happen often. I was terrified that Ren would want her friend Mary to spend the night. Mary was vegetarian and I had no idea about what I would cook for her. Debra, it seemed, handled these impromptu dinners or overnights with much more equanimity, or so I'd observed when we lived together.

Our separation wasn't all gloom and doom, though. I found my strengths as a parent, and unsurprisingly, they were similar to the ones my parents had. I found things to do with them when they were with me on the weekends, taking them to the aquarium, the zoo, the movies, and even live theater. They also joined me on errands like grocery shopping and clothes shopping. And I took them to church. Debra's parents were southern Baptist, and the church had played a large role in their lives. They'd had Debra and me promise to take the girls to church. They said it didn't have to be southern Baptist, but they wanted religion to be part of Ren and Sara's lives. I took my promise seriously. Since I had them more often on Sundays than Debra did, the onus fell to me to carry out that pledge.

As a sophomore in high school, Ren delighted in her discoveries about cells and plant and animal life. She found in her biology class what she wanted to do with the rest of her life. As a family, we had visited many Pacific Northwest beaches looking at tidepools and the tiny resident microorganisms that popped up when the tidewater receded. Debra, always the teacher, would explain what we were seeing and foster Ren's interest in marine biology. I helped Ren with her English and Advanced US History classes. Ren began to volunteer at the Seattle Aquarium in the summers as a guide for summer campers. She was always eager to go and loved the man who coordinated the young volunteers. Her avocation of marine biology was further confirmed when she chose biology as her college major and spent a semester abroad on one of the Turks and Caicos Islands studying marine life. While she didn't like the bugs or the hot tropical climate, she loved the warm water and what was contained in it.

Shortly after she started her first weeks of college, she called me.

"Mom, I think I'm going to try to get on the crew team."

"Why? How?" I asked.

"You can walk onto the team here. They have few women rowers, because they don't even offer scholarships. I think rowing would be good for me."

Three days later, she called again, excited that she had made the team. I was thrilled. Both Debra and I had taken rowing lessons with a local club in Seattle and on Green Lake. We had reveled in rowing as part of an eight-person team. I thought this sport was a way better fit for Ren than taking part in sorority rush, something Ren also planned to do.

My own sorority experience made me less than enthusiastic about Ren's desire to join. I didn't discourage her, but I struggled to share her interest. But being part of a rowing crew—that I could definitely get behind. Ren was one of those naturally gifted athletes who excelled at almost any sport. I'd had instructors pull me aside after a tennis lesson, a riding lesson, and a golf lesson, even, to tell me she was a natural. Who knew? Maybe crew would turn out to be her college thing.

Many freshmen try to find their group or sense of belonging. Forty years earlier at Whitman, in addition to being in a sorority, I'd played basketball and tennis. I enjoyed the practices a lot more than the actual matches and games. I wasn't competitive enough—much to my mother's dismay. Her own competitiveness was often on display when she came home from her twice-weekly golf matches with two different leagues during the summer. She would groan about her score and go over each shot. She was so hard on herself that I often wondered if she even enjoyed playing.

Ren called again to say she had joined a sorority in addition to being part of the freshman crew team. Soon I was hearing not only about her classes but about the godawful hours she was devoting to crew as well as her studies, her work-study job, and the sorority. In order to maintain her GPA for her grant money, Ren decided in her sophomore year that something had to give. I wasn't surprised the sorority was the first to go. Ren's heart was in crew.

Occasionally, I would go down to Tacoma to watch her home crew meets. But my favorite one occurred in the spring on the Montlake Cut in Seattle. Schools from all over the Pacific Northwest competed and it was thrilling to hover close enough by the water to see the rowers' determined faces and the bright sweep of school colors on display. I would bring my camera and take action shots of Ren and her teammates. I was close enough to hear the cox yell, "power ten!" and watch Ren and her teammates rev up their stroke rate harder and faster to match.

One thing that didn't change was Ren's request that I edit her papers. I don't recall when it started. I would be reminded of those times with my mother and her green chair. During these emailed exchanges I would use computer generated track changes instead of my mother's blue marking pencil. I noticed this similarity between my mother and me. But unlike my mother, I was generous in praising Ren. Still, I worried about whatever legacy I might be passing on to my own daughter. I was glad to remember my mother then and know the weight of what I might be handing down.

The spring of her junior year, both Debra and I attended the meet at the Montlake Cut. We each arrived separately. Our divorce had been dragging on with all of the attendant hostilities. Ren and I had chatted about meeting up, but we'd floated it more as vague idea than definitive plan. I watched when Ren's race was over and they were getting ready to pull the shell out of the water and walk back over to the crew house. I found the spot where they were pulling out. Debra had beat me there. Ren said, "Hi," and I said, "Good race." Debra barely acknowledged me but mentioned going to meet the crew over at the crew house and I said I would eventually wander over myself. Debra turned away, as though indicating she didn't care one way or the other. I'd been trying to limit my contact with Debra. Our meetings were often cold and I was feeling fragile. She, by contrast, looked and acted like she belonged there.

Various rowing shells rested on the pavement in the parking lot and young women in their college colors were bunched up with their teammates. I was madly trying to find the familiar maroon-and-white uniforms for Ren's team and finally eyed her and Debra. I wanted to see if Ren needed a hand and if she was going back to school or spending the day in Seattle.

I was trying to figure out how to get this information, but Ren looked busy preparing the shells for trailer loading and I didn't want to get in the way. I stood lost in my thoughts, suddenly aware of a quick blur of maroon and white and someone with long black hair in my periphery.

"Mom," I heard Ren say. "I . . . I just wanted to tell you that Kayla and I are more than friends."

"What? What are you saying?" I said to Ren. She looked nervous and was half-hopping from foot to foot. "Are you saying what I think you're saying? Why are you telling me here like this?" The moment seemed surreal. Dozens of girls with their parents and friends whirled this way and that around us, car engines hummed and horns squawked, accompanied by the scrape of rowing hulls against pavement. We couldn't be in a more public place. I asked myself again, *why was she telling me this? Why here in this location amid all this commotion?*

"I wanted to tell you and Mom at the same time and this just seemed the best place," Ren said, and then she was off.

"Wait, wait," I tried to say, but I don't think any words came out. I didn't even know who Kayla was, but I was sure Debra would know. Debra had gone to more team meets and seemed to know the names of Ren's friends. I knew the names of her roommate and her best friend but that was it. I couldn't even remember if I'd heard of Kayla before that moment. My ears were ringing. I felt like I'd just been torpedoed. It wasn't the news itself that was so surprising but the way Ren had told me. Yes, it was true that Debra and Ren and I were never really together at the same time in the same place anymore, but to divulge this rather critical, important piece of news with such haste. It wasn't the news itself. That wasn't it. It was the *how* of it.

I thought back to my own coming out, my parents squashed into my tin-can car, my palms sweating at the wheel. My big moment had been so different—so carefully planned—and yes, agonizing. With Ren, I felt blindsided. I would have preferred a private conversation than being told in a crowd of near-strangers. As far as I knew, this was Ren's first romantic relationship. She'd offered no signs or any indication of her interest in girls, and certainly hadn't talked with me about her sexual identity or about romance in general. This was a big deal, and I hadn't had a chance to react or tell her how happy I was for her before she dashed off. Hearing the news in this way made me feel unimportant—which I knew wasn't true—but I was having trouble grasping this piece of information. I wanted to get away from the crowd and think. I needed time, not to process Ren's news, but to ponder my reaction to it. *Why was I having such a big reaction?*

I wondered what Debra thought and I went over to where she stood talking to these other parents I didn't know. "Debra," I said, trying to catch her attention and draw her away from the other parents. "What do you think?"

"About what?" she said.

"About what Ren just told us. She told you, didn't she?" I needed to talk to Debra and get her reaction about the strangeness of Ren's news. I wanted something. Maybe some kinship, some connection with this woman I had spent seventeen years with.

Debra scowled as if trying to get rid of an annoying fly. "We're going to go to lunch. Do you want to come?"

"But what about what Ren just told us? What's your reaction?" But Debra just looked at me, or rather through me, and didn't respond. No, I didn't want to go to lunch with Debra and these parents I didn't know. I wanted to be alone, so I declined with some made-up excuse. Debra looked fine. She didn't look rattled. *Why was I so rattled?*

I made my way slowly back across the campus to where my car was parked. I ambled through the parking lot, my head made of cotton, the distance to my car never-ending as a myriad of feelings swirled through me. *Is this how my mother felt when I came out to her? Like this*? But no, her reaction had been swift. Violent. I didn't feel violent or hysterical, but I did wonder if I knew my daughter at all and that part of my wondering hurt. My daughter had made a decision on her own about her own life that had nothing to do with either Debra or me. She was growing up, finding herself, and making her decisions. That separation of parent and child was beginning, and I just wasn't ready for it.

I got back to my car and drove home. I didn't see Ren for the rest of the weekend. I learned later that she and a few crewmates had stayed at some Seattle friend's house and gone back to Tacoma. The next weekend, Ren came up to Seattle and brought Kayla with her. She brought Kayla over to my house to meet me, which I was pleased about.

I was pleased she had made the effort. When Ren came to Seattle for the holidays or the occasional weekend, it was me who made the effort to seek her out. And, that usually meant me going over to Debra's for a family dinner, or just me going over there on my own. And although Debra only lived fifteen minutes from me, during those times, I might as well have lived in Oregon. The gulf seemed too wide. I finally decided to say something to Ren about this arrangement.

On one such visit home, I asked her if she would take a walk with me. A slight breeze brushed against the side of my face on this fall day. It was clear the weather was turning. We walked away from Debra's house along the all-too-familiar, tree-lined, northeast Seattle streets. We passed the houses of people I used to nod to and speak with about the weather or their children. It was a single-family neighborhood full of well-kept yards where people mowed their lawns in the summer and raked their leaves in the fall. I missed the neighborhood and I missed my family unit.

I needed to talk to her about a subject that I didn't think I should have to spell out. But apparently if I wanted to see more of Ren one-on-one, I needed to have this talk. I waved at Donna and Mike as they drove by and took a deep breath. "Ren, this relationship you and I have is a two-way street. If you want to see me, you need to make an effort to seek me out. You need to come to my house on your own initiative. I don't want to beg you for one-on-one time. The pain of having to visit you at Debra's house is still very real."

I continued. "Debra has moved on, but visiting this house is painful and stirs up a lot of memories for me." I wondered how Ren was receiving this little speech. I'd fretted about being this vulnerable with my twenty-year-old. Ren had always been an empathetic, intuitive child, but I wasn't sure if she got it.

Ren nodded her head yes. "I think I understand Mom," she said. "I'll try to do that." I didn't tell her that not visiting me made me feel like a beggar and unimportant. *How shameful,* I thought, *that I should have to plead with her to come visit me.* So, yes, I welcomed her response. I was pleased she felt it was important for me to meet this woman she was in love with.

They came over one Sunday, and Ren had called first to say they were coming over. I greeted them at the door, and after fulfilling requests for beverages, we sat down in my small living room to chat. Kayla shifted slightly in her chair and I realized she was nervous. The scene reminded me of TV shows where the dad met his daughter's date for the first time and immediately started grilling him. I didn't want that scene but wasn't sure how to put this young, well-meaning girl at ease.

Our conversation was stilted. I lobbed softball questions at Kayla about where she was from and her college major. The discussion lagged. Ren seemed equally nervous and often answered for Kayla. These answers were short, offering little for me to work with. Eventually, they left, and while I now had a face to match the name, I had no sense of this young woman whom Ren had fallen in love with and wanted to bring home. Ren and I never talked about the strange way she had announced her news, but over the phone, we talked about how she and Kayla had met and how long their affair had been going on. Apparently, they'd been seeing each other for a few months. I told Ren again I was happy for her.

Shortly after the visit with Kayla, I began to hear from Ren about this thing called the "Enneagram." This term was unfamiliar to me. I soon learned that the Enneagram was a model of the human psyche based on nine personality types. It was popular in Christian circles and offered a window into one's identity. Ren began cajoling me in earnest to buy the 2016 book *The Road Back to You*, which she told me would explain everything. She was eager to know my personality type. *Where was all this coming from?* I wondered. Ren certainly didn't identify as Christian. In fact, she had resisted all my best efforts to introduce her to the spiritual world. I didn't exactly identify as Christian either, but I believed in something out there greater than me, something like the "higher power" concept that I had learned about in AA meetings.

I then remembered so distinctly one particular conversation I'd had with Ren while she was in high school. We were driving one Sunday to the Presbyterian church we attended. Ren did not like the church's high school group, so we compromised: she agreed to attend the service with me while Sara attended the Sunday elementary school class. "Mom, why do you go to church?"

Wow, I thought. *How do I answer this question?* She wanted an answer as to why she was being dragged, albeit compliantly, every Sunday to this institution that she clearly did not identify with. I took a deep breath. Her question was difficult to answer, because the church that Debra and I were attending did not condone homosexuality, and yet we went to this church anyway. While no one was preaching anti-homosexuality sentiments from the pulpit, the Presbyterian orthodoxy were clearly unsupportive of homosexual couplings. But Ren didn't need to know any of that. We went there because friends went and I had grown up regularly attending a Presbyterian church and Debra was happy with any church other than southern Baptist, the church she had grown up in. "We go . . ." I started and stopped and started again. ". . . I go, because I think it's important to expose you to the idea of something greater beyond our own, self-centered lives."

"I get that in nature," Ren said. I smiled at her simple statement, because she, Debra, and I agreed with this idea wholeheartedly, and our many camping and hiking trips had fostered Ren's appreciation. I was glad she'd found her spiritual connection in nature.

"I go because church and what they talk about in the service reassures me that when the chips are down, something is out there that I can turn to," I said. "It's important for me to have hope. Debra and I are just trying to introduce you to this idea."

"If it's not for you and you're not getting anything out of it, you don't have to go any more," I concluded.

There, I thought. *I've done my job. I've exposed her to these ideas and she is old enough now to decide for herself.* I didn't want to torture her. I'd done what I could. I had no idea, however, how I would get her little sister, Sara, to continue going to church without Ren accompanying her, but I would deal with that later.

Now here was that same child wanting us to do the Enneagram, some personality test that apparently had its roots in Christianity. She wanted all of us to do the test: Debra, Sara, and me. Ren's enthusiasms were contagious, and I, of course, was interested—as I thought any mother should be in a subject that her daughter was so keen on. I remembered back to my own high school and college years where I had tried so hard to connect with my mother. I wanted to know her as a person and not just as my mother. Personality tests seemed to pop up with some regularity in the only women's magazine my mother read, the *Ladies' Home Journal*. I was fascinated by these quizzes and tried to enlist my mother's participation in taking them—not just so that I could better know her, but also so she could truly know me. I bought her books as another tactic, books that I hoped she would read and we could talk about together. All of these efforts would meet with dismal results.

I did manage to garner Mom's interest in one book: Nancy Friday's classic *My Mother/My Self*, which came out in 1977 when I was twenty-two. I devoured it and passed it on to my mother to read. It marked the milestones of a mother's life and explored the mother-daughter relationship in detail. The book's premise was that daughters needed separation from their mothers in order to discover their sexuality and identity. I hoped that she would see me in that book and gain insight into my own travails. I saw her reading it. I worked up the courage and finally asked, "So, what did you think, Mom? Do you think we're alike?" I was hoping for approval or recognition or even a spark of connection. She lifted her reading glasses and peered over their tops. "Why on earth would you think I would read it with you in mind? I thought of my own mother." This response would make total sense to me later, but at twenty-two, I was baffled. I hadn't even lived through some of the decades that the book spoke to. Years later, I would realize that my mother didn't want to be seen by me and she certainly didn't appreciate that critical separation between mother and daughter that Nancy Friday talked about—most especially when it came to the identity I was busy pursuing.

I tried to connect with my mother through other books but never met with any success. I gave her what I thought was a humorous, but affirming, poetic book about getting older titled *Warning: When I Am an Old Woman I Shall Wear Purple*. "Why would you give me this?" she said as she unwrapped the book. Apparently, she thought I was insinuating she was old and did not like that. The book sat forever on the bookshelf untouched. She was in her fifties at the time. It became clear that my mother and I would not bond over any of my book suggestions.

She who had introduced me to books and thoughtfully provided one every Christmas was now on a different wavelength from me, now that I was a young woman getting older myself. She gave me one book that I'm sure she had read and treasured herself. It was Anne Morrow Lindbergh's *Gift from the Sea*. We never talked about why she gave me that book, but I loved it for its beautiful writing and self-reflection.

Perhaps that was why I was more willing to read this book from Ren about the Enneagram. If nothing else, reading it would be a way to connect with my recent college graduate who was rightly and rapidly moving out of my orbit and into her adult life. I could only assume that this new fascination of Ren's was coming from Kayla. I knew Ren wasn't taking any psychology classes. Ren confirmed this assumption. Throughout the summer and the following year, Ren's fascination with the Enneagram continued. She seemed to have discovered the key to the universe and was on a mission to convert the nonbelievers. I speculated on my own—but only half seriously—that she secretly hoped Debra and I might learn how to communicate better based on an appreciation of our personality types and thus get back together. But that was not to be.

I discovered I was either a "four" or a "nine" personality type, based on the Enneagram model. Ren said she identified with being a nine. In highly simplified terms, those who identified as a nine were peacemakers who wrestled with making decisions. If you identified as a four, you struggled with self-acceptance. These revelations were not a surprise to me. I was still in therapy, trying to accept who I was and the fact that being me was okay and acceptable. I fell prey to self-judgment and worried about other people judging me. And, now that I had children, I worried not only about what they thought of me, but also my place in this broken family unit. That even Ren knew I was a four showed her insight, and yet, made me feel exposed in some way.

Ren explained that I really needed to read the book she was reading to understand it all. I didn't quite understand her obsession, but I was interested in learning new things about myself. And if it brought my daughter and me closer together, I was all for it. When I asked Ren about her zeal, she said, "Mom, I just think the world would be a better place if we could all learn how to communicate better with each other." Ren was expanding this concept well beyond the singular lens of her self-growth. I marveled to myself.

The Enneagram wasn't the only thing that occupied Ren during her senior year. She was finishing up her requirements for her biology degree. I had loved watching Ren's growing passion for the world's water-bound plants and creatures, and I enjoyed how she shared it with those she loved. It was as if someone had pushed a button and she couldn't stop talking about water pollution, coral, plankton, different fish species, and conservation. It wasn't long before she announced that what she wanted to become was an aquarist, preferably with the Seattle Aquarium, considered one of the most significant aquariums on the west coast of the United States and a competitive locale. The stiff competition, however, did little to deter Ren.

When she graduated, Ren needed more experience before she could even apply for aquarist jobs and ended up one summer as a camp counselor in marine biology on Catalina Island. But the camp was a Boy Scout camp and she was one of few female staff. Times had changed. Ren endured bugle calls and having to wear a uniform with regulation socks and khaki shorts and having to sing silly camp songs and perform in camp skits just to gain more experience. Her persistence displayed my daughter's tenacity in pursuing her dream job.

Along the way, the relationship with Kayla ended despite the in-depth Enneagram plunge. Ren began a relationship with Zuri, a friend and crewmate. This time Ren remained more private about her new romance, and I was more prepared but still felt a jolt. I wasn't ready to let go, to accept my daughter had another, more important person in her life. I could blame my insecurities on my perception that neither of my children fully accepted me as a full-time parent. The divorce played a role in limiting my time with my children, but I harbored my own unease around my place in the family unit. Without this family unit, my identity felt further stripped, as if a part of me had been torn away.

Yes, I had chosen a role that seemed more dad-like where I went to work and provided financial security, but I wanted, as Debra suggested, "to have my cake and eat it too." *Couldn't that be possible in a lesbian couple?* I mused. *Why was I hewing to the hetero-normative stereotype?* That wasn't what I had hoped for when I came out. My decision to leave not only my marriage but our family home meant severing my association with the house where the kids grew up and continued to live the majority of the time. I'd flown the coop—abandoned the proverbial family nest—that divorce lawyers claim remains the foundation for nurturing young children. I hadn't foreseen the fallout when I made my decision to leave. I didn't want the physical house, but I desperately longed to hug and to observe and to interact routinely with my children. I couldn't imagine the huge hole their absence would create in my life—how my less-than-part-time parenting would get in the way of building those connections with them as they grew into adults.

Sara, now fifteen, continued to shuttle between my house and Debra's. Sara was eight when we'd separated, and where Ren was stoic at the news of our separation, Sara had cried. She hadn't understood at all. How could she? I wasn't even sure I understood it myself. Gathering in the living room with Debra and the girls on the sofa and me perched on the coffee table, I told them I was moving out. The decision was mutual, but I felt like the homewrecker. Just the way we were all sitting illustrated how the family dynamics worked, but the girls didn't know that, and I didn't come to grips with it for years. I was the outsider. While Debra and I had agreed on that artificial division of roles and labor, it hadn't worked.

We now had to create a new blueprint for family, and I recalled how with Sara in tow, the two of us looked together for my new living quarters. Sara, surprisingly, was excited about this task of finding Mommy a new place to live that she would get also get to stay in for a few days a week. After each viewing, we came out and discussed the possibilities. Sara thought the bedroom too small and I thought the kitchen didn't have enough storage space. After several appointments at various types of residences, we looked at a new townhouse in North Seattle. Townhouses were sprouting up all over North Seattle.

The neighborhood was a far cry from the single-family, green lawn plots of the neighborhood I was leaving, but I didn't take into account the absence of a sense of permanency. I needed to find something quickly as my apartment lease was coming to an end. I wanted to own, not rent. The townhouse offered a park with a playground nearby and a big playfield about two blocks in the other direction. We walked out together, and I turned to Sara and said, "What do you think?'

"I liked it, Mommy," she said. And, with that, our future was set. It was important to me that Sara like the place. She would be there at least five years longer than her older sister.

That seemed a long time ago now as Sara sat in my kitchen wanting to know when dinner would be ready. She was on her phone, focused on little else but being fed. Maybe that's how I had felt at fifteen, but instead of telling me, she rarely shared her thoughts except in texts to friends. She often said, in her own way, that I didn't know her—let alone understand her. How could that happen when I worked full time, rushed home to pick her and Ren up, and then had to get dinner and homework done? I had no idea how Debra was faring or if she understood Sara any better, because Debra and I didn't talk much. I suspect Sara was putting her other mother through the paces as well—as most healthy, individuating teenagers do. And at some level, I knew that Sara would outgrow her moody silences—just not soon enough for me not to spend years berating myself for creating those imagined emotional distances with her.

Once Ren was away at college and then living on her own in Tacoma, she may not have appeared on my doorstep as much as I would have liked. But she called me a lot. If I couldn't have her physical presence, the next best thing was talking to her on the phone. She was always full of news about her work, Zuri, boosting her qualifications, and finding full-time employment as an aquarist.

One day in September 2021, midway through the pandemic, my cell phone buzzed next to me on my desk at home. I turned it over and was pleased to see Ren's number pop up. "Guess what, Mom?" she said as soon as I picked up. "I got a job as a full-time aquarist at the Baltimore Aquarium."

"But . . . but that's all the way across the country," I said. "I thought you wanted to stay in the Pacific Northwest."

"I do, I do. But I also need more experience and working at this aquarium will give it to me," she said.

"I assume Zuri is going with you?" I said. I meant, they must be. I didn't think Ren would go all the way across the country by herself. But she had talked to professional aquarists and learned that she needed a full-time job somewhere to get more experience. What better place to do that than at one of the top aquariums in the country? Wow, I thought, she's doing it. Even if it means moving all the way across the country during a COVID-19 pandemic where she knows no one. Good thing Zuri is going with her.

As if reading my mind, Ren said, "Well, Mom, that's the thing: Zuri is not going to come with me. They have their own dream job here being a physical therapist for children. But they're going to help me drive across the country and I was wondering if you would come too."

Me? I thought. Why me? Why was she asking me and not Debra? I would have thought Debra would be her first choice. I also wondered why she needed me to go along, because she had Zuri, after all, to help her drive to Baltimore and get settled there. But I didn't want to ask Ren why. I just wanted to relish the fact that she was asking me.

When I had moved across the country from Evanston, Illinois, to my first full-time job in Los Angeles, the last thing I would have done was ask one of my parents to come with me. I wanted to put them and Evanston behind me. One thing Ed and Shirli Vanneman had done well was to raise an independent daughter. I can still remember my mother reflecting those words back to me. "We wanted you to be independent and you have shown us that you are that." I don't remember if she said that after I found my way at sixteen to the Versailles in Paris when my high school summer study group had accidentally left me behind or when I managed to survive being lost on my own for two-and-a-half days after getting separated from my hiking friends in the Sierra Nevadas, or when I left for Whitman College. But it was true: I was self-sufficient and I liked that about myself. I think my mother valued independence and fostered it in her children because she had left her family and roots in Seattle at twenty-two. I suppose I had to learn how to stand on my own two feet for real during the years my parents withdrew from me establishing myself in a lesbian community and learning to accept and even embrace who I was—though I doubt that's what my mom had in mind when she taught me independence.

I withdrew myself from these thoughts so I could continue my phone conversation with Ren. I asked her when we were leaving. "In three weeks," she answered. That's fast, I thought. I needed to get permission to take time off from work and book a one-way flight back to Seattle. I was worried about flying during the pandemic—vaccinations were still under development—but Ren had asked. How could I say no?

Twenty-one days later, we embarked on our trip in Ren's 2009 Honda van. I still didn't know quite what I was doing here—would I end up being a third wheel?—but I was happy to be there just the same. We planned to do the drive over four, ten-hour days. This was not a vacation. Almost all indoor dining was limited during the pandemic: our meals would probably be takeout. The extra hassles were worth it, though, since Ren would have both of us on hand for the hardest part of the trip: unpacking and settling into her new place.

During our second day on the road from Montana to Minnesota, we stopped for gas and Ren and I stood near the back of her open van. Zuri had gone to pay for the gas. I still couldn't figure out why I was there and I was embarrassed that I didn't know the answer to that question. I turned and asked Ren, "Why am I here? Why did you ask me to come?" She looked at me in amazement and said, "You're my mom. This is a big step for me. It's like going to college and I need a parent with me." Her look conveyed that she couldn't even believe I was asking this question.

In that moment, I realized that Ren saw and acknowledged me as her parent and although I was surely not perfect, I had done "good enough." And maybe, just maybe, I was good enough, whether anyone else told me that or the Enneagram told me that. Ren wanted me there as I had been there throughout her life, allowing her to be who she needed to be—which is her own, authentic self. It seemed like a reasonable conclusion that I could do that for myself: accept me for me. My child did. I no longer needed to be perfect and I didn't need to meet anyone's expectations. I settled back into the rear passenger seat, briefly tipping my head back and closing my eyes, and as I did, I blacked out the image of that old betterment campaign manual I once imagined my parents had written for me.

EPILOGUE

I WISH I COULD say that was the end of my story and that shame has disappeared from my life. It hasn't. Does it ever? Even my hero, motivational speaker and shame researcher Brené Brown, talks frequently and openly about her imperfections and lapses of self-compassion. Life is a series of casting offs. In the play *Death of a Salesman*, Linda Loman more succinctly tells her husband, Willy, "Life is a casting off." I have cast off the notion that I need to be made better. I no longer see a therapist to fix me but to get help with my ongoing struggle with self-compassion. My therapist is always asking me, "Would you say that to Sara or Ren?" I reply, "No, of course not." But for some reason I persist in saying unkind things to myself about myself.

My therapist Kaitlyn will then say, "Why do you say that to yourself, then?" She usually says this after my inner critic has thrown a knock-out punch and I am down for the count. Along with compassion for myself I know that empathy is also important. If I share my shame with someone, allowing myself to be vulnerable, then the shame shrinks. The tricky part is taking the risk, because the person I share with may not be empathetic. That's just the risk I have to take. Coming out to my parents was a risk, but I grew from that experience. I learned how to take other risks. I also learned how to parent in a different way than my parents had.

I believe my parents loved me and thought they were generally acting in my best interests. But amid the perfection-seeking 1950s and '60s, our house harbored a lot of shame. My parents felt that the best way to combat that shame was to avoid talking about our imperfections and anything that made us different from anyone else. I have learned that the opposite is true: shame thrives in the dark. It's a lesson I've tried to pass on to my children, the idea that honesty and vulnerability is the fastest route to self-forgiveness; I can only hope they arrive there more quickly than I have.

ACKNOWLEDGMENTS

IT IS OFTEN said that it takes a village to raise a child. What is true in my case is that it took a village to shepherd this book to the volume you hold in your hands.

Little did I know how fortunate I was to stumble upon Cami Ostman and The Narrative Project at the 2019 Chuckanut Writers Conference in Bellingham, Washington. I couldn't wait to begin and thus when the world shut down in March 2020 a door opened through The Narrative Project. Cami and my many critique partners throughout my three years in The Narrative Project helped immensely in the shaping of this book. Thank you to my coaches Nancy Canyon, Cami Ostman, and Jeanne Rawdin. Thank you to my critique partners, Mary Jo Campbell, Francie Allen, Erica Goodkind, Kimberly Brown, Melanie Cool, Noelle Davenport, Jean Wells, Holly Miller, and Randye Sundel. Others from The Narrative Project who provided support and guidance include Colleen Haggerty, Anneliese Kamola, Isabel Castro, and Dana Tye Rally.

Dana Tye Rally provided a thorough and incisive developmental edit. Her belief in me and the importance of this book are immeasurable. She continues to be a steady influence in my writerly life.

A huge thank you to two very special companions on this journey: Kaitlyn Braile and Naomi Stenberg, who provided support, encouragement, and acceptance.

I sincerely thank Brooke Warner and the She Writes team for their shepherding me through the publication process.

And last but far from least my two daughters, Ren and Sara, who believed in me and encouraged this project.

It is my hope that by sharing my story fewer people will not feel so alone with their feelings of shame.

ABOUT THE AUTHOR

Author photo © Fontaine Photography

JILL VANNEMAN is a former prosecutor and police legal adviser, as well as a legal consultant for a major city's planning and development department. She holds a BA in American studies from Whitman College, a master's in journalism from Northwestern University, and a JD from the University of Puget Sound. Her short fiction has been featured in *True Stories* and *Oaxaca: A Wayfaring Writers' Anthology*; her nonfiction work has appeared in the *Citizen Patriot*, *Miles City Tribune*, and elsewhere. She resides in the Seattle area with her aging tuxedo cat, Pablo, and her rescue dog, Honey.

Looking for your next great read?

We can help!

Visit www.shewritespress.com/next-read
or scan the QR code below for a list
of our recommended titles.

She Writes Press is an award-winning
independent publishing company founded to
serve women writers everywhere.